seeing is b

selected writings on cinema

CHIDANANDA DAS GUPTA

seeing is believing
selected writings on cinema

PENGUIN
VIKING

VIKING
Published by the Penguin Group
Penguin Books India Pvt. Ltd, 11 Community Centre, Panchsheel Park, New Delhi 110 017, India
Penguin Group (USA) Inc., 375 Hudson Street, New York, New York 10014, USA
Penguin Group (Canada), 90 Eglinton Avenue East, Suite 700, Toronto, Ontario, M4P 2Y3, Canada (a division of Pearson Penguin Canada Inc.)
Penguin Books Ltd, 80 Strand, London WC2R 0RL, England
Penguin Ireland, 25 St Stephen's Green, Dublin 2, Ireland (a division of Penguin Books Ltd)
Penguin Group (Australia), 250 Camberwell Road, Camberwell, Victoria 3124, Australia (a division of Pearson Australia Group Pty Ltd)
Penguin Group (NZ), 67 Apollo Drive, Rosedale, North Shore 0632, New Zealand (a division of Pearson New Zealand Ltd)
Penguin Group (South Africa) (Pty) Ltd, 24 Sturdee Avenue, Rosebank, Johannesburg 2196, South Africa

Penguin Books Ltd, Registered Offices: 80 Strand, London WC2R 0RL, England

This arrangement first published in Viking by Penguin Books India 2008

10 9 8 7 6 5 4 3 2 1

Typeset by Eleven Arts, New Delhi

Printed at Gopsons Papers Ltd, Noida

CONTENTS

INTRODUCTION

I wrote my first piece of film criticism sometime in 1946, a year before India's independence, also a year before we started the Calcutta Film Society. Political independence and the beginnings of film appreciation are thus fused in my memory. Indeed there was more than a trace of messianic fervour in our attitude to film. A new cinema, we thought, would come inevitably with a new political life, and film would emerge as an art and a social force. A country like India, with its honeycomb of identities defined by language, religion and a host of other criteria, would need social engineering of some scale to weld itself into a nation, and cinema would be the ideal force to supply the motivation. Needless to say, cinema as it existed in colonial India failed to meet the requirements of the situation as we saw it. Nothing but a new cinema would suffice. The thoughts of the leaders of the country were not radically different from ours, for within four years of Independence the central government set up a high-powered Film Enquiry Committee in 1951 with a cabinet minister at its helm. The Committee concluded that 'the film industry was incapable of reforming itself' and proposed far-reaching changes through new institutions.

My own writing was inevitably coloured by these predilections. Cinema had been born in the industrialized West, I argued, and had achieved its heights there. The course of Indian cinema would be linked to industrialization in what was now predominantly an agricultural economy. The form Indian popular cinema had acquired was a distortion. It would correct itself as the country industrialized itself. For formal growth, we should look to the West, and for understanding the workings of popular Indian cinema of the time we would have to take recourse to sociology.

By and large India's art cinema has derived its inspiration from the West—American storytelling, Russian revolutionary innovations, Italian neo-realism, French New Wave, and so on.

For a hundred years Bollywood has expressed, experimented with and explored social concerns affecting a country caught in the throes of change. This perception is far removed from the equation of popular cinema with pure entertainment. This book brings together many of my writings of this nature. Thus the chapter on cinema and politics ('Cinema Takes Over the State') analyses the unique way, unparalleled in the world, politicians have used cinema consciously and deliberately in Tamil Nadu and Andhra Pradesh. It explains how this experience is different from that of Ronald Reagan in the United States. Social concerns have also paralleled the political throughout India. These are amply reflected in 'Cinema Takes Over the State', 'Seeing Is Believing', 'Why the Films Sing' and other chapters. Some of the films are so involved with social problems that it is hardly possible to describe them as entertainment. No wonder sociologists have been increasingly drawn into discussions on popular cinema. Indeed, their deliberations on social concerns of this cinema have been singularly unrelated to their artistic aspirations. It is odd to find that the so-called art cinema should wear social problems on its sleeve while pure entertainment should conceal its social concerns in a secret chamber of its heart.

Sixty years is a long time, and an active scribe can turn out a considerable amount of writing during this period. The problem is often one of making a representative selection. I am immensely grateful to Kalyan Ray for helping me in this task. Like many commentators on cinema Kalyan is a professor of English literature (I myself began life that way). I am no less indebted to Diya Kar Hazra of Penguin Books for her steady interest in bringing this effort to fruition.

May 2008 Chidananda Das Gupta

1

OF MARGI AND DESI
The Traditional Divide

In Indian tradition there has been a clear awareness of the elite (unpopular) strand in art as distinct from the popular. Perhaps the clearest articulation of this awareness is to be found in Sarangadeva's thirteenth-century treatise, the *Sangeeta Ratnakara*, which makes a clear distinction between divine (courtly?) and popular music in the following words:

> Vocal melody, instrumental music, and dancing are known as *Sangita* which is two-fold, viz., *Margi* and *Desi*. That which was discovered by Brahma and (first) practised by Bharata and others in the audience of Lord Siva is *Margi* . . . while the *Sangita* that entertains people according to their taste in different regions . . . is known as *Desi*.

There are certain obvious implications of this statement, one of them pointed out by the English translator—that '*margi* means classical and *desi* means regional practice'. Of the implications not noted by the translator/editor, one is that margi, that is, classical, having been the discovery of Brahma and first performed before Lord Shiva by Bharata (of the *Natyashastra*) himself, is divine and thus superior, and is meant for the initiated, that is, those capable of attuning themselves to classical music. There is also the implication that classical is the opposite of regional, suggesting that regional was equated with the not-divine and therefore the inferior. Furthermore, the inescapable suggestion is that the classical is regarded as the standard, the central, the courtly, as it were. Conversely, it also means that the desi's existence—and need—was accepted; it was not thrown overboard or denied space in the category of music. It appears to have corresponded well with what is today called *lokasangeeta* or folk music rather than regional variations of the classical. The coexistence of margi and desi and the view of margi as the central, the superior, are thus basic to the Indian traditional attitude to music. To this day, the term *Margasangeeta* is often used to denote classical music.

There seems to be no reason for not applying this distinction to cinema. It would help to define the terms of coexistence for the two categories, popular and elite (unpopular), given that it is a division that exists in literature and the arts. No free society demands that all literature and all art be totally accessible to the masses. In fact, most new currents are denounced for years before they come to be understood. The poetry of Rabindranath Tagore and Jibanananda Das are prime examples in Bengali. Both had been received with hostility that, over the years, gave way to adulation. New cinema, like new writing, may be denounced before it is adored. A famous example is of Jean Renoir's *Rules of the Game* (France, 1937) which was first condemned and later hailed as a masterpiece.

Simplistic Solutions

There are only two kinds of film—the good and the bad—say those who look for simple solutions. But good films are not always popular nor the bad ones invariably unpopular; so the problem of deciding what is good and what is not cannot be measured by the money they make or do not make. That judgement remains beyond the test of the box office. Outstanding examples in India are some of Guru Dutt's films like *Kaagaz Ke Phool* (1959) or *Sahib Bibi Aur Ghulam* (1962). Many of his lesser films, such as *Chaudhvin Ka Chand* (1960), did well. In fact, as far as national and international awards go, the unpopular clearly wins.

Not unnaturally, the distribution and exhibition set-up is oriented so firmly towards the popular film that the good but unpopular has hardly a chance for a look-in. The film industry has not shown any particular inclination towards creating an artistic vanguard that would ultimately serve its own interests. Steps towards building an infrastructure for the qualitative growth of cinema have always been taken by the government or by committed adherents of 'Art'. There have been virtually no signs of creation of a space for the other cinema within the film industry's scheme of things. What osmosis has taken place between the two rather watertight identities—art cinema and commercial cinema—has been fortuitous and unintended.

One advantage of accepting the age-old division between margi and desi, or classical and folk (more correctly pop, in the urban context),[1] is that neither category can then demand the non-existence of the other. The Film Enquiry Committee of 1951 harboured the illusion of purifying all cinema one day as an article of faith; fifty years on, it is the need for the margi cinema that is being questioned. Proposals for the winding up of the growth centres built then—the Film and Television Institute of India (FTII), the National Film Archive of India (NFAI), the India International Film Festival, the National Film Development Corporation (NFDC)—are mooted every now and then. Once the margi–desi coexistence is granted, one can proceed to examine the two categories separately, without feeling guilty about either.

Besides, the acceptance of the margi–desi coexistence assures a much healthier give and take between the two. Some such symbiosis has indeed occurred but not to an adequate degree. New cinema often introduces elements that later become useful to popular films. Thus the jump cuts and freezes that shocked the audiences of Jean-Luc Godard and François Truffaut at the Cannes Film Festival in 1959 became commonplace within a few years. In India, new actors and actresses discovered by unpopular cinema have later made it big in the popular. An outstanding example is of Sharmila Tagore, who made her debut in Satyajit Ray's *Apur Sansar* (The World of Apu, 1959) and later became a big star of the popular cinema. Mithun Chakravarty was discovered by Mrinal Sen and made it big in the mainstream. Of Shyam Benegal it can be said that he ran a veritable factory for the manufacture of stars—Shabana Azmi, Smita Patil, Naseeruddin Shah, Om Puri, Kulbhushan Kharbanda and many others. Similarly, outstanding cameramen and other technicians graduating from the FTII have served to raise immeasurably the production qualities of popular cinema. On the other hand, major actors from the mainstream have acted in the unpopular cinema for a pittance, attracted by the opportunity to flex their acting muscles, develop a character and explore its psychology, participate in the excitements of innovation.

Defining Unpopular Cinema

There are semantic problems in defining unpopular cinema. First of all, there are the hordes of commercial films that have been resounding failures at the box office (124 flops out of 132 films made by Bollywood in 2002).[2] Indeed, they constitute the overwhelming majority, in spite of being made with all the experience and expertise of the film industry. But they conform to the set patterns of cinema favoured by financiers in quest of big money and are therefore categorized as 'commercial' cinema. A study of these films could be educative but is not the object of this essay, which is primarily concerned with margi cinema.

The low-budget, realistic, artistically advanced body of films using the universal language of cinema, rather than the uniquely melodramatic, operatic form developed in India, has been defined under a multiplicity of rubrics. Of these, the common ones are: Alternative Cinema, New Cinema, Parallel Cinema, Art Cinema, The Other Cinema, Personal Cinema, Auteur Cinema and so on.[3] Margi would have been the ideal term with the merit of being recruited from Indian tradition, but may be dismissed as elitist. But of all the characteristics these nomenclatures summon up, the most commonly shared is their failure at the box office.

The failure is not absolute, one might protest. There have been quite a few films that have recovered their low cost and even those that have shown a profit. Satyajit Ray's exquisitely made *Charulata* (1964) was the second biggest box-office hit of its year in Bengal. There are many other examples of such success in Bengal, Kerala and other regional cinemas. Mrinal Sen's *Bhuvan Shome* (1969), made in Hindi with much panache but without stars, did well. Nevertheless, the failure to make big money is common to these films as a category. Hence, in these pages, no matter which of the variously unsatisfactory labels is used, the reader will know what is meant; that they all stand in their different ways for the same thing—the creative personal cinema that appeared on the scene soon after Independence in the work and in the wake of Satyajit Ray and others who put art and social commitment in the forefront of their scheme of things.

At the same time it is worthwhile to remember that experiments in showing film classics to new rural audiences have been surprisingly successful. Heggodu, a small village close to Bangalore, made Indian film history in 1979 with its festival of film classics. Neenasam, a cultural association, showed films like *Rashomon* (1950), *Pather Panchali* (1955) and *Wild Strawberries* (1957). The response from the villagers was perceptive and enthusiastic. A similar experiment in another set of villages by a group called Artha yielded similar response, suggesting that if the first exposure to cinema takes place with classics, new audiences respond very differently from what is normally assumed. The divide between mainstream and parallel cinemas is thus not as natural as one might think. But the relationship between manufacturer and consumer in the mass production system is so organized that small is hardly ever beautiful.

Motion pictures, like any other product of mass consumption, are manufactured in mega cities by corporate bodies of the official or extramural kind through an intricate network of advanced technology, large-scale manufacture, distribution and exhibition. They are, if anything, less capable than other media, of challenging the stereotypes held dear by the audiences. Minority wishes would be of no consequence. Popular cinema, in other words, must be populist.

It becomes inevitable, in these circumstances, for the minority view to seek to organize itself on a scale viable for such resources as can be marshalled by a few committed adherents to its ideology. Low budgets are a sine qua non. Especially organized audiences (such as film clubs, art houses, film festivals and any international consolidation of such resources) are their inevitable pastures. Thus, France financed Satyajit Ray's last but one film; when Akira Kurosawa was unable to get money for his films, groups in France, USA and Russia provided the finance to him; Japan funded a film by Adoor Gopalakrishnan, France a few by Nagisa Oshima, one by Shaji Karun.

In the national context, it is equally inevitable that artistically inclined cinema should need support from the powers that be to ensure its continued existence. Cinema is by no means unique in this respect. Serious theatre, dance, music, literature, folk forms—all survive today on the strength of varying degrees of governmental and private help. Delhi has governmental academies for the support of almost every art form. In Kolkata, ITC sponsors a large Sangeet Research Academy; in Mumbai, there is the Tata-supported National Centre of Performing Arts and so on. In Japan, no traditional art could survive without large-scale imperial patronage.

The Marxist Agenda

Marxism set a model for large-scale state patronage of the arts, giving primacy to cinema. But it imposed upon the artist's freedom in no uncertain manner. Nehruvian India tried to steer a path between the two, not without some success. India has, by and large, been able to support art without dictating its content.

Nonetheless, the Russian model, being the central one for the Marxist ideology, played an important role for several decades in the history of unpopular cinema. Its influence still provides the leavening to many a film, years after the collapse of the Soviet edifice and its satellite states. It flowed into the reformist channel and enlarged the agenda of social change in independent India. The history of unpopular cinema is largely a tale of the often self-imposed struggle of the individual artist with the dictates of the collective, that is, the Party. Even to formidable individualists like Adoor Gopalakrishnan it has been an important point of reference, for instance in *Mukhamukham* (1984). Ritwik Ghatak was tormented by the struggle. Mrinal Sen, Ketan Mehta, Saeed Mirza, M.S. Sathyu, Buddhadev Dasgupta, Goutam Ghose and many others contended with it for decades in their diverse ways. But the Marxist-reformist legacy in cinema ran into a frustrating inability to communicate with the people.

Marxists would give their right hand to reach the mass audience that popular cinema commands. But alas, most of the films driven by the Marxist ideological engine did not, do not, reach the people for whom they are meant. First of all, cinema is an urban medium. It calls for stable, high-voltage power not available in most villages. That leaves out the peasantry. It does leave in the urban working class, largely a class of migrants to the city. The cinema audience also comprises the urban unemployed, the destitute, the lumpen, who live by their wits and are not nearly as amenable to Marxist preaching as the organized worker. The popular cinema product is designed for this large urban configuration to which the middle class is an adjunct. Due to the paucity of films custom-built for them, educated middle-class men and women become interlopers to this audience and remain so until they are slowly sucked into the vortex of its culture. From the Marxist point of view even this section is not a good recruiting ground of revolution. Popular commercial cinema is primarily interested in making money, not in the overthrow of bourgeois governments. The revolutionary artist sworn to the promotion of class struggle is therefore left in the void, and has to be content with the crème de la crème of an intelligentsia thinly spread across the cities.

Not that this dilemma is solely India's. There is the outstanding international example of Bertolt Brecht which ran into the same quagmire in Germany. His artistically outstanding plays became instrumental in rousing the intellectual's conscience without making contact with the masses. Furthermore, they consciously cultivated the mode of alienation from the illusion of storytelling and the Aristotelian notion of catharsis (purgation) through pity and terror brought about by the enactment of tragedy. They relied solely on appeals to the intellect at the expense of emotion. Needless to say, his work did not endear itself to the people and ended in preaching to the converted. It is the same syndrome that troubled the mind of the Marxist film-maker moulding messages for the common man that fail to reach him. Nearer home, the same predicament befell leftist poets in Bengal whose frustration was most acutely felt in Samar Sen. His realization of the problem was deep enough to lead him to the conscious decision to stop writing poetry altogether. It must have brought him enormous relief from attitudinizing.

In Indian cinema the Catch-22 was most manifest in Ritwik Ghatak (see the essay *Ritwik Ghatak: Cinema, Marxism and the Mother Goddess*). It is an important issue because Marxism has been one of the important strands running through the history of unpopular cinema. Apart from the known exponents of it like Khwaja Ahmed Abbas (whose scripts coloured the work of Raj Kapoor), Ritwik Ghatak, Saeed Mirza, Govind Nihalani, Goutam Ghose and others, there is a host of directors for whose work Marxist ideology has provided an important leavening. These include Bimal Roy, Raj Kapoor, Chetan Anand, Nemai Ghosh, Satyajit Ray, Shyam Benegal, Mrinal Sen, Adoor Gopalakrishnan, Buddhadev Dasgupta—all of whom had (some still have) proletarian sympathies derived from the Marxist experience if not directly from the Soviet model.

For many of these film-makers, especially the ones with a commitment to the values of parallel cinema, there existed the problem of making films for proletarian audiences which the proletarian hardly ever saw. They had to be content with exposure only to the urban middle class, sometimes not even that. Avowed Marxists Mani Kaul and Kumar Shahani never got any of their films released in public theatres.

The problem afflicted not only the film director but the painter or the theatre director or literary writer as well. In Mrinal Sen's *Calcutta 71* (1972), there is an episode showing a rich man giving a sumptuous dinner. As the delicacies are swallowed, the host pontificates on the merits of a painting showing a starving man. The scene can be read in the exact reverse mode of Mrinal Sen's rags-and-riches contrast in caricature. For, it shows up the predicament of the sensitive painter whose whole existence would fall apart without the rich buyer and his hangers-on.

It is the realization of this inevitability that makes the Marxist film-maker give up and address himself to the middle class, the class to which he belongs and which he understands. Mrinal Sen, with his characteristic candour, has voiced this condition many a time.

Art and Social Engineering

The significance of parallel cinema in India far outstrips its number of films, the absence of large audiences or the money it does not make. It often reaches into the conscience of the educated middle class—professionals, teachers, lawyers, bureaucrats—reminding them of how the other half lives and what's wrong with things as they are. It disturbs their complacency. A large section of the complacent suffered acute discomfort when confronted with the stark poverty, or rather the humanness amidst poverty, in *Pather Panchali.* They tried to prevent it from being shown abroad and, if they could have had their way, would have been content to ban it altogether. It was rescued from bureaucratic vandalism only at the personal intervention of Prime Minister Jawaharlal Nehru. What happened in the case of *Pather Panchali* affected many other films concerned with poverty and oppression in modern India. Shyam Benegal's *Ankur* (The Seedling, 1974) was allowed to be shown at the Berlin International Film Festival only after it declared, at the insistence of the Indian ambassador to Germany, that the things shown in the film belonged to the past and do not happen any more.

The persistent international recognition of some of these films, and repeated acts of high-level rescue, reconciled these hostile forces to a grudging tolerance. Their embarrassment was shared by many Indians abroad because the films compromised their assumption of equality with the westerners among whom they lived. Evidently, to these Indians, Vivekananda's call to the more fortunate Indians to declare the poor, illiterate masses their own brothers and sisters, would fall on deaf ears. All that these forces were concerned with was hiding the reality from international knowledge. Film star and nominated Member of Parliament Nargis's famous diatribe in Parliament against Satyajit Ray for 'exhibiting India's poverty abroad' revealed the depth of the hostility of the industry she represented towards the by then much-acclaimed new cinema.

What this new cinema achieved for India was neither an exhibition of poverty nor merely a proof of its film-making skills. Apart from shaking up middle-class complacency, it made a sensitive section of the international community aware of India's own effort to face up to its condition. Most of the films of the new cinema sent out an important message: that the country was keenly aware of the poverty and illiteracy of its masses, and was trying to pull itself up by its bootstraps. This coincided exactly with the Nehru era's mindset—its emphasis on self-reliance, on laying down an infrastructure for industrial development, on a legal framework to ensure the growth of equal rights, on the liberation of the country from the binds of superstition and of its women from slavery to men. All these movements, concerns, were dependent on awareness and were reflected in the films thrown up by that awareness.

Indeed, the inspiration behind this cinema stretched back beyond Nehru to Gandhi and Tagore, and, going further back in time, to the nineteenth-century Renaissance. However much the subalterns might denigrate the Indian Renaissance for being confined to the middle class, there is no doubt that it laid the foundations of the Constitution of independent India, its legal structure of human rights and its concept of equality before the law. No doubt changing society is more difficult than changing the law; but it is obvious that changes in the law eventually do change society. It is equally obvious that reformist minds group together to facilitate the process of converting legal edicts into social goals if not all of social practice. One of the most effective means of this social engineering is cinema. With its clearly established faith in these objectives, parallel cinema can be seen as a direct descendant of the social reform movements of the nineteenth and early twentieth centuries. In literature and the arts, the ferment of ideas, the interface between personal expression and social engineering, had already started in the writings of Premchand, Krishen Chander, Subramanyam Bharati, Josh Malihabadi, Kaifi Azmi, the dance dramas of Uday Shankar, the paintings of Amrita Sher-Gil, Jamini Roy and so on. Sher-Gil's figurative works brought out the innate dignity and the contemplative calm in the faces and stances of the common people; Jamini Roy's reasserted the traditional two-dimensionality of Indian art, rejecting the colonial overtone imposed on Indian mythology by Raja Ravi Varma's oleographs. Uday Shankar reinvented classical dancing in the context of modern India, matching what Rabindranath Tagore did to music with his two thousand songs, modern in their sensibility yet umbilically connected to the system of Indian myths.

The new cinema followed in a direction set by them and sought to bring the medium up to the level of the rest of the arts. Much of this is evident in the films of Satyajit Ray, which absorbed the narrative mode of the European novel and Hollywood cinema, investing the outcome with a contemplative quality of spiritual calm. Hence it is that there is a frenetic, un-Indian pace in our mainstream films, and characteristically calm body rhythm, based on Indian rural life, in the products of unpopular cinema even when they deal with contemporary urban reality.

The exposure of real social conditions was by no means the sole concern of the new film-makers. They were equally occupied with personal expression of both content and form, and strove to engage with a more universal language of cinema. It was important to break out of the confines of convention so culture specific that they could not be understood outside their circumference. Despite the occasional acceptance by Western consumerist society of some films like *Lagaan* (2001), the gulf between the international mode and the Indian, between consistent narrative and the variety show, however rambunctious, persists. Also it is uncertain as to how long the partial acceptance of Indian cinema in the West will last; for all we know, it can, like other fashions and waves, vanish into thin air. How far it is tied to the apron strings of the non-resident Indian is also a moot question.

In recent decades, parallel cinema has encountered other hostilities besides the ones Nargis represented. With their cynical rejection of all utopias and notions of transcendence or mediated change typical of a consumerist hegemony, sections of the postmodernist constituency are drawn powerfully to an alliance with popular culture. No wonder the study of popular culture draws scholars today like moths to flame. Without denying the need to understand the workings and objectives of popular culture, one has to note that much of the writing on it is tantamount to justifying philosophies for whatever sells. Essentially, one of the traits of postmodernism is existentialist. It refuses to see the causal patterns behind the manipulation of society by the manufacturer with his control of the nature of consumption. It brushes aside all issues relating to the power of the underworld dons over the style and substance of the films they finance. The more the evidence of the nexus between the underworld and the film industry surfaces, the less is written on it by the scribes of newspapers and magazines or scholarly apologists of popular culture. For this constituency rejects all social engineering agendas of the vanguard of the middle class as the grievous sin of modernism. Its championing of the desi as subaltern by implication rejects the margi as comprador and questions its right to exist.

Text and Subtext

It is well known that the incidence of sex and violence in cinema has increased many times over despite the cogitations of pundits and the earnest labours of the censor board for more than half a century. Yet when society censors a subject, it becomes inadmissible. A really confrontational film on caste conflicts is virtually impossible to make within the mainstream cinema; it will be asphyxiated at birth or aborted beforehand. Similarly, Hindu–Muslim marriages are taboo. Mani Ratnam defied that fatwa with *Bombay* (1995) but he got away with it largely because he is not Bollywood; his resource base is in Tamil Nadu whose political and social equations are different in character. Not surprisingly, he has not had imitators.

However, it is not as though mainstream cinema does not have social concerns. It does, in plenty. Only it does not wear them on its sleeve. Behind the escapist sugar-coating, there is a set of social objectives and there are debates over issues it cannot decide on. The mainstream is troubled by challenges to the status quo and to traditional hierarchies, systems of social loyalty cemented by religion.[4]

Exceptions are worth examining because they can prove the rule. An outstanding example is Mani Ratnam's *Bombay*, which presents, indeed advocates, marriage between Hindus and Muslims, a subject normally anathema to the mainstream. The marriage, sealed under the law despite equal opposition from both families, yields identical twins, one of whom is brought up as a Muslim, the other as a Hindu. They go through the experience of communal riots to emerge as indivisible brothers who win over not only their grandparents but the society around them, shaming them into peace and brotherhood. Just the message the country needs today, one might conclude.

But the subtext says something else. The relationships between the lover and the beloved as well as their parents are treated as fantasy; the riots are for real. We clearly get the subterranean message that the fantasy parts depict what should happen but cannot. The realism is reserved for what does happen. The fantasy is reinforced in the case of the lovers by the beauty of the landscape and the speed with which they fall in love. There is no attempt to build up that process bit by bit. The other dimension that adds to the unreality is the highly unreal symmetry in the attitudes and actions of the parents. One set of parents is ardent Hindu and the other equally devout Muslim. Each family reacts to every situation in exactly the same manner, like mirror images; the director does not sense the need for any variation. As in most mainstream films, unreality is created through the device of total and absolute symmetry. Now, we know that nature abhors mechanical symmetry; artists, following the principle of nature, strive to achieve an asymmetrical balance in structure and design. In *Bombay*, when we come to the riots, the film-making is, if anything, more realistic and elaborately detailed than in parallel cinema. Symmetry is thrown to the winds because we are now dealing with what could actually happen (the Hindu–Muslim riots), not with what should but actually cannot happen (Hindu–Muslim marriage). But when it comes to the two families getting together to arrange the marriage, exact parallels are shown on both sides; if there are four people on one side, the other side must have four of the same size and age and must sit in exactly the same formation as the other. Such symmetry denies the dynamics of living reality.

Contrast with this the story and treatment of Aparna Sen's *Mr & Mrs Iyer* (2002). A married Hindu woman travelling with a child is attracted to a fellow passenger, a Muslim, in the context of a communal riot. Sen's style is of course asymmetrical and fully realistic. Schematic fantasy never enters the frame at all. The accent is on multiplicity. The people in the bus are a motley crowd.

However, where the riot is concerned, Mani Ratnam is much more forceful in his realism. Sen concentrates on the development of character, event and relationship. In other words what this film seeks to make plausible is not what should happen but what could actually happen. It therefore gives a body blow to the presumption of total unacceptability of a Muslim man and a married Hindu woman's attraction towards each other. At the end of the film the two have become just two human beings, without labels loaded with prejudice. So one film says it could actually happen, the other that it could not. And the style is what makes the difference.

The comparison also shows up some of the standard differences in story treatment between commercial cinema and its parallel equivalent.

A detailed examination of these would not be germane to an essay on unpopular cinema. Let it suffice here to say that by and large, mainstream cinema still upholds tradition against forces of change; it confirms rather than challenges the clutch of basic attitudes making up the mindset of the large audience. It extends across a wide range of issues: father's right over children, husband's right over wife, son's duties towards father, wife's towards husband's, lower castes' towards the higher, loyalty to the country (my country right or wrong), inter-community marriage—and almost all such basic issues and their standard resolutions.

From D.G. Phalke (the 'Father of India Cinema') onwards, the trend in the bulk of films has been towards conformity to conventions, unquestioning faith in gods and goddesses, in fixed forms of their worship. Exceptions exist in some Bhakti-based films such as *Sant Tukaram* (Maharashtra, 1936) featuring Vishnupant Pagnis which express a uniquely individual passion. But in the majority of the products, there has been no opposition to institutions like sati, the sacrifice of children and animals, or to traditional binds in marriage such as those of caste or dowry. Conspicuous by its absence is any continuity with the reformist movements of the nineteenth and early twentieth centuries and the edicts of Gandhi.

There is no doubt that from the beginning there has been an avant-garde that broke away from conventions and stood up for reform sometimes even in direct confrontations as in V. Shantaram and Master Vinayak, but these have been dissident rather than dominant trends. With Independence, cinema appears to have abandoned its socially proactive role, leaving it to the government. Gross commercialization of cinema set in in the post-Independence period. With the growing divide between the art film and the commercial product, initiatives of this nature passed into the domain of the parallel cinema which acquired certain characteristics that increasingly defined its ideology and moulded its creative propensities.

NON-VIOLENCE

There is more than a leavening of Gandhism that served to make parallel cinema unpopular. Its rejection of violence, in spite of Marxism's canonization of violence as a means of changing the social order, divested it of one means of easy access to the emotions of the populace. Non-violence is central to social reform because the aim of reform is to keep resolving conflicts within the body of traditions, allowing it to flow into the modern, absorbing its organic needs from the time and space through which it meanders. As the inheritor of the mantle of social reform, parallel cinema got wedded to non-violence. Even with directors of leftist persuasion, for whom revolution is a declared aim, its visions seldom erupt into graphic violence. In films like Ray's *Devi* (1960), Pattabhi Rama Reddy's *Samskara* (1970), Girish Kasaravalli's *Ghatashraddha* (1977) or Prema Karanth's *Phaniyamma* (1983), the pressure brought to bear upon society is of persuasion towards reform. More common is the expose of social injustice. Even the cold anger of Ray's *Sadgati* (1981) does not provoke an urge for violent intervention.

Indeed, non-violence has been an article of faith with parallel cinema. Visions of revolution have seldom erupted into violence on the screen except as perpetrated by the rich on the poor in the pre-revolutionary context (Shyam Benegal's *Ankur*). With very few exceptions, the texts and subtexts of parallel cinema have endorsed non-violence as the central mode of behaviour. Govind Nihalani's is the only name that springs to mind in looking for a deliberate use of violence to state an idea. Within the compass of parallel cinema, violence takes such precedence in *Hazaar Chaurasi Ki Maa* (1998) that the human relation between the two mothers gets pushed into the background. The violence germane to the statement of most films in parallel cinema is generally treated in a non-participatory manner, with few close-ups and none of the 'Kill him!' passion aroused in the audience typically in mainstream handling of violence. Almost invariably the mainstream tradition has been one of the invocation of a spirit of revenge abounding in gory close-ups. For a striking contrast take the recent films of Buddhadev Dasgupta; in most of them, violence is seen from a distance that makes the audience think rather than feel involved.

The centrality of non-violence in the utopias nurtured in the heart of society in an age of atomic or all-destroying warfare is obvious. But it remains outside the popular cinema's discourses, where the immediate box-office gains from violence exercise greater attraction.

The gross exaggeration of muscular prowess, with the lone hero felling dozens of thugs, in the majority of mainstream films cannot be dismissed as fantasy. It can, in Peking Opera or Kung-Fu fight films for they declare their fantasy premise from the word go. Unlike Bollywood, these Far Eastern forms can sustain their fantasy level from beginning to end; such consistency is not germane to the Bollywood product which must make a patchwork quilt of genres.

SEXUALITY

Puritanism in matters of sex has been a dominant characteristic of parallel cinema. Perhaps this inhibition is born of an amalgam of socio-religious postures, not always very determinate. There is the direct derivation from Christianity's doctrine of the original sin that regards sex as the source of evil—a necessary evil for the propagation of the species. Any interest in it in excess of that requirement is sinful. What is more, the assertion of sexuality in woman is more sinful than it is in man. The woman is more responsible for the nurturing of children and provides the major force that binds the family together. She is basically the object of sex perpetrated on her by man. The idea that it can give physical pleasure to the woman as well would make sex even more sinful. Sexual freedom in man is less harmful.

Thus, the orthodoxy of St Paul and St Augustine bears antagonism towards female sexuality and its assertion. What brings it closer to the Indian mindset, especially that of the English educated, is the Christian attitude formally upheld by the British ruling class and insinuated into the body of Indian beliefs by Mahatma Gandhi, who did not feel any affinity with ancient India's freedom from a sense of guilt over the pursuit of sexual pleasure. Dharma (righteousness), artha (wealth), kama (desire) and moksha (deliverance) were the four defined and approved purposes of life in ancient India. Gandhi's dissent from this view was so marked that he once proposed the destruction of all erotic sculpture on temple walls and was prevented from carrying out his purpose by the hue and cry of artists.

The prudery of unpopular cinema is somewhat Gandhian (Christian). Since parallel cinema is markedly influenced by Western models, it is not unnatural that it should inherit some Christian ambiguities from that source. However, it may also have descended from the modernist nineteenth-century reformers who had themselves imbibed shades of Puritanism from the Western impact. Conformity to the beliefs of the colonizer offered an array of advantages, including the ruler's tacit approval. All this also had to do with the rejection of superstitious ritualism that often led to the throwing out of the baby with the bathwater. Tradition was sometimes thrown out in the process of its reform.

Although *Pather Panchali*'s Sarbajaya is still young and good looking, she is only the mother, never the wife. When her husband is with her, their relationship is oriented entirely towards the children. In Ray's *Devi*, Doyamoyee is always covered from head to toe. There is one kiss seen through the sanitizing mist of a mosquito net. In his *Ghare Baire* (1984), the kisses are mechanical, devoid of sensuality. The same is true of the adulterous mother in *Pikoo* (1981). There is the same shying away from sensuality or suggestion of nudity in Ritwik Ghatak (except for moments in *Titas*). In Mrinal Sen's *Antareen* (1993), Dimple Kapadia's form is carefully hidden from the eye, even when she is completely alone in her room, lying in bed and talking on the telephone. There is nothing casual about the way her clothes are draped over her up to her ankles. Shyam Benegal's *Ankur* is somewhat formal in showing master and maidservant coming together; so is the actress going boldly from man to man in *Bhumika* (1977). There was sensuousness but not sensuality in his *Manthan* (1976). Adoor Gopalakrishnan avoids the need to face a choice in the matter. In *Swayamvaram* (1972), a film noted for breaking out of conventions, a man and a woman have eloped but whenever intimacy needs to be suggested, the director takes recourse to mainstream cinema's oldest devices—cavorting by the seaside or lying demurely side by side. G. Aravindan's eye could have celebrated the poetry of the nude, but one doubts if the possibility ever crossed his mind.

Only in supposedly realistic depiction of classical times has some sensuous exposure of the body been validated as in Girish Karnad's *Utsav* (1984) or Nachiket and Jayoo Patwardhan's *Anantayatra* (1985). In M.S. Sathyu's *Garam Hawa* (1973) there is a moment of genuine sexuality in the boat scene when a hand pushes the clothes up to reveal the thigh. In Goutam Ghose's *Paar* (1984), the close relationship of husband and wife comes through in a palpable way despite the absence of sensual contact as such. In Aparna Sen's *36 Chowringhee Lane* (1981) and *Parama* (1984), the kisses are warm and passionate—a rare phenomenon in Indian cinema so far. In Rituparno Ghosh's *Chokher Bali* (2003), the body comes into its own in a way hardly ever seen in parallel cinema. While Rituparno's creative technique is markedly Ray derived, his treatment of sexuality, like Aparna Sen's, may spell the end of sanitized sex in post-Ray Bengali cinema. But by and large the reticence over sensuality is a marked characteristic of parallel cinema's mix of attitudes. It is distinctly more puritanical than the mainstream.

Mainstream cinema is less hostile to the expression of sexuality; sex sells and therefore cannot be rejected. In the mainstream, sexual enthusiasm is aroused in a kind of mass effect without emphasizing individuality. Leg-kicking en masse, however short of clothing, has the effect of stylizing the action and de-individualizing it. Sexual enthusiasm in man is to be winked at as an unavoidable, eminently forgivable, fact of life. The vigorous sexual horseplay in the dances lies strictly outside marriage; it celebrates the young man's need to sow his wild oats before he marries for money. The underlying justification is bestowed by the mythological pranks of Krishna with the gopis. The woman's (Radha) role is to take part, with mandatory enthusiasm, in the man's wild oat sowing. Her acquiescence is the subtext of what looks like romance. To acquire sexual freedom, a woman must be at best a tawaif (geisha-like); you could fall in love with her but not marry her. In essence, a woman who enjoys sex is a whore. Here the mainstream has inherited the mores of the near past, the courtly sexual etiquette of the Mughal era.

Neither mainstream nor parallel cinema takes cognizance of the mores of ancient India. In mainstream cinema nudity is out; semi-nudity is the order of the day. Here parallel cinema's implicit stand is clear; it would rather have nudity, beautifully portrayed (take Mani Kaul's *Erotic Tales*—made abroad—for instance), than semi-nudity, reminiscent of Titian's paintings of sacred and profane love (the sacred being completely nude and the profane half-clad).

The Marxist streak in India also took on a puritan colour, condemning sexual frankness as a sign of bourgeois decline. Sometimes the pupil overtook the teacher; nudity and sexual intimacies in Russian films often upset Indian Marxist audiences. There was commotion in Calcutta over nudity in a Soviet ballet show sometime during the last years of the USSR. Could this have been due to British communist predilections that were the main source of Indian Marxist ideology, one wonders.

The ploys in mainstream have variety. You can have a man on his knees embracing a woman with his mouth dangerously close to her crotch; but you are not supposed to see that. You must see not the flesh-and-blood reality before you but the idea of devar and bhabhi or mother and son they are enacting. On seeing Shekhar Kapur's *Bandit Queen* (1994), a semi-literate man from a Bihar village remarked, '*Ghatiya film hai* (It's a bad film).' Asked whether such incidents of enforced nudity never happened in or around his village, he said that they did happen but they should not be shown.

Not very different was the wife of a former minister of information and broadcasting who vented her spleen on me because in an I.V. Sasi film I had liked, the woman decides her sexual life herself, choosing men as she pleases. The minister's spouse would have objected equally hard to Shyam Benegal's *Bhumika* for the same reason. Had the men chosen their women she would have considered it the natural order of things. Obviously she had much the same world view as the half-educated Bihari and took the same dim view of parallel cinema. Even in the educated middle class, similar attitudes often prevail. Loyalty to the new cinema's mores is by no means universal.

Recent generations of Hindus (the majority in the population and the audience) are ashamed of ancient sexual mores that are in conflict with those overlaid by the Islamic–Christian rulers and perpetuated to the present day. They seek to keep these racial memories safely hidden within the confines of mythology. Indeed, in contemporary times, militant Hindu groups aggressively posit Islamic–Christian sexual mores as their own.

Neither the censors nor the producers in the mainstream or parallel constituency feel or seek any link with ancient Indian tradition. Until the coming of the Muslims, India's attitude to sex was open, positive, free from a sense of guilt. Sex was recognized as a life-giving force, a source of legitimate pleasure. There is a genuine problem of cultural continuity here for both the cinemas and their audiences. Confronted with evidence that in ancient India women went topless, a minister of the Maharashtra government roared: 'What should I therefore do? Send my daughter to school without any clothes on?' Popular cinema legitimizes it by recourse to dance a la the Krishna myth; unpopular cinema by turning away from sex.

Given the stranglehold of the Judeo-Christian-Islamic code of sexual morality over contemporary Indian society, the extent to which mainstream cinema is able to celebrate the joys of sex without transgressing the line of control is astonishing.

However, it took a long time for the kiss to pass muster in Indian cinema. Even now, there is something evasive about it; it is used more to prove a point than to please the eye of the beholder. The lip-to-lip contact is so individualized and real that it cannot be stylized like the leg-kicking, navel-displaying, hip-wiggling dances.

Modernity, Family Life and Male Domination

As in all traditional societies buffeted by the winds of change, in India too the integrity of the family has been central to the struggle to cope with the aggression of unwelcome new ideas. This is one of the issues that lie at the heart of India's popular cinema. The typical polarity has had the mother trying to hold the family together amidst the forces of modernity—the liberation of women, the pressures of consumerism pushing the younger generations towards the nuclear family and individual development. The pressures towards modernity and tradition have been reflected by the two cinemas almost exactly. Both have been somewhat simplistic in their treatment of the family; one iconizes the mother and ignores her role in resisting change, the other fails to see the cohesive strength of the joint family structure in trying to protect tradition. Mrinal Sen's *Matira Manisha* (1966) sees the essential part played by agriculture in holding the family together while also projecting the family as an obstacle to individual development. Shyam Benegal's *Trikaal* (1985) takes a sad, last look at the family in colonial India. The Apu trilogy traces the emergence of an individual from the heart of a traditional family. At the end of Bibhutibhusan's original story, Apu deserts his son in order to go off to Tahiti, without any indication of when he might return. Indeed, we are left entitled to speculate whether he would return at all. Ray changes that ending but in essence retains the writer's ending on a note of freedom from all family bonds. Although the feeling here is of the freedom of the hermit, in Ray's retelling, the shade of modern, Western development of individuality cannot be ignored altogether. In *Devi*, the son is at war with the father whose authority over the family is absolute and includes the right to overrule his son's wishes and his wife's. When they try to leave home, it is by stealth.

One of the dimensions of modernity evident in unpopular cinema is its espousal of the liberation of women, itself a guarantee of unpopularity, since the majority of men and women in society are opposed to it. The tacit approval of male dominance is proverbially transmitted by women from generation to generation. No wonder it has been, compulsively, a subject for unpopular cinema. Take the films of Shyam Benegal, for instance. In *Ankur* and *Nishant* (1975), the sexual enslavement of women is coeval with the feudal system and indeed its symbol. Sometimes women earn their independence by wielding the power of sex as in *Bhumika* and *Mandi* (1983). In film after film, Amrish Puri is the stereotype of the tyrant male ruling over the lives of the daughter, wife and (unofficial) concubines. Virtually all outstanding films from Karnataka—*Samskara*, *Grahana*, *Ghatashraddha*, *Phaniyamma*—deal with some aspect of the enslavement.

It is easy for cinema to be unpopular when it eschews the standard ingredients of popularity—sex and violence, songs and dances, fights and chases. For a medium mostly seen as entertainment, parallel cinema's approach is very ascetic, minimalist. Budgets are low, financiers and production controllers make sure that expenses are kept on a tight leash so that they do not exceed expectable incomes.

What is more, the directors must depend upon tight storytelling, creating an illusion that must hold the audience's attention right till the end without interruption; the audience must forget that it is watching a film—anything that makes it aware must be avoided. Believability depends on realism, which is therefore important.

More often than not, the director in the parallel cinema will dictate the placement of the camera, its height, the use of the lens and many such 'technical' details in order to make sure that the technique remains subservient to the purpose, mood and spirit of a scene and its believability is not impaired. Creative technique must be solely derived from the needs of the story. The geography of a place, the continuity of lighting, the naturalness of the skin tone in people must be strictly maintained.

The human dimension too must stay within limits; the figures must not be so big that they seem, in the words of Satyajit Ray, to 'fall off the screen'.[5] This discipline in humility is in consonance with concepts of non-violence, empathy with the rights of the poor and of women and children. It is best seen in Ray's early work, particularly in the Apu trilogy but it is traceable in the work of many other directors and has become part of standard technique. Indeed, departures from it stand out forcefully, for instance in Girish Kasaravalli's *Tabarana Kathe* (1986) or Rituparno Ghosh's *Chokher Bali* in which the figures sometimes become larger than life and tend to get de-contextualized. They often seem to 'fall off the screen'. Ritwik Ghatak dramatizes the imposition of the characters by placing them against vast backgrounds expanded by the use of wide-angle lenses, without distorting the human dimension. Shyam Benegal, Adoor Gopalakrishnan, Mrinal Sen, G. Aravindan, Aparna Sen, Goutam Ghose, Buddhadev Dasgupta and the majority of directors of the unpopular cinema maintain this humility of the human figure in their work as a matter of course, without undue deliberation.

In the mainstream film, the storyline has to be thin because it must be open to interruptions by song and dance, fight and chase sequences which have a life of their own and are in fact often directed by specialists other than the director of the film as a whole. This reduces the role of the director to what A.V. Meiappan, head of AVM Studios, Chennai, once described as 'floor manager'. Meiappan went on to elaborate this by saying that he visited each floor of his studios regularly to tell the director what to do. He once asked Satyajit Ray to make a film for him but hastily withdrew the offer when he was told, in no uncertain terms, that the director must have complete creative control.

The coming of the new century has seen some of these creative mores of the parallel cinema insinuate their way into the mainstream as well, bringing the two modes closer than ever before. Indeed, the first half of *Parineeta* (2005) could well have been made by the director of *Chokher Bali* which itself could have been partly the work of the director of *Parineeta.* These signs of symbiosis are in good part the contribution of graduates of the FTII, in other words, the infrastructure created with much foresight by the government in the 1960s. For decades these blithe spirits had put in their technical best in films with which they felt little oneness; now virtuoso technique and conceptual sophistication are coming together to fire their imagination. The tribe AVM Studios would once call 'floor managers' are finally emerging as directors. The mainstream is possibly inventing its own parallel, its avant-garde, its 'margi'.

2

SEEING IS BELIEVING

One remarkable outcome of grafting the technological art of cinema on to India's pre-industrial society is that the adage 'seeing is believing' has acquired a new significance. In industrial societies, the audio-visual media, whether on an optical or electronic base, is trusted as well as distrusted. News stories on television are by and large believed; love stories on the cinema screen may affect the emotions yet are recognized as fiction. Fictional films may influence attitudes but are not believed as fact. The situation in India is different and the differences are not always easy to understand.

When films began in earnest in India, with Phalke's *Harishchandra* in 1913, suddenly the gods and godlike men of mythology came to life. The 3,700-foot film on a mythological personification of noble sacrifice was an overwhelming success (it was remade twenty times in eight languages in fifty years). Its successors, Phalke's own *Mohini Bhasmasur*, *Satyavan Savitri*, *Lanka Dahan*, were equally popular and established the 'mythological' as a long-lasting genre of Indian cinema. Hitherto the Hindus had seen the trinity and pantheon in their minds and in images of clay, wood and stone; now they saw them walking, flying in space, throwing flaming discuses (Vishnu's Sudarshana Chakra), setting offenders aflame with a burning look, making the dead come alive, appearing out of, and vanishing into, nowhere. This is how the gods had dwelt in the mind's recesses, held aloft by a network of myths and legends spawned by the epics and the Puranas. The loves and hates of the gods had been seen as leela, divine play, evoked by the bhakta or devotee in his imagination. These now became reality; here was Raja Harishchandra walking barefoot through the brambles, giving away his son Rohita, his wife Taramati, for the sake of charity; and there, Rama roaming the Dandakaranya forest with Sita. Inside the cinema theatre, the devout took off their shoes, sat with folded hands and even threw offerings at the screen.

Ramrajya, the ideal kingdom ruled by Rama, King of Ayodhya, had always lived in the Hindu mind unrelated to historical time—a utopia the Hindu hid in his heart through a millennium of alien domination, first by the Islamic kingdoms expanded into an Indianized empire, then by the Christian British. It is to this deep-seated nostalgic dream of Ramrajya, sanctified into divine myth, that Gandhi appealed in support of his non-violent struggle against the British when he declared in a moving speech, at King Edward Hostel in 1920: 'This is Ravan-Raj.' No wonder Gandhi made a kind of contact before the days of mass communication technology that leaders of later generation could not.

Naturally, the early films were mostly mythologicals. Until 1923, 70 per cent of the films made in India had mythological themes. They ensured large audiences and their appeal was firmly addressed to diverse groups linked by a common undercurrent of religious belief. Besides, they helped to hide the moral and social stigma of the performer, traditionally a member of one of the lowest castes, especially if it was a woman behind the divine garb. It also served the deeper purpose of confirming faith in an age of alien challenge.

The British conquerors were preceded and followed by the missionaries of their faith. They were ever ready to bribe the native believer with their education, guaranteeing advancement in the new world of their making, full of marvellous innovations such as railway trains, buses and trams, post offices, the telegraph and ships. The advantages of embracing the conqueror's faith were many and, at poorer intellectual and social levels, difficult to resist. It was even more difficult to separate the self into behavioural compartments outwardly in consonance with the conqueror's norms, and inwardly conforming to traditional faiths. For the urban majority exposed to cinema, the act of seeing the gods became a subtle aid in propping up the belief in them. The fact that humans were dressed up as gods mattered little. Rich people took Prem Adib (Rama) and Shobhana Samarth (Sita) in the full glory of their make-up, straight from the studio floor to their homes, and offered puja to them.

This was different from seeing them in the folk theatre. The gods of Jatra (Bengal) or Yakshagana (Karnataka) could not actually fly or burn or vanish. The leela of the gods was visually manifest only in cinema, therefore difficult, impossible, to disregard. The actors in the folk theatre were too real; too often you knew where they lived, and saw them paint their faces before they entered the arena. In cinema they were real yet shadowy, not gross enough to lose their distance and dignity. The folk form was (still is, despite its decline) based on what we today call Brechtian alienation, that film-makers like Ketan Mehta invoke in their films. As the screen lit up in the vast night in the open air or inside the dark womb of the theatre, before their eyes a primeval dream unfolded in which the gods lived and had their being, emerging from an ancient communal memory secreted within the self. The thrill was no less than that of audiences in Europe, trembling as the train approached the station in the tiny fragments the Lumières showed everywhere at the close of one century and the beginning of the next. For the devout Hindu, it was almost like the traditional glimpse of God in a dream that directly influenced action—something enshrined, decades later, through the sympathetic but sceptical eye of Satyajit Ray in *Devi*.

The medium of cinema works against the stylization of folk forms. When it is stylized today, in the works of a Mani Kaul or a Nirad Mahapatra, it loses the popular reach of the folk form. In pre-industrial society, production was individualized, regionally fixed; its art was largely an anonymous by-product of religion and regional culture enclosed within the narrow limits of social and geographical mobility. The difference between art and craft was marginal. The maker of an image or a water pot knew the buyer of it personally and sold it through direct encounter. The folk theatre reflected this reality. Its performers were known entities of flesh and blood and belonged to well-defined geographical areas. It drew both its religious and secular content from the prevailing tradition of the area, sometimes fusing them, sometimes treating them separately. It projected them in a way suitable for open spaces and dim lights.

Naturalism in acting and staging was hardly possible; the voice had to be raised in order to be heard, the gesture had to be magnified in order to be seen. It is this style that was at first directly transferred to cinema but modified over the years to acquire a greater degree of naturalism. In any case, compared to folk theatre, the illusion of reality in cinema was greater even at the beginning. For one thing, the miracles wrought in Phalke's mythological, with the innovative flair of a Georges Méliès, came to life far more vividly than they could ever have on either the newfangled proscenium stage or the traditional folk theatre.

In an interview in 1979, Kamalabai Gokhale, reminiscing on her acting in the early mythologicals of Dadasaheb Phalke around 1914, commented on cinema's disconcerting immediacy: 'Theatre acting is done within the norms of restraint. It is symbolic, particularly in love scenes. On the stage you keep your distance, decide your limit and say that I would go no further than holding hands . . . But in a love scene in a film, you have to embrace—really embrace—the other fellow in front of the camera. Otherwise it would make no sense.' This was not long after the period when even prostitutes found it socially embarrassing to appear in cinema, and men often had to play the part of women.

II

Cinema has a lot to do with materialism. The apprehension of individual and collective life, and the factors surrounding or determining them, must be made, in industrial society, through a new ability to understand material things. Cinema was invented by scientists who sought to fashion an instrument for gauging the optical illusion of movement (persistence of vision) or animal locomotion or the transit of a planet. Charles Babbage was a mathematician, John William Herschel an astronomer, Etiénne Jules-Marey an anatomist; Eadweard Muybridge, photographer, may be considered the only artist among the inventors of cinema. The rest were scientists or, like Thomas Edison and William Dickson, technologists.

The very need for an additional dimension to man's communicative abilities arose out of conditions created by the Industrial Revolution. Modern technology, urbanization, high mobility and rapid communication introduced a whole new set of sights, sounds, symbols and their material interrelationships which demanded interpretation. A jet fighter shooting up in the sky leaving a vapour trail, or a man walking along the street seen from a hundred floors above can be evoked in writing, but when they are seen in the cinema, they carry a different kind of conviction of materiality. It is to this instrument of belief that the latter-day gods of Indian politics, produced by the mythical world of cinema, repaired to induce conviction in their divinity and eligibility for elections.

Men do become gods in cinema; but some of cinema's gods too have become men of power on earth—avatars of Krishna or Rama. Indeed, two of them who promised, and created, something of the illusion of realizing Ramrajya, both bear his name—Marudur Gopala Ramachandran in Tamil Nadu and Nandamuri Taraka Rama Rao in Andhra Pradesh. The process of equation of myth with fact, the easy movement of the mind between the two, is helped by the nature of visual perception in pre-industrial societies. For the servant just arrived from a village a painting by Jamini Roy was exactly like a photograph: the illusion of verisimilitude was easy. The morphological perceptions of industrial man, tempered by a scientific assessment of what appears real, are sharper; they instantly verify the form in terms of geometry, gauging its solidity, comparing it to others of the species and, through inductive logic, moving from experiences of the particular to some general gestalt.

The appearance of any element depends upon its place and function in the pattern as a whole. 'Far from being a mechanical recording of sensory elements, vision turned out to be a truly creative grasp of reality.' Thinking within the orbit of Baconian science, one would conclude that all vision is grasped by a struggle for an orderly conception of natural form, proceeding in a logical development from the perceptually simplest patterns to increasing complexity. 'When we look at one side of a ball, we also "see" the other, i.e. not a partial but a complete sphere.'[1]

But to the average Hindu, the elephant-headed god Ganesha is not a representation of an abstract idea; he exists even though he cannot be encountered in the flesh. So is Jamini Roy's impossibly long-necked, extra-wide-eyed woman the same as a photographic image. The question of the purely *material* existence of a form is unimportant, because in traditional Indian art, as opposed to the academic art born of a scientific awareness of materiality in post-Renaissance Europe, the form is seen in the mind, not in reality. Yet it exists. Thus the form of the seated Buddha is a representation of the *idea* of meditation; the dancing Nataraja (Shiva, the king of dance) embodies the *idea* of cosmic rhythm. The idea assumes human form, thus manifesting itself in material terms. In post-Baconian European perception, the material form comes from nature and is then informed by an idea. There is a process of reversal from this in post-industrial society's 'art'; but that is confined to a small minority producing a market commodity rather than the whole of society yielding art as a by-product of essential socio-economic processes as in pre-industrial societies. Even so, modern art remains a scientific perception; it analyses light, or density, or assembles aspects of material reality; the point of reference from which it withdraws, and eliminates, is the naturalistic image.

III

But far from inducing a 'modern', sceptical, secular spirit, early cinema gave the Hindu pantheon access to this powerful instrument of belief; instead of retreating before science, as in the West (where are Zeus and Apollo or Athena today?), the Indian gods obtained new life from it.

The realistic illusion-making power of cinema therefore works in favour of the merging of myth and fact rather than their separation as evidenced in pre-industrial societies. Even after seventy years of films, gullible members of the audience were seen prostrating themselves before the screen deity in motion picture theatres everywhere when *Jai Santoshi Maa* (1975) was shown.[2] For the bulk of the population of India, the process of perception has not been metamorphosed by science into a way of grasping the material existence of an object. Only in high-literacy areas subjected to Western thought structures, especially rationalism and Marxist materialism, such as the states of Kerala and West Bengal, do cinema audiences have a ready ability to separate myth from fact. As an actor, Prem Nazir held the Guinness Book record for having acted in the largest number of films in the world (more than 600), but when he developed political ambitions, the people of Kerala made it quite clear that their matinee idol in the cinema would not be acceptable as their political chief. This is in direct contrast to M.G. Ramachandran in Tamil Nadu or N.T. Rama Rao in Andhra Pradesh.

But cinema is the product of a new need for grasping the material reality of the industrial–scientific world. It represents a pressure, within the evolution of the popular arts, towards greater naturalism, farther and farther reaches of conviction of materiality. Indian cinema, developing on a large scale within a mainly agricultural population with myth-laden minds, countered this pressure in the land of elephant-headed Ganesha and the stone lingam by mythologizing the present. With the expansion of the industrial–urban sector, the mythological as a genre has beaten a retreat;[3] it cannot deal with the manifest phenomena of modern society and therefore becomes inadequate, despite exceptions like *Jai Santoshi Maa*, an enormously successful film which spread nationally and spawned a cult.[4] What happens then is that cars, skyscrapers, jet planes and gunfights are used to endorse the same basic faiths as the 'mythologicals' without denying the audience its visual experience of the new phenomena.

Amar Akbar Anthony (1977) has its three brothers, estranged in childhood, grow up under surrogate fathers of the three major religions of contemporary India—Hinduism, Islam and Christianity—and brings them together again at the end in a realization of their (Hindu) unity. The brothers, coincidentally together throughout, have their mother present among them without being aware of her identity. They treat her as their surrogate mother. She has lost her eyesight in an accident, but regains her vision in a dramatic moment in the dargah of the Shirdi Sai Baba. While Akbar sings to the statue of the saint, two blobs of light (you can see them, they are *there*) issue from the eyes of the saint and travel across the screen in a panning shot over the congregation, stop at the mother's eyes and get into them. Now she can see. Other manifestations in the film—clothes, houses, cars, trains—are modern; but the faith invoked is no different from that in *Bhakta Prahlada* (1926) or *Bharat Milap* or any of the professed 'mythological' films of old.

In films like *Trishul* (1978), dead mothers call upon their sons from the other world to take revenge on their enemies. They power the muscles of the protagonists with a divine maternal boon, enabling them to perform miracles such as defeating thirty strong men with their bare hands. In *Karz* (1980), the mix of the modern and the traditional peaks in the reincarnation of the hero, whom a sexy but evil woman had run over with a car near a shrine of Goddess Kali. Divine retribution consists of the villainess being run over by a car near the same shrine. Thus is the present constantly mythologized and the currents of traditional belief kept alive beneath a modern exterior.

Except for the core of religious doctrine and ritual, all other physical manifestations are jazzily modern in these films; perhaps the object is to emphasize the means of resolution of conflicts as divine and eternal, above the purview of social change. Traditional faith is not allowed to be subverted by the freedom to doubt old beliefs and the spirit of scientific enquiry that led to the invention of modern industrial products parading across screen space.

Closely related to this is the way certain new visual models came to dominate the mythological. Raja Ravi Varma's imitative English academicism recreated Indian gods and goddesses, transforming them from the superbly idealized figures of the Ajanta frescoes and the stone images of Vishnu or Shiva into florid bazaar oleographs in crude homage to the naturalistic idiom of the colonial ruler's art. Today, any treatment of the gods in cinema that does not follow Ravi Varma's prescription in image-making may be in trouble with the audience. The prescriptions of the medieval *Vishnudharmottara Purana* would not be understood. In cinema this is the model of mythology that has retreated under the pressing need for encounters with the modern. Interestingly, it has reasserted itself through television, where the driving spirit behind its appearance is a certain view of tradition uninformed by either a historical sensibility or an understanding of Indian art traditions.

It is interesting to compare all this with the 'superman' mythology of American cinema. Laser weapons melt human flesh and encasements of steel; lethal weapons unleash spectacles of colossal disaster, projecting not only the possibility of conquest of the denizens of outer space, but of Armageddon on earth. It is as though two tracks laid on the visions of the future of a super-industrial society travel through its mental space, one of conquest, the other of destruction, while the impatient present can no longer wait for either. It is a mythologization of the future arising from the compulsions of the nineteenth-century dream of man's conquest of all he perceives, whose fulfilment seems almost possible.

India's age-old society, faced with the spectre of modern science, baulks at the prospect of being dominated by it and shaken out of the security of traditional faiths. The significant but small minority whose body and soul have both entered the industrial stage and adopted the rule of science, produces the 'new cinema'; the vast pre-industrial sector mythologizes both the past and the present, perhaps propelled by a fear that calls for a return to the womb.[5] The city is where the modern and the traditional meet and where the dream factories are located. The ways in which the cities of modern India are related to the moral sector determine the nature of the battleground of ideas that cinema represents.

3

WHY THE FILMS SING

There are a number of ways in which the popular film in India struggles to overcome the built-in naturalism of cinema, and to bend this medium, developed in a Western technological society, towards its own pre-industrial, mythical style of discourse.

A beard on Valmiki in the Ramayana—whether on film or on television—is not a photographic record of a real beard on a real man; it is a photograph, but of the beard symbol of someone who is supposed, by tacit agreement between film-maker and audience, to be a traditional sage. Many a film in Telugu or Malayalam paint the hero's face white (fair) but leave his limbs dark and not paint the minor characters at all. The idea is a little like painting the faces of Kathakali dancers; there are specific colours and iconographic features by which Bhima or Dushashana are recognized, by common agreement as in the case of the meaning of a word. The camera is thus made to record a symbol instead of a fact. Fact is turned into myth. There is a complete subversion here of the purpose of invention of motion picture photography in the industrial age, which is the promotion of a superior apprehension and judgement of the geometry of movement of shapes and sizes, distances and differences, through which the mind understands the materiality of matter.

The instrument, however, which achieves this turning of fact into fiction, of the present tense of the camera eye into the past and the future, is the song. It is the transcendental element in the language of popular cinema. It expounds philosophies; proposes inductive and deductive syllogisms on the truths of individual life in relation to the social universe; explains hidden meanings; comments, like a chorus, on the worth or consequences of an action, besides providing aural enchantment to the otherwise music-less urban world at its rural grassroots. Take the title song of Raj Khosla's *Do Raaste* (1969):

There are two types of people in the world, two roads,
Two forms of life; in order to live
Step out carefully . . .
Make it clear to every crazy fellow
One road takes you to the temple
The other takes you to the tavern;
Don't lose your way, traveller,
Don't let yourself be duped.

If ever there was a passionate romantic in Hindi cinema, it was Guru Dutt. He was perhaps the only one to create something of a personal cinema within the commercial format, complete with song and dance. He is the one who came nearest to a form fashioned out of drama, story and song, with one complementing rather than interrupting the other. He also combined the most romantic elements of both Urdu–Muslim and Bengali–Hindu culture. Here is a rough translation of one of his most popular songs from the film *Pyaasa* (Thirst, 1957), written by Sahir Ludhianvi:

What will I gain if I win this world,
Of palaces and thrones and crowns,
Of society that is the enemy of man,
Of rich rulers hungry for wealth?

What will I gain if I win this world
Of wounded bodies and thirsty souls,
Of confused eyes and sad hearts?

What will I gain if I win this world,
Where life is but a toy,
Where walking skeletons bow before death,
Where death is cheaper than life?

What will I gain if I win this world,
Where youths loaf around shiftless,
Where young bodies are decked out for sale,
Where love is but a business deal?

What will I gain if I win this world
Where loyalty means nothing,
Where friendship stands for nothing,
Where love counts for nothing?

Oh, this world, destroy it,
Take it away from me, from my sight
It is yours, and you can keep it—
I have no use for it, none any more.

(translated by Mani Mistri and Chidananda Das Gupta)

The lyrics and melodies of today exemplify a withdrawal from the middle-class Urdu-shairi of even the somewhat woolly philosophic level of Guru Dutt in the 1950s; but the song continues to function as a transcendental device, even in films full of nightclubs and street fights. The inveterate didacticism of Indian cinema, both in its high art and pop forms, finds an outlet in the latter's songs. Invariably, they spout facile philosophy, giving vent to the Indian predilection, even among the illiterate, for moralizing and generalizing on every event. The oral convention runs deep within the process of transmission of popular wisdom from one generation to the next, just as the Brahminical tradition is able to retain canonical texts in Sanskrit in pristine form. In popular cinema's survey of contemporary sins and search for ways of returning to tradition, the song holds centre stage, giving it wings to soar above the fights and chases, the melodrama of heroes and villains, the nightclubs and slinky dances, to declare the meaning of life and the nature of duty.

It is because of this transcendental imperative that the cultural level of the song is often strikingly different from that of the rest of the film. The words are skilfully written by mature poets, the melodies composed by talented musicians, often forming an individual, harmonious whole, utterly different from the fragmented variety show of repetitive types and situations that make up the action and dialogue sequences. From the illiterate lumpen level of entertainment, there is a leap into creativity more typical of urban high art. Even if the sentiments expressed are sometimes trite, the songs are often written in felicitous language and perfect syntax, and their eclectic melodies come from folk traditions, the Urdu ghazal, even classical music or Rabindra Sangeet and Western pop music. It is only in the 1980s that one begins to come across a mindless streak, in the songs of Anand Bakshi, Bappi Lahiri and their ilk, that refuses to take off from the low average level of the action and dialogue sequences. They celebrate a new ugliness that has invaded the screen. Music, like other elements of a film, has changed its character with the shift of emphasis from the middle to the working class and other illiterate or semi-literate urban groups since Independence. In the 1930s and the 1940s, film melodies were largely derived from a classical base; the dilution began in the 1950s and by the 1960s, the mixture of all possible sources, with fresh innovations in the blending of disparate elements, was complete.

The manner in which the song is treated reinforces the film's power to ignore the demands of realism. The convention is that there should be no tonal perspective; whether the person singing is far from or near the camera allows no difference in the volume or depth of the sound. Invariably, the voice of the same playback singers emanates from all the characters in film after film. Instead of appearing absurd, the sameness of the voice in different characters seems to provide a comforting sense of security. Whenever a song is played, the projectionist immediately pushes the volume to its loudest. The only concession to verisimilitude is in the difference of singing voices for different characters within the same film.

The song is like divine speech, filling the firmament, and all vacant space on earth. It flows into the pores of the mind, like balm on wounds inflicted by the daily battles of existence. It represents an experience shared by a vast, varied, divided populace in the cinema theatres, in roadside restaurants for the poor, at fairs, festivals, temple yards, weddings and all celebrations. There are no music halls in the cities; traditional folk forms do not satisfy the needs of a changing situation in which people want ways to resolve new conflicts raging within themselves. Music for the common people in urban areas and the rural periphery means, by and large, film music. Some traditional music survives on the streets at night when people may gather around a fire in winter, but this is mainly among rurally oriented migrants, markedly different from the urban lumpen. Film music blares forth everywhere for everyone, including the unwilling ears of those who are used to high art. This imminence of the film song shared by all lifts it way above the bounds of realism required by particular films and gives it an autonomous, transcendental presence in society. It has been said that the predominance of the song dimension has thwarted the growth of more cinematic elements and the development of a cinematic grammar. However, this has been offset to some extent by the sophistication of 'song picturization', a unique feature of Indian cinema that revels in quick cuts and fast movements, slow motion and other special effects. The song steps forward suddenly from the context of the film; the visuals underline and frame the song rather than the opposite. The concept of finding a choreographic action correlative to the music may have been taken from Hollywood musicals, but its development has become peculiarly Indian. This is true despite occasional suggestions of the childish and the aesthetically awkward when judged by absolute standards derived from the grammar of dancing and its formal unity both in classical and folk manifestations.

Film music derives from traditional music in at least one respect. The high-pitched three-octave range of Lata Mangeshkar's or Asha Bhonsle's voice is thrown at the audience in the same way as an itinerant folk singer's in the open spaces of the countryside. It is always on a high enough scale to be heard across streets and buildings and over the noises of the city. Within the theatre itself, it descends to a loud whisper; it is as though it is coming not through powerful if distorted speakers, but directly from a human being with a miraculous pair of lungs. The quality of folk music performed out in the open has been transferred into the enclosed space of the theatre with the reproductive outfall in the city's spaces very similar to music in the countryside.

Folk theatre, such as Jatra in Bengal, Yakshagana in Karnataka, Tamasha in Maharashtra or Nautanki in Uttar Pradesh and so on, has traditionally relied on lung power. The need to be heard raised the scale in a medium that functioned in open spaces for people of all ages and levels of culture. The village teacher or priest could be a sophisticated person who normally spoke in low tones; but when he went to a folk performance he would accept the high pitch and the forces of voice throw. The pressure on the voice, of course, affected the style of acting and promoted the melodramatic technique of declaiming the surfaces of an emotion rather than exploring the motivations that led to it, much as the need to be seen from a distance imposed a breadth of gesture on acting. Thus the conditions of performance dictated its very nature and artistic content. What I am suggesting here is that in theatrical rather than dance forms, the melodramatic element is not due to the heightened gestures and stylization of, say, Kathakali, which has its own imperative of choreography, but at least partly due to the physical circumstances of performance. Hence it is interesting that an essentially folk theatrical style should be transferred to a medium that does not need it since it provides its own amplification of both the aural and the visual dimensions (occasional variations in soft tones provide the exception rather than the rule).

A parallel can be drawn from acting to provide a clue. When Dilip Kumar answered Prithviraj Kapoor's melodramatic declamation (in films like *Mughal-e-Azam*, 1960) in the low tones of normal speech, he took Indian cinema to a new level of realism within the commercial format. Audiences overjoyed by the recognition of familiar instead of mannered speech made Dilip Kumar the new hero, dubbing Prithviraj old fashioned. What this indicates is that, in pre-industrial societies, the audience's concept of verisimilitude changes from a primitive likeness of reality to a closer approximation of it. This is possible primarily through the training the film-maker imparts as his own ability to close in on reality improves. Cinema as a 'scientific' medium then comes into its own. Perhaps this leads us once more to the rural base of what is, at least physically, an urban medium. One must remember here that early Indian cinema derived from the Parsi theatre, which presented a variety show of song, dance and drama in a melodramatic style designed to meet the same needs of an urban audience, alienated from folk drama.

The blending of music, dance and drama in both the classical and folk traditions has led many to the facile conclusion that popular cinema is their legitimate heir. In actual fact, the staging of Sanskrit plays like Bhasa's *Madhyama Vyayoga* or Shudraka's *Mritchchakatika* shows a vastly superior degree of artistic unity in the blending of song, dance and drama than the popular cinema has ever achieved. The same is true of folk performances because they represent a social harmony, whereas popular cinema struggles with alienation from traditional faiths and modes of living. Afflicted by doubts and fears born of the clashes of faith and unable to come to terms with a technological mode of apprehending reality, the popular film emerges in the form of a variety show of disparate elements rather than a unified whole. What gives this form its only significant core is the song. Belonging to a different cultural level from the rest of the film, dismissing the demands of dramatic continuity and defying the inbuilt realism of the medium, the song acquires an autonomous presence rising above the disparateness of the other elements in a film. In some of the playbacks of Kishore Kumar, the singing is free even from the inappropriateness of an outdoor style of rendering (in any case, this has been less of a problem with male singers); it has an element of the private, the inner monologue. The fact that such songs as '*Chingari koi bharke*' or '*Kabhie kabhie*' are popular shows that audiences are prepared to accept a sophistication in music that they are deemed unable to take in the idioms of cinema. The privacy of the song monologue, one must note, is often destroyed by their overloud and over-constant assault on the ears all over urban space. Even so, it is obvious that in songs, this cinema is able to raise the level of audience consciousness; in the rest, it lowers that level. There is a tacit agreement between film-maker and viewer that the song is for transcendence.

The autonomy of the film song is felt inside the theatre as much as outside it. With each song, the attitude of the audience changes instantly. Even the slight suspension of disbelief the narrative demands is suddenly relaxed. During this interlude of philosophic or lyrical comment, the theatregoer can go out for a cigarette or a cup of tea and still hear in the foyer the song he has probably heard many times before. Mothers, so long wrapped up in the story, can turn to the children to see if they need anything. If a feeding bottle or a change of nappies is called for, this is the time, the intermezzo, in which to do it before the story is resumed.

Inescapably, the interruption of narrative by song has an effect on the acting. One must remember here that the song is not the sole interrupter; there are the dances, the fights (directed by the dance or fight director), the clowning and the chases, all of which are played in an exaggerated, larger-than-life style in the operatic sense. The dialogue, like the characters, falls into clear stereotyped progressions, which the audience can normally predict. The actor knows that the lines he speaks are meant to lead up to a climax marked by a song or a dance or a fight. The acting therefore becomes a charade, a little game played between actor and audience, full of flourishes signifying little. These flourishes, and not what the acting expresses, determine the success of the actor. The novelty, appropriateness and the dramatic (as in a dance) effect of the stances and looks and manner are what matter. Expression of meaning is left to the song. The song romanticizes, philosophizes, comments. It is the most 'serious' element in the content of the film. Here is a song that moralizes on the duty of woman:

Man: A woman must be like this
Even if she learns English in sweet Tamil Nadu
Woman: Tell me and I will do as you say
Change me this way and that as you wish.
Man: Here chastity and modesty are the clothes of women
hence woman must be like this
She must not show off her body for public admiration and
She mustn't let her clothes expose her belly
She mustn't paint her lips red.

This can also be read as an ode to regionalism; in sweet Tamil Nadu women are chaste and modest (at least they are expected to be); elsewhere they are, by implication, bad, especially the ones that have learnt English or expose their bellies like northerners.

Songs have an important climactic, orgasmic function as well, Indian cinema being the most erotic in the world behind its puritanical facade. Ever since the kiss was banned by the censors in the late 1930s, Indian cinema has been in search of a sexual climax to replace it. It has never found one. The world's largest film industry is also subject to its strictest censorship. A boy meets a girl, they realize they are meant for each other and rush into an embrace; but what then? The film must back away from the oncoming kiss, usually by sublimating it with a song. Suddenly the heroine will fly from the impending meeting of the lips and start singing while entwining herself round a tree or rolling down a hill slope with the hero in hot pursuit. The onrush of the 'Big Sound' orchestra combining Western and Indian instruments and the loud voice bursting forth is very orgasmic in its sudden release. The constraints of the plot are suddenly removed; avoiding the kiss is no longer a problem, the figure-of-eight walk, the rolling on the grass, the big breast shake, the quick jerk of the hips to the rhythm of music from a hundred-piece orchestra all suddenly, magically, come into their own, climaxing in an intimate orgasmic experience wrapped up in fantasy unique to Indian cinema.

The total ban on the kiss has now been removed; but neither actresses nor audiences favour the lip kiss. When used, it is somewhat perfunctory, puritanical; it remains within the charade, never suggesting the satisfactions of a real, wet kiss exploring the entire body as it were through the mouth—all of which would be too overt for the audience. Driven underground, eroticism therefore becomes compulsive and pervades the entire film. It builds up a subterranean energy in the sequences of love play full of physical proximity and innuendoes that must be allowed to erupt from time to time. As the sexual tension builds up and yet backs away from the actual union, it erupts into song. Thus it takes some of the frustration out of what might be called the recurrent coitus interruptus of Indian cinema.

In traditional rural communities music was, and still is—though to a lesser extent—presented at religious assemblies, fairs and festivals where folk plays are performed occasionally by itinerant players, and folk songs sung. For people as inward looking, emotional, philosophically minded and mortality conscious as Indians, music is necessary in large doses and high frequency. The social system that supported the structure of rural music has eroded with the phasing out of the big landlord who presided over it in the past. Where he still exists in defiance of state policy (of abolishing landlordism and its concomitants), he no longer cares. The state has largely taken over the patronage of the arts in the cities but not in the vast rural areas where 75 per cent of the people live. There is thus a vacuum in art patronage in most of India's 575,000 villages. Besides, the winds of change are ruffling the villagers' traditional lives in even the smallest hamlet. They, too, want to know, and to understand, something of the change taking place in the cities and in the country at large. In this the film song, wafted across the countryside from the cities, helps in some broad and general way.

But Indian cinema, one must repeat, is an urban phenomenon. The country's 13,000-odd cinema theatres are situated overwhelmingly in towns and cities where electricity is available. Villagers go to the cinema only when they visit the nearest town to buy or sell or to pray in a temple, or for some such purpose. In the four southern Indian states, there are some touring cinemas that go to the villages. But the people who live in the towns and cities were themselves villagers not so long ago. The large majority of urban people today, including some of the rich and the educated, came from the village one or two generations earlier. The need for music of these urbanites is met solely by the cinema; only the rich and culturally advanced have the access to, or the inclination for, the high art of concert halls, cassettes and records. Reproductions are expensive, making even folk songs a property of the rich. Folk songs may be heard on the radio, but who wants to hear them, anyway, after escaping from the drudgery of the village into the excitement of the city? It is the interpretation of the new values of city life, the artefacts of science, the wealth of consumer goods, and the complex new relationship of these things within the society revolving around them that is necessary to provide some emotional adjustment to the migrant labourer working alone in the city, the nuclear family broken off from the extended one back in the village, the industrial worker with the ever-pregnant wife, the young student who must be the saviour of his family one day but sees no prospect of employment at the end of his studies. For all these variously frustrated people trying to cope with a relatively new environment, the cinema provides an interpretation of the environment, however crude, as well as an escape from it. Nothing symbolizes either the interpretation or the escape more than the songs. And in the absence of any other forum for popular music, the cinema is its only source. While in many other parts of the world the change in musical taste affects the kind of music that goes into films, here the position is reversed. It is film music which sets the trend and moulds musical tastes.

Hindi cinema would not have had its all-India acceptability, nor popular regional films their own without songs. A wordy drama would tax the non-Hindi audience to the extent of discouraging it; and entirely action-oriented cinema would be unable to explore the issues of tradition and modernity that exercise the minds of most Indians and form an important underlay to the texture of India's popular cinema. No wonder popular films are sold to distributors before they are made—on the strength of the stars and the songs. The bottom would fall out of the present kind of commercial film, very probably, if an alternative, inexpensive source of popular song and dance were to be built up along with visual accompaniment, as in music halls in the West.

4

CINEMA
The Realist Imperative

As the twentieth century draws to a close, cinema too nears a century of its life. The first film show was given by the Lumière brothers in France, and in other countries including India, in 1896.

How cinema was invented has been recounted times without number and need not be repeated here. Look up a book and you will know all about the Thaumotrope and Praxinoscope and Phenakistiscope and innumerable other scopes which led to the cinema as we know it—a celluloid reel going through a projector which casts an image on the screen. The question to ask is why. Why was it invented? What was the need that prompted the arrival of cinema at the turn of the twentieth century? Literature and drama, painting and sculpture, music and dance were all there. Why a new medium?

Part of the answer does lie in the story of the cinema's birth, whose details I have decided to skip. Cinema was invented by scientists. Peter Mark Roget and Michael Faraday discovered the principle of 'persistence of vision' which is the basis of the cinematic illusion. Babbage, a mathematician, and Herschel, an astronomer, invented the Thaumotrope in order to establish the principle that Roget and Faraday had enunciated. Etiénne Jules-Marey was an anatomist dedicated to the study of animal locomotion, Jansen the astronomer was interested in recording the transit of Venus. Eadweard Muybridge was a professional photographer but he had been engaged to study the motions of a racehorse to find out if at any time all four of its legs left the ground. In other words none of the many people who developed the concept and the means of recording movement had any idea of the ulterior use of their findings as art or entertainment, whatever you choose to call it. The fact that technologists like Edison, Dickson, Friese-Green and a host of others turned the discoveries and inventions of scientists into an instrument of show business is not a material part of our present proposition.

The proposition is that we needed the cinema at the time it came. The Industrial Revolution had introduced a whole new set of sights and sounds and their interrelationships which became embedded in the perceptions of technological society. When T.S. Eliot compared the evening spread out against the sky to a patient etherized upon the table or the heart to a ticking meter of a waiting taxi, he expressed a fragment of the network of new relationships that had changed the visible and audible patterns of the urban world. Modern literature has explored these relationships and vastly extended the area of expressiveness of the language of words in our time. Similarly, modern painters delved into the new world of form and analysed the geometry at its base and the nature of the light that brought the form to the human eye.

Impressionism and post-Impressionism were both thoroughly impregnated with the scientific urge to analyse reality and to reassemble the fragments in the many ways of pointillism, cubism, surrealism and the many other art movements. Some of them tried to analyse and capture movement itself, like Duchamps in *Nude Descending a Staircase*, to quote one of the innumerable examples of kinetic art in Western Europe and the Soviet Union immediately after the revolution. Indeed, it can be said that almost all art since then has been informed by a new awareness of movement. When Amrita Sher-Gil's paintings of traditional India celebrate stillness, they do so in contrast to a European sense of movement which may be her point of reference. But I am straying into a territory where I am an interloper and might easily lose my way. The trouble is that cinema too is a visual art and can hardly be discussed without reference to painting.

Of course, the awareness of movement in art goes back much further. Indeed, it can be traced to prehistoric caves on whose walls primeval man strove to capture the animal in motion that he was going to kill. To him painting was not an act but Frazer's imitative magic; he believed that if he could capture the animal in painting, he would be able to do so in real life. It was the movement of the animal that frustrated the hunter's aim, so it was an important element of his perception. Much later, in the murals of Ajanta or Sittanavasal, we see an acute awareness of movement. (I am of course talking here about the physical movement of objects and not about the movements of the beholder's eye guided by the painter, or the implied dynamics in the placement of figures and objects on a canvas.) Similarly the low reliefs of Bharhut and Sanchi suggest complex orchestrations of movement. So what's new about movement in cinema?

Right from the beginning, it seems, there has been a pressure towards realism within art. Primitive man did not think he was not producing a likeness. Perhaps the search for naturalism was restrained in medieval Europe where God was in heaven and all was in order on earth. Everything was clearly deducible from God and there were no questions left. It was Francis Bacon's inductive logic that reversed the process. With the Renaissance, everything was no longer deduced from God; the truth of a general statement was established only by the observation of particular facts that led to it. Hence the new realism, naturalism if you like, in painting and sculpture from the Renaissance on. I read somewhere that Michelangelo would add muscles to actual anatomy in order to stress the physicality, the roundness of the figure. There was a strenuous effort to apprehend the actual existence of material things, including the human body.

In the West, painting set out on a quest of realism, reaching its high water mark in portraiture. But with the invention of photography, the need for the redemption of physical reality through painting eroded fast. Industrial society destroyed the last vestiges of the craft-based village-centred society in which almost all functions had a certain creative character and relations between individuals had a directness and organic integrity. Mass production made factory workers and clerks out of most people, separating the artist from the rest and putting a stock exchange value on his work. A successful artist could now practise his vocation and earn a superior living without bending to the will of God or man. It was no longer necessary for him to be understood by the majority of people, as it was during the days of the Elizabethan theatre or religious music or secular portraiture. The language of painting today enshrines the artist's private vision of the world, and seeks to communicate it to the spectator at a level beyond the reach of words through the organization of lines, masses and colour which have their own evocative powers.

In the Western world, classical music, painting and theatre had thus retired from the service of the masses at various stages during the nineteenth and the early twentieth centuries. By the time of the World War this retirement into a high cerebration minority was already complete, leaving the mass audience in a vacuum to be filled by cinema—the common man's new language in a technological world coming to him out of a machine, in a tin can.

Some five hundred years ago, in *Henry V*, Shakespeare had lamented his inability to show physically the battlefield with its clanging swords and prancing horses.

> O for a Muse of fire, that would ascend
> The brightest heaven of invention . . .
> Can this cockpit hold the vasty fields of France?
> Or may we cram
> Within this wooden o the very casques
> That did affright the air at Agincourt?
> . . .
> Suppose within the girdle of these walls
> Are now confin'd two mighty monarchies,
> Whose high upreared and abutting fronts
> The perilous narrow ocean parts asunder.
>
> Piece out our imperfections with your thoughts;
> into a thousand parts divide one man,
> And make imaginary puissance
> Think, when we talk of horses, that you see them
> printing their proud hoofs i' th' receiving earth,
> for 'tis your thoughts that now must deck our kings
> Carry them here and there, jumping o' er times
> Turning the accomplishment of many years
> Into an hour-glass;

One need not doubt that Shakespeare knew the value of the imagination and its power to call up images. Yet there is a ring of truth in his prayer for 'Muse of Fire, that would ascend/the brightest heaven of invention'. No one with Shakespeare's ability to command an audience would spurn such an invention. Raleigh tells the story of how Shakespeare's producer told him that the plays he wrote were useless: 'Write me a play with bloody murder in it.' So Shakespeare wrote *Hamlet*. It had more than one killing in it; besides it had a ghost, a madwoman, swordfights, incest, and what have you.

Am I saying then that that Muse of Fire is the cinema? Yes, I am. At no time was it more needed than it has been in our time. The approximations to reality represented by the language of words or of painting were not enough for humanity. It wanted to see the real thing. A railway engine steaming away against the sunset, a jet fighter diving through the clouds leaving vapour trails across the sky, a man seen walking along a street from the top floor of a skyscraper, the sound of a horn stuck in a motor car in the middle of the night, the wail of an ambulance speeding through the traffic—these are perceptions pre-industrial man was not familiar with. The very process of perception was speeded up in the industrial world, because there was so much more to perceive. When two high-speed trains pass each other, the flickers of light and the sudden doubling of sound call for a speed of perception that the bullock cart never demanded. In such an environment the apprehension of reality takes on a heightened understanding of material things. The eye and the mind quickly assess a moving object: is it flat or round, square or circular, triangular or hexagonal, what is its line of approach—is it coming at me or will it pass me? These judgements are made rapidly in today's urban world and they are much more exact than that of pre-industrial man.

In turn, as Rudolf Arnheim pointed out as early as 1954, 'The motion picture has broadened not only our knowledge but also our experience of life by making it possible to see motion that is either too fast or too slow for our perception . . . The single-frame camera revealed that all organic behaviour is distinguished by the expressive and meaningful gestures we formerly considered the privilege of man and animal . . . We see the vine searching around, fumbling, reaching and finally taking hold of a suitable support with exactly the kind of motion we considered indicative of anxiety, desire and happy fulfilment.'

Decades ago, when Jamini Roy had not become an icon, his paintings used to cause middle-class people to shake their needs in dismay: How can a woman's neck be so long? How can her eyes extend out of their sockets? I had just bought a painting of his and some of my relatives pelted these questions at me. In despair I asked my servant, an illiterate young man from a village in Medinipur, what he thought of it. He took a long look and said: 'It is exactly like a photograph.' I am quoting this for just one reason—to show the difference between the judgement of verisimilitude between industrial and pre-industrial man. Talking about Jamini Roy, I once asked him what he thought of cinema. He said: It is full of shadows and ghosts.

The degree of realism keeps growing with time. What satisfies one generation or one level of sophistication seems simplistic to another. Take this reaction to India's first fully fictional film, D.G. Phalke's *Harishchandra* in 1913:

> All the movements and expressions of the characters on the screen were so realistic that the spectators felt that those moving characters were also speaking. Harishchandra and Taramati of the screen bring tears to the eyes of the spectators. This would perhaps not happen if one saw them in flesh and blood on the stage. The scenes of the forest, the forest fire, the river, the hangman's house, the hen pecking around—all these are unrivalled . . .
>
> —Letter to the editor, *Kesari*, Pune, 6 May 1913

Looking at *Harishchandra* today, experienced filmgoers are unlikely to react the same way. The search for increased realism seems endless in popular media.

The modern urbanite in industrial countries has been influenced by Freud and Marx even if he has not read them or does not have the capacity to understand them. Their concepts have spread in ripples across society's vast expanse through popular media and formed backgrounds of enhanced awareness of the self in relation to others. Like a child understanding its identity from its image in the mirror, society has developed self-awareness from the myriad reflections in the multiple mirrors that surround urban man. I must hasten to add here that I am not using the term self-awareness in a spiritual sense or judging its quality. It is merely a statement of a material process that has enabled human beings in the modern world to distinguish myth from fact, to penetrate the fallacy of imitative magic to a much larger extent than in the case of pre-industrial man.

An odd illumination of this fact can be found in the history of the mythological film. Until cinema came along, the country of the gods had existed only in the mind's eye, sustained by a network of myths, legends and static visual representations like the oleographs. The passionate loves and hates of the gods had been seen as play (leela) evoked by the devotee in his imagination. When cinema, a product of science, began in earnest in India, with D.G. Phalke's *Harishchandra*, suddenly the gods and the godlike men of mythology came to overwhelmingly visible life: The bereft king Harishchandra giving away his wife and son, or Rama wandering in exile with Sita. The devout in the audience sat barefoot, entranced as if before mobile idols, occasionally making obeisance or offerings. Science had reinforced faith and blurred the distinction between myth and fact. Today, coinciding with the rise of religious fundamentalism, Arun Govil and Deepika, Rama and Sita of the *Ramayana* series on television, are again being besieged for darshan and worshipped by the gullible.

To man's traditional means of expressing his complex underworld of thoughts and dreams, emotions and feelings, the twentieth century brought a crisis. I.A. Richards pointed out how the materialist logical outlook induced by science tended to make people suspicious of the magic of poetry. That suspicion was best met for most people by the creation of poetry out of the palpable—the sight, not the description, of a girl standing at a window, of the wind swaying the casuarinas at the seaside. Cinema tells people less than it asks them to find out for themselves from the fragments of reality shown with documentary conviction. Seeing is believing.

A great deal of poetry has been created in the cinema around the railway train. In a film like Basil Wright and Harry Watt's *Night Mail* (1936) the fusion of this product of science and nature is complete. The sounds and sights of the railway train clattering away through the night and arriving at Edinburgh in the grey dawn, the lives of the postmen waiting in it through the night, yielded film poetry of a high order. Trains have always attracted film-makers far more than writers. Renoir played with trains in *La Bête Humaine* (1938); David Lean's *Brief Encounter* (1945) takes place in a railway station in the background of trains coming and trains going; the first Russian sound film, Nikolai Ekk's *Road to Life* (1931), makes marvellous use of trains. Through a century of their use, trains have been absorbed into our new consciousness of nature. We are no longer aware of the fact that they are man-made products of science and the landscape through which they wend their way is pure nature; because in our daily lives, within our familiar environment they represent speed, 'conquest of nature'. They remind us of the fact that we no longer need to be afraid of nature. In Mark Donskoy's *The Rainbow* (1944), the end of a long, weary, wintry battle with the Germans is heralded by the sound of approaching Russian aircraft. It is a musical sound, like the drone of a bee, which slowly approaches and fills the sky, and our ears with a message of hope.

The extent to which an Eliot or a Joyce, a Picasso or a Stravinsky can perform this interpretative function is limited, as far as the majority of people are concerned, by their demand for a near-impossible degree of intellectual development for the common man who therefore began to need a medium of greater realism in the visual arts, continuing a trend which had existed from the very beginning of primitive painting. At the same time, the age of the radio and the telegraph, the aeroplane and the photograph, the gramophone and the telephone and the tape recorder increasingly called for an audio-visual civilization to supplement if not supplant the tyranny of the older 'print civilization'. Even among the educated young, impatience with the academic world of slow and indirect perception is marked. It is said that much of the campus unrest in industrially developed countries stems from the tyranny of the printed word in an age which acquires a good part of its education from audio-visual sources. Many young people in sophisticated environments revolt against the over-explicitness of much of the verbal communication they come across and prefer the more direct and less interpreted, less intellectualized non-verbal response which audio-visual representation of reality makes possible. The contemplation of a photograph may be more attractive to a sensitive intellectual. A film with few words and much action may be preferable to a factory worker, or to both, sometimes for different reasons.

Technological development generates popular pressures not only towards this audio-visual civilization but also towards a synthesis and condensation of the older arts—literature, painting, sculpture, music and dancing—into a new, more quickly assimilable medium. Since such a medium must be designed primarily for those who do not have the intellectual ability, the training of sensibility, or the time and patience for enjoying the older arts, it is forced to seek greater and greater approximation to the recognizable surface of reality. The camera records what is before it. In the cinema, at least, a horse must look like a horse, a girl like a girl. Besides, they move; therefore they are as good as living things. You don't have to think. Just watch—and listen.

Of course, by the time sound arrived on the scene, cinema had not only fashioned its language but thrown up a number of masterpieces which still remain highly effective when seen today. The American cinema had established its basic genres of comedy and the western; post-revolutionary Russia had produced classics of purposeful cinema; Germany had produced some grandeur in films of originality and imagination. In the 1920s France already had an avant-garde film movement. By 1928, there were twelve art cinema houses in Paris, serious film magazines were analysing international cinema and its relationship with the other arts; classic works of film criticism had appeared.

Yet, in its essence, cinema remained a medium for the masses. Whether it was American comedy or western, German macabre, or Russian revolutionary zeal, the films were made for the masses and the masses went to see them. If the pressures were financial in the United States, they were political in the USSR. If the artists were fighting the financiers to express themselves, they were mostly doing so in the manner in which great portrait painters painted a likeness which pleased their client and yet said a great deal of their own in the language of painting. In the grand Shakespearean manner, art and the private vision were hidden behind something the audience needed or was at least prepared to see. Artists seized hold of the medium as much as the businessmen did; they passed off art as entertainment while the moneybags passed off entertainment as art. Sometimes the conflict surfaced. Erich von Stroheim could hardly make a film without the studio hacking it to a third of its length; Sergei Eisenstein suffered at the hands of the state, yet, by and large, cinema managed to maintain an uneasy peace between the artist and the financier.

Silent Cinema: Stylization

The mass media's search for a greater approximation to physical reality began with the silent cinema; but the lack of sound forced it to stylize itself either into slapstick comedy, seen at its best in America in the cinema of Charlie Chaplin and Buster Keaton, or into the intellectual abstractions of the post-revolutionary Russian silent cinema, and the grand gestures of the silent cinema of Germany between the two wars. In spite of the blaring of the orchestra, the ingenuity of the projectionist in creating effect sounds (iron sheets for thunderstorms and coconut shells for galloping horses) and the audience's practice in lip-reading, the absence of the voice when the lips moved remained a severe limitation on realism. Today's sound film often brings out the most intimate moments through very little dialogue (Michelangelo Antonioni, Satyajit Ray) but its depth is created by the very act of holding dialogue back. The use of silence in a sound film is a qualitatively different proposition from silence (despite music and effect added in the theatre) in the silent film. The net result in the mature sound film is a more realistic unfolding of the narrative, the absorption of the audience into an illusion which it enters at the beginning of the film and disengages from only at the end. Technical devices in the sound film had to change, the grand manner had to come down to earth, the editing had to be more skilful and the art less obvious in order that the audience should not become conscious of the camera or of other behind-the-scenes techniques which would break the spell of the illusion.

The closer cinema came to the representation of surface reality, the more its apprehension became like the apprehension of life itself. To quote Michael Rohmer, 'All of us bring to every situation, whether it is a business meeting or a love affair, a social and psychological awareness which helps us to understand complex motivations and relationships. This kind of perception, much of it non-verbal and based on insignificant clues, is not limited to the educated or the gifted. We all depend on it for our understanding of other people and have become extremely proficient in the interpretation of subtle signs—a shading in the voice, an averted glance. This nuanced awareness however is not easily called upon by the arts, for it is predicated upon a far more immediate and total experience than can be provided by literature and the theatre with their dependence on the word, or by the visual arts with their dependence on the image. *Only film renders experience with enough immediacy and totality to call into play the perpetual processes we employ in life itself.*' (Italics mine.)

It is obvious here that we are talking about the sound film in which the verbal and the non-verbal interpenetrate to offer a totality of immediate experience. Hence the major part of cinema today is devoted to the creation of an illusion of reality, whether its language is used to create a spectacle of art, poetry or prose, 'entertainment' or 'education' or any other compartments in which we may seek to divide film-making. (It is only very recently, after the advent of television, that a small group of film-makers whose work is seen only by cineastes have sought to create a new cinema of awareness in which the illusion of reality is deliberately broken and the audience is made to realize that it is watching a film.)

In the industrially developed countries, where cinema was born and bred, narrative cinema of the naturalistic surface and a dramatic–novelistic structure was thus perfected. Throughout this period, the more the cinema sought to serve the common man's requirement by creating simple formulae of entertainment, and reflected the surfaces of reality, the more the artists in it found ways of expressing the reality beneath the surface, rather like the portrait painters who had to produce a likeness but managed to express something of themselves underneath the verisimilitude.

In this the box office has served as a useful melting pot, a guarantee of the cinema's universality, a terrifying giant with whom the musclemen and the artists had to come to some kind of understanding, finding some way of communication with the vast mass audience raising, in Graham Greene's words, its 'Wembley roar'. The minority cinema, with its festivals, institutes and academies, film clubs and learned periodicals, has been able to exist only as the apex of a vast triangle, the cream at the top that cannot exist without the mass below. No cine club, however esoteric, can completely reject the commercial cinema for then the baby gets thrown out with the bathwater. The vulgar and lusty aspects of cinema have been as vital to it as the most refined and one has not only had to put up with the other but also needed it in order to find its own identity.

With the rise of television, the polarization between the artist and the mass audience sharpened, creating the cinema of personal vision which becomes viable mostly on an international plane on which all intellectuals and cineastes come together in a shrinking world. The artist in the cinema was no longer hiding behind entertainment but asking for acceptance in terms of art. This coincided with the rise of television and the gradual decline of the cinema, a sharp fall in the number of cinema theatres and films produced practically all over the industrial world except lately in the United States. Western cinema is certainly not dying, it is possibly only carrying out Jean Renoir's dictum that 'Television will take over all rubbish from the cinema and leave it pure'. Certainly television carries an even greater sense of immediacy in a high-speed world than cinema.

The situation in India is sharply different from this world picture in important ways.

The transplantation of a technological art to a predominantly agricultural society created massive problems of absorption and led to distortions in form, preventing the narrative cinema from emerging within the mass entertainment format. The commercial cinema in India has, by and large, acquired the character of a variety performance. It has developed unique characteristics unknown to the industrially advanced countries;

even its vocabulary is often not understood abroad. A good part of the minority cinema which is sponsored by government agencies is struggling to get the narrative cinema form accepted by a wide enough audience to make its production viable. Only *Salaam Bombay* (1988), made by an expatriate Indian with foreign technicians, has succeeded in doing so in the all-India Hindi film; that it has done so with a fully narrative form, using highly realistic means unembellished by song and dance interludes may point to the future direction of popular cinema in India. If it does, our cinema may follow the same process as in Western countries, for the same reason, namely, the industrialization of the country.

5

WOMAN, NON-VIOLENCE AND INDIAN CINEMA

In the Valmiki Ramayana, Sita, eternal model of the submissive Hindu wife, says something about non-violence that should become a beacon light to the postmodernist world. When they are in exile in the forest, she objects to Rama's going about wearing arms. Why? What's wrong? asks Rama. Sita's reply: The fact that you wear arms will make you violent. The rakshasas have not done us any harm; if you kill them without cause, it will not reflect credit upon you. If you and your brother roam around here with bow and arrow, you might end up doing just that. Such things are known to have happened in olden times. Because of my love and regard for you, I want to *teach* you this lesson of history.

When I first read these lines of Valmiki, I was stunned. Sita seems to be the first known person in history to understand the meaning of the words 'have gun, will kill'. It is a lesson humanity has yet to learn. Because you have the means to kill, you will become violent. The means create the end. Could a woman be more of a catalyst for non-violence than the Valmiki Sita we encounter here? This episode, as far as I can remember, does not occur in later Ramayanas—Kamban's, Tulsidas's, or Krittibasa's. Ramanand Sagar's television serial makes no mention of it either. All of them take away Sita's intelligence and reduce her to an inert shadow of her husband, true to the medieval ideal still valid for the major part of the country's non-tribal population in the plains, especially among the middle classes. As an assertion of women's intelligence, Sita's pronouncement in the Valmiki episode I have quoted is unique.

If you agree with me that Sita's statement here is unique in its intelligence, then the question arises, why? Why is it so rarely that we come across evidence of independent thinking in women in our late ancient and medieval literature? We know that women rishis like Viswavara, Apala,

Ghosa and Indrani composed some of the *suktas* of the *Rig Veda* (Sukta numbers 5/28, 8/91, 10/145, etc.). In the early Vedic period women priests participated in yagnas, wore the sacred thread themselves and performed the sacred thread ceremony for others, had the right to marry by their own choice, and to remarry. By the time of the *Manu Samhita* (circa second century AD), she was not allowed to recite the Vedas (see Manu 9.18), nor to take part in sacrifice (Manu 4.205–6 and 11.36–7), and she had to be dependent on man in all stages of her life (Manu 5.148 and 9.3 in which he says *na stree swatantryam arhati* or woman is not fit to be independent). To Manu, killing a woman was a petty crime. He also decreed early marriage for girls: thirty-year-old men should marry twelve-year-old girls. In other words, woman had lost all her rights of the Vedic period by the beginning of the Christian era. Where does one position Sita in this sequence of things? It is impossible to say, because our epics were expanded, rewritten and riddled with interpolations for several hundred years according to what was acceptable to later ages. All one can presume is that a few passages, like the one I have quoted above, escaped the censors.

Even in Buddhism, one of the least oppressive faiths ever, woman was denigrated. The Buddha himself told Ananda, who persuaded him to open an order for women, that women are stupid, full of passion, envious; one should not even speak to them. And if they should speak to a man, 'Keep awake, Ananda!'

It was after the completion of the patriarchal revolution that the idealization of women in the scriptures and in literature as wife and mother began. Manu wants women to be honoured; Kalidasa's women are beautiful, delicate, but have no will of their own. They are not lovers, but beloveds. Idealization sanitizes them, deprives them of their own sex drive and makes them into objects manipulated by man.

In this patriarchalization, which in most countries took place at the dawn of the Iron Age, India was in good company. For instance, it happened with Zoroaster in Persia. Scholars have noted that before the arrival of the Aryans, the original inhabitants of Iran had been matrilineally organized and that this was reversed by Zoroaster, who achieved a complete overthrow of the cyclical fertility cults associated with seasonal changes paralleling the female reproductive process. In Zoroastrianism, the woman is seen as an ally of Ahriman, the 'Demon Whore'; although she had been originally created for Ormazd or God as the upholder of the good, she later fled to his enemy. From her satanic embrace of Ahriman sprang menstruation, which Persian men of the time, like many others, considered a defilement.

An originally female orientation was evident also among the Hebrews who were strongly influenced by the Persians. Polyandry was rampant among both the Hebrews and Persians before the patriarchal revolution began, even though the position of the woman was not as formidable as in Egypt, where the wife was often the head of the family or in Babylon, where she could acquire property, take legal action, sign contracts and hold a share in her husband's estate. The worship of the Goddess in polytheistic fashion was the prevailing religion.

In early Christianity we find a resurgence of the female. As St Mark says, the risen Christ appeared first before Mary Magdalene; in Matthew, she is the one who keeps watch at the Crucifixion, helps to bury Jesus and later returns to the tomb, where an angel tells her that Christ has risen. Earlier she had anointed him, washed his feet in her tears while he was eating, much to the disgust of the Pharisee who considered it defilement. Indeed, the suggestion of a love relationship between Christ and Mary Magdalene was celebrated by the Gnostics in the second century. But this female-friendly attitude of Christianity was quickly removed by St Paul, St Augustine and St Jerome. Paul asked women to cover their heads in church as a token of their inferiority to men; Augustine hated the idea of sexual union as the means of reproduction; Jerome was outraged by the very thought of menstruation which he thought was an evil thing. The Church eventually wiped out the women priests common among the Cathars in the south of France, killed off the only woman pope ever, Pope Joan, expunged the records of her two years as the head of the Vatican and unleashed the Inquisition to eradicate knowledge among women. A knowledgeable woman was a witch.

The patriarchal revolution came to the Arabs nearly a thousand years after other civilizations. Before it, in many parts of Arabia, matrilineality, polyandry, polytheistic worship of female deities was the order of the day. Prophet Muhammad would not marry a woman of the Ansar clan because among them women dominated the men. His father, Abdalla, used to visit his mother at her parents' home after marriage in what is called an uxorilocal marriage. All traces of such matrilineal structures disappeared completely within a century of the Prophet. Indeed, it has been remarked that one reason for the rapid propagation of Islam was the appeal that the downgrading of women's power in society held for the concourses of men. The time, it would seem, was ripe for the patriarchal revolution at the time the Prophet appeared.

II

All this is very well, you might say, but what does it have to do with cinema and with women today? Is non-violence relevant today at all? I do not know; I can only share some thoughts with you on a subject that haunts all of us: violence.

The escalation of violence to the point where the perpetrator of violence is himself destroyed by the force he unleashes compels us to think of its opposite: that is, non-violence. No matter how difficult non-violence may be to achieve, we have to consider it. In order to do so today, we have to sail into virtually uncharted seas, for reasons I will go into later.

It would be true to say that if Mahatma Gandhi had not appeared, the West, the inventor of the atomic bomb, the ultimate weapon of violence, would have had to invent him. What the Mahatma had to say acquired overwhelming importance after Hiroshima and Nagasaki and the invention of even more lethal weapons, leading to the ever-increasing possibility of the destruction of the planet we inhabit. The destroyer becomes one with the destroyed. The heat that violence radiates surrounds us, begins to scald our daily lives, makes life unsustainable. How to switch off the heat becomes the prime question.

We can no longer turn away from the fact that violence on the cinema screen is overflowing on to real life. Those who live by the gun are fated to die by it. It is idle to pretend today that violence in reality has nothing to do with the violence we are showing more and more on the screen.

One is clearly the consequence of the other. Violence in society fathers violence on the screen; the illusion then inflates the violence in reality. The cycle repeats itself in a constantly expanding spiral until the whole thing bursts and takes us all with it.

Today it has become almost impossible to think of a popular film without violence. Dealing with a medium that costs a lot of money, we become its slaves; economy of scale dictates that one film should be seen by all kinds of people, that it should not be necessary to build small holes for small pigeons and big ones for big pigeons as Newton is reputed to have done. Hence the search for the lowest common denominators acceptable to all. The star system which we borrowed from Hollywood in its heyday of studio production has burgeoned in about fifty years of 'independent' production to an impossible size, demanding quantums of money that a country one-third of whose population lives below the poverty line can ill afford. To go against the grain of what is considered 'safe' for the box office is pretty much impossible.

The low-budget film may be able to challenge the stereotypes of the audience but the big commercial film must confirm them in order to play safe. Studios at one time could try out a variety of things at the same time and get away with it by making a profit on some and losing on others; in one-time throws of the dice that is an impossible thought.

III

But is it relevant to talk about non-violence today? And what do women have to do with violence or non-violence?

Traditionally, in India, the woman has been associated with non-violence and passivity. The perception has been: man is active, aggressive; woman, non-violent, nurturing, soft, yielding, patient, capable of bearing pain to bring forth life. Religions enforced this patriarchal view and made it a part of woman's own creed of non-violence. Yet it is from this traditional view that Mahatma Gandhi created the idea of non-violence as a weapon; what would be normally called 'effeminacy', he elevated into a form of strength. In the conflict with the British ruler, this strategy worked to perfection; by altering the terms of the conflict, by positing passive femininity against manly aggression, by turning the other cheek in Christian fashion, he struck at the roots of the double dilemma of the British in their aggression upon unarmed people by a supposedly Christian nation and in their self-contradictory principle of democracy at home, imperialism abroad. Ashis Nandy presented this elucidation to us in an almost revelatory fashion in his famous essay on Nathuram Godse, Gandhi's assassin. Nathuram was called by that name because he was a boy brought up as a girl to ward off the evil eye. He wore a *nath* in his nose and was dressed in female clothes till the age of fifteen, when he was liberated from the prison of femininity into his manhood. This made him a violent enemy of the effeminate. In his speech at the trial he praised Gandhi on many counts but said that he had to kill the man because he could not forgive him his effeminacy.

Here, let me mention a film that reflects the Gandhian method in cinema as early as 1937. V. Shantaram's *Duniya Na Maane* is an astonishing example of non-violent non-cooperation or passive resistance, defying the norms of society. As we know, his Nirmala, married off for money to a man old enough to be her father, refuses to consummate her marriage and survives every trick, every blandishment and punishment. In this enterprise, she is aided by her husband's daughter Sushila, who is a social worker. After a long and dramatic struggle over all this, her husband has a change of heart and kills himself, asking her to marry a man more suitable. There is a direct reflection here of the contemporary Gandhian concept of non-violent resistance.

Rabindranath Tagore had many differences with Gandhi but in non-violence they were one. In his earlier years Tagore did write some narrative verses which included tales of military prowess, but the totality of his work radiates the spirit of non-violence not only towards man but animals as well. Like Gandhi he realized that the imperatives of the nation state called for unnecessary conflicts in order to predominate over others and, for that reason among others, rejected the notion of nationalism. Only on a world scale could non-violence overcome the aggressiveness of the nation state. Of course, the world has not achieved that condition but it has probably realized the truth of this idea more than ever before in human history. One can say that it was the peak of violence reached in Hiroshima and Nagasaki that brought forth the United Nations and its manifold worldwide operations affecting multiple dimensions of national life. No matter how far from complete and how fraught with intractable problems of hegemonism they may be, they still represent a condition never before achieved in the world as a whole. We may find many faults with UNHCR but at least it exists and a few things on a supranational scale do get done. No country is quite as free to oppress its own citizens as it was before. At least whatever it does has to be under the glare of worldwide publicity and that itself is a deterrent. It is already evident that the rejection of nationalism by Gandhi and Tagore and others was not entirely in vain, even though the full potential of that idea is as yet very far from being realized.

IV

The Tagorean world view deeply affected succeeding generations of writers, artists and thinkers particularly in Bengal. Among those who inherited that world view was Satyajit Ray and a number of those who came in his wake. The heights of cinema were at last integrated fully into the mainstream of advanced literature and the arts. At one stage in Bengal, cinema seemed to be ahead of all the arts in the projection of the most introspective levels of thought and feeling. Among the subjects it embraced in no uncertain manner was the condition of women.

But the Gandhian view was essentially one-sided and incomplete; woman as the embodiment of non-violence was predicated upon sexual passivity. Like St Augustine (and St Paul before him), Mahatma Gandhi could not bear the thought of sexual union as an act of pleasure which enabled the reproduction of the species or the ugly birth of man from the womb of woman in a welter of blood and grime and amniotic fluid. He saw women as the passive receivers of lustful male sexual aggression. The only light in the darkness of sex is the passivity of women. To quote his own words: 'Ahimsa means infinite love, which again means infinite capacity for suffering. Who but woman, the mother of man, shows this capacity in the largest measure?'

Even in Tagore, acceptance of the sexual expressiveness of the woman was somewhat muted. He trod that ground in rather gingerly fashion, unsure of himself, except when dealing with classical myths as in the glorious poem on Urvasi which, as it were, laments the loss of her bold and unashamed nakedness with the end of classical times. He makes tentative forays in a character like Ela in *Char Adhyay* in a social atmosphere far from ready for her. As a result, many of his bold and dissident women acquire an arguably more symbolic than immediate character, as in Nandini in *Rakta Karabi*.

In this context it is interesting to discern the tonal differences in the treatment of the passive and expressive aspects of the sexuality of women in the films of Satyajit Ray. Take the case of the Apu trilogy. Since the story is obviously placed somewhere in the late nineteenth or early twentieth century, the natural dress for Sarbajaya would have been a sari without a petticoat or blouse. The petticoat, being worn under the sari, would have made less of a visual difference but that blouse does, as it was introduced to the Bengali woman by Gnanadanandini Devi, wife of Satyendranath Tagore, Rabindranath's eldest brother, around 1890. It took decades for the custom to spread through urban society. What Sarbajaya wears is in Bengal a chemise (French word for shirt), a loose garment covering her from the shoulder to the feet, highly improbable in rural Bengal of the period.

It should be noted that there was in fact a socio-religious injunction among Bengali Hindus against the wearing of stitched clothes, to which an exception had been made for men who served the government in any way or were in business or belonged to the zamindar class. The probable reason for this prohibition could be the fact that according to tradition (and the majority of historians) the 'Aryans' wore unstitched silk clothes. To this day Hindus are enjoined to wear unstitched silk clothing at all religious ceremonies. Cotton, although traditionally associated with the 'non-Aryan', was allowed for daily use perhaps because silk was too expensive. Especially among Brahmins, stitched clothing was rarely worn. As a Brahmin wife, it would have been improper for Sarbajaya to be in anything other than a sari, and a wrapper for the torso. It is interesting to ask why Ray, who was quite meticulous about the accuracy of such period detail, chose to dress Sarbajaya in clothing that belonged to a later period.

In *Pather Panchali* and the early part of *Aparajito*, Sarbajaya is still an attractive young woman. But in his anxiety to depict her as only the mother, Ray denies her the sexuality natural to her age and circumstance as a married woman. A bare back and bare shoulders and arms would emphasize not her maternal presence but her femininity and sexual presence. She does her wifely duties towards Harihar but there is never the faintest suggestion that the two have a marital life in physical terms. It can of course be argued that the pressures on the couple are so heavy that suggestions of sexuality would be irrelevant and in fact disturbing. Yet one is obliged to note the total absence of even an intimate look exchanged between husband and wife even at a happy moment of their lives such as when Harihar brings news that he might get a job. Indeed, one might say that Ray makes their sexuality even more improbable by inventing Harihar's physical unattractiveness.

Similarly in *Apur Sansar*, Aparna must be seen as the innocent young girl. The warmth of her sexual life we are allowed to deduce, but to show her arms and back bare would bring out her sexuality too stridently for Ray's taste. She is to him an embodiment of the mythical Aparna, Shiva's wife, whose death would later find her forlorn husband wandering in the forest like Shiva himself. She is an idea manifested in a temporal and spatial context. Stressing her flesh-and-blood presence would take away from the mythicality, her embodiment as the traditional wife with whom her husband would fall in love after marriage. It would make her too much of an individual, appropriate her excessively into a particular time and space and destroy her status as an ideal being, a type embodying the entire history of the ideal feminine in the context of a race and a civilization. We have to look further afield to discuss the secret of Ray's attitude which so far conforms to the Gandhian.

With the mother in *Pikoo*, we come to Ray's coarsest image of the sexually active woman. For one whose compassion for the human being had made it impossible for him to portray a villain except towards the end of his career in *Ghare Baire*, Ray's condemnation of her sexuality is so outright, so Gandhian and Augustinian as to deny her all humanity. Being outside the law, her relationship with her lover is necessarily ugly; her concern for her son is almost a contradiction in terms. She is, as it were, a sex machine; no tenderness, no emotionality is allowed in the relationship. As in *Ghare Baire*, the kisses are like two birds with long beaks pecking at each other. In *Pikoo*, the husband too is not affected by his wife's 'betrayal'; it is merely a fact that condemns her and justifies his total disregard of her. If the film had not reached great depth in the poignancy of the relationship between old age and childhood, *Pikoo* would have been a rather disagreeable product. One must remember here, however, that the film is not primarily about illicit love; it is about childhood, which Ray understood, as always, with uncommon acuteness.

A surprising depth of understanding of sexuality manifested itself in *Asani Sanket* (1973). The women come together in a secret comradeship which forms perhaps the most remarkable aspect of the film. The blood of the rapist colours the stream flowing through the woods and seals a secret bond among the women. Not a word of the incident is ever uttered; nor of Chhutki's surrender to an ugly labourer from the city for a handful of rice. As she declares that she would rather do that than go hungry, there is a subtle hint in her body language that the hunger is not exclusively for food. Ananga, the Brahmin priest's preciously beautiful wife, has a handsome husband and exudes physical satisfaction; yet she wordlessly understands Chhutki's need for fulfilment. This aspect of the film is not essential to the narrative; it is an offshoot that seems to have grown on its own, taking Ray closest to a complex perception of sexuality without condemnation. I am not entering into a discussion of the sexual peccadilloes of the restless wives in *Shatranj Ke Khiladi* (1977) partly because the episodes are treated as farce to emphasize the impotence of their men and partly because it would take us too far afield from the subject of non-violence. In Ray's early films, the woman is asexual, sanitized and idealized.

In Ghatak, who is otherwise fairly puritanical, the film I find most interesting is *Titas Ekti Nadir Naam* (1973) where there is a strong, triumphant assertion of female sexuality. His earlier films seem more concerned with woman as the focus of human suffering, in the Gandhian passive mode which dominates many of the films of the early post-Tagore period.

V

Fortunately, as Tagore himself recognized in his classical poems, Indian tradition did not confine itself to the one-sided, Gandhian view of women. Nandalal Bose was shocked when Gandhi called for the destruction of the Bandhakama figures, or the explicit Mithuna sculptures in Indian art. They belong to a strand in Indian classical tradition of bold affirmation of woman's sexuality. In the Mahabharata, Bhishma, lying on his bed of arrows, answers a question on who enjoys sexual union more, man or woman. He has no hesitation in giving an un-Gandhian answer: woman. But then the Mahabharata takes, unlike almost any other ancient text, a realistic, not an idealized view of life. Irrawaty Karve has pointed out how Kalidasa, for instance, idealizes the story of Dushyanta and Shakuntala through the usual device of curses and boons to make it into one of all sweetness and glory; the Mahabharata exposes the greed and nonchalance of both. Dushyanta has had his fling with the girl in the forest and does not want to pay for it; Shakuntala wants to extract her due and wins—her son becomes King Bharata after whom our country is named. Her bold figure stands at the fountainhead of our history.

As we know, the glories of sexual union are celebrated in temples like Konarka. The Sun God, the giver of life, is the fecund father of the variety of living beings that proliferate on the earth. There are sculptures in temples of Orissa and elsewhere that clearly depict woman's pleasure in sex in every possible position and manner. These sculpted women hold their heads high and thrust their naked breasts out against the sky. They are not coy maidens archly eyeing their lovers. The entranced nobility and joy of life carved in the faces of the Mithuna figures in Konarka, give the lie to cowardly theories about the need to survey sin before entering God's abode, theories hatched to camouflage and explain away the joy in sex which later generations grew ashamed of under the influence of West

Asian Zoroastrian-Judeo-Christian-Islamic religions. Gandhi himself was a prime victim of this influence.

There is no question about it that from Bharhut and Amaravati in the second century BC to Vijayanagar in the fifteenth century AD, in miniature paintings of later eras, and some folk paintings of almost contemporary times, the female form is treated with complete candour and with respect. There is absolutely no sense of guilt to be traced anywhere. The painters and sculptors were invariably men. Some commentators might see in this an element of male self-fulfilment; but this would be an error because if society were censorious about it, the artists could not have indulged their own whims to the extent they did. Men, women and children of all ages were and are, to this day, constantly exposed to the temple exteriors. Also, artists have displayed in olden times as well as our own, a certain androgyny, an *ardhanarishwara* ability to understand and express both male and female feelings in their work. We see it even in cinema today; film-makers concerned with art do not make sex objects of women, it is the money-at-all-costs commercial cinema which does. Parallel cinema has displayed a great deal of interest in the true condition of women, irrespective of whether the film-maker is a man or a woman. It is also possible to conclude that over the ages the artist has not traditionally disapproved of sexual expressiveness on the part of women a la Gandhi; that the Gandhian mindset is in fact an imported attitude, markedly different from the traditional Indian as expressed in art and as a reflection of social attitudes of the times.

VI

If we agree that non-violence is important to the world today, we have to face up to the question: Is the practice of non-violence dependent upon the passivity of the woman or is it compatible with the acceptance of sexual expressiveness on her part? How has this so far been expressed in cinema?

Let us look at a classic example of aggressive womanhood in Master Vinayak's *Brahmachari*, made in the same year as *Duniya Na Maane*. The film jokes about celibacy, makes fun of both Hanuman and Gandhi; its heroine relentlessly chases the man she wants and wins him in the end—

all of this without causing any harm to society. A film like it has hardly ever been made again. In fact between the two, Shantaram's film and Master Vinayak's, they celebrate two sets of feminine behaviour, both perfectly valid, both non-violent.

Some of the films of Shyam Benegal are interesting for a discussion of non-violence with and without sexuality. Two such films feature Smita Patil and give me an opportunity to salute her memory, her talent and her extraordinary screen presence. In *Manthan*, she wordlessly, delicately and unknowingly suggests a sexual projection towards Dr Rao (Girish Karnad), the man from the city, who is building the milk cooperative. This creates tension between the educated, city-bred do-gooder and the village milkmaid, two categories of people who seem to want to know each other in every sense, and spells danger to her idle but hefty husband. In *Bhumika*, Smita, with all her mercurial flow and her turbulent search, in the midst of all the pressures that buffet her restless life, has an overt sexuality without becoming a sex object herself. This to me, or rather to my memory of the film which I have not seen for a long time, is a remarkable aspect that gives it life, tension, drama. I remember it as perhaps the first celebration of female sexuality in Indian cinema. Yet both *Manthan* and *Bhumika* stay within the area of catalytic non-violence.

Mrinal Sen's *Ek Din Pratidin* (1979) seems to me a seminal film in showing up the refusal to recognize the identity of woman and her right to sexuality. When the working girl returns home very late one night, her family, her mother and her neighbours all assume one thing. Only her sister rises to a spirited defence of her in a magnificent piece of writing, mounting and acting. The working girl is totally non-violent; the violence is directed by society towards her.

Ketan Mehta's *Maya Memsahib* (1993) is a sort of celebration of the modern Indian woman but her sexuality is not defined in social terms and tends to come through as slightly arbitrary. His earlier *Mirch Masala* (1985) has more of a ring of truth to it and a focus on woman's refusal to surrender to sexual subjugation.

Many of the films by women concentrate on woman's traditional role of passive suffering in a man's dominion. Among those that do not there is Deepa Mehta's path-breaking *Fire* (1996), a subtly articulated defence of female homosexuality as an outcome of male maltreatment. It is perhaps an Indian trait that makes her seek justification for the lesbian relationship, unlike in the West, where it seems to be flaunted with an unnecessary aggressiveness which only puts a question mark on itself.

However, I have no interest in cataloguing films about women made by men or women. What concerns me more is the un-Gandhian idea that if we recognize sexuality in woman we do not necessarily nullify her nurturing role as a catalyst of non-violence. One of the things that struck me anew as I was watching Pasolini's *Oedipus Rex* (1967) for the fifth or sixth time is that the love of a woman for her man is not qualitatively as different from her love for her son as is normally supposed. It is a matter of a shift of a few degrees. In a very fundamental sense, she is the mother of both her son and her husband. The organs of sexual love are also the organs of birth and nurture. In all sexual and birth relationships there is an indeterminate mix of affection and desire whose precise nature we will probably never know but which is recognized very subtly in the Indian concept of androgyny in Shiva as *ardhanarishwara*, half-woman, half-man, representing the continuous spectrum from the male to the female. Deep within tribal societies there is an awareness of this too. The word for God in the Khasi language in Meghalaya translates into English as She-He. 'And then She-He said . . .'

VII

How does one define, or classify, violence in cinema? With so much violence in life it cannot be decreed that there should be none on the screen. And in fact there is not and cannot be any such decree. Indeed, the extent of violence sanctioned by the censors shows that they themselves live in fear of it. Besides, banning violence today would be tantamount to closing down cinema as an institution. It is no use complaining that the commercial cinema is violent, why can't it be non-violent like the 'art' film? It is the commercial film that keeps the institution of cinema going. If there were no popular cinema, art films would not be made for there would be no cameras, studios or laboratories for them. There always was and will be a pop cinema. If this pop cinema cannot do without violence, then there will be violence. However, the level of violence has been escalating; people must have more and more of it all the time so that they are not bored by it. It is now overflowing into reality for all to see, hear, and for many to die of. Cinema is becoming a weapon of destruction both inside and outside the screen. When the scale of violence outside the screen begins to match what is on the screen, cinema might become a weapon of mass destruction. When that happens, it will become self-defeating, self-destructive, and there may have to be a recoil from it. Non-violence will then be not merely a laudable idea but a necessity. It is like the growth of the cities into festering wounds. The next century might recoil from the concept of the city itself; the car carrying a single individual as an extension of his foot and a boost to his ego may become an utter nuisance with nowhere to dump it. The city itself may have to disappear, being no longer necessary in an age of instant communication. The atomic bomb, as we know, is not a recoilless weapon; indeed, its recoil is almost as bad as the damage it visits upon its target.

It is relatively easy to specify two kinds of violence in cinema. There is the one that raises the adrenalin level in you and urges you to kill. This is the urge that is most manipulated. Your hero gets beating after beating and then one day he avenges himself upon his tormentors. You are then like putty in the hands of the director, like the spectator in the boxing ring screaming: Kill him! kill him! You are helpless; you cannot distance yourself from the violence but must become a participant in it, excited by the heightened sensation of hatred, of vicarious pleasure. You come out of the cinema filled with the macho urge to hurt someone. This is the screen violence that overflows on to reality, poisoning mind and body systems. Then there is the other kind, as seen in *Mother India* (1957) where the mother kills the son but does so without hatred; for that reason it is not an infectious type of violence. Sometimes violence on the screen is shown without close-ups, shot from a long distance which makes the violence seem ridiculous. If our censors had any sense, they would ban violence in close-up, violence that involves the audience and does not distance it from the hatred which informs the scene.

Finally, if sexuality does not take away from the nurturing, non-violent aspect of the woman, is there anything she can do? After all, even in countries that have achieved a great deal of equality of the sexes and made gender roles highly flexible, the number of male criminals is overwhelmingly greater than of women. Perhaps liberation does not necessarily kill off the nurturing, non-violent aspect of a woman.

It may be simply a question of the woman within us; both men and women.

6

PRECURSORS OF UNPOPULAR CINEMA
A Parallel View of Indian Film History

The beginnings of Indian cinema saw the release of forces that led to a tradition in socially committed, realistic, reformist films. In a capital-intensive, technological medium that needs economies of scale and a large, homogenized set of consumers, it is difficult for the lone voice of the dissident to be heard in the din of industry. Yet its existence became indubitable early in the day. Since the camera records what is set before it, realism has been a natural corollary to the medium from the beginning. It became a potential, natural, ally of the maverick artist who wanted to speak his mind, to expose the true nature of reality. With the rise of myth-making as a powerful force, the strand of realism was to couple itself with the penchant for personal cinema. That this unlikely, perhaps inchoate, combination was present almost from the birth of the medium in India is apparent from its history. Together they laid the foundations of what was to demonstrate the inevitability of a cinema prepared to address itself to a minority, that is, to be unpopular.

The arrival of cinema at the turn of the century in India was at first hailed as a new wonder of the Industrial Revolution. But when operatives of the Lumière brothers displayed their fragments of actuality on screen at Watson's Hotel in Bombay on 7 July 1896, they sowed the seeds of one of the most enduring strands of cinema—the realistic spectacle.

By 1899, the first realistic films had already been made by Harishchandra Bhatvadekar, better known as Save (pronounced Saavay) Dada. One was called *The Wrestlers*; another was about the training of monkeys. Other actuality films included a record of Muharram in Delhi, the flight of the (then) Dalai Lama from Tibet, and, most notably, the Delhi Durbar of Emperor George V in 1911. Thus the beginning was made with the documentary recording of actualities. The Lumière tradition of films reflecting reality was established early in the day.

The early years of the new century saw a spate of realistic film-making by Indians. Save Dada continued making them in Bombay. F.B. Thanawala, also of Bombay, began shooting by mid-1900, with *Splendid New Views of Bombay* and *Taboot Procession*, the latter recording a Muslim religious pageant. In 1903, Hiralal Sen of Calcutta, who first filmed local stage plays and imported foreign films, made *Indian Life & Scenes*, an ambitious project that included scenes from both Indian mythology and realistic portrayals. Bengal registered its penchant for social activism in Jyotish Sarkar's *Great Bengal Partition Movement*. It was made in protest against Lord Curzon's decision to divide Bengal into two provinces.

Meanwhile, Georges Méliès had made a triumphant entry with his fantastic *Trip to the Moon*. Between Lumière and Méliès, the seeds of realism and myth-making had both been planted. The archetypal polarity between the two may be questionable in principle, but seems to be valid in the history of Indian cinema where mythology has traditionally occupied so much space.

When Save Dada resolved to make India's first feature film, he chose the miracle-laden story of (God) Krishna's birth. But the death of his brother made him give up the plan and yield his place to D.G. Phalke, 'the Father of India Cinema', who was to make India's first feature film, *Raja Harishchandra*, in 1913.

The surviving fragments of Phalke's film show a Méliès-like interest in the magic aspects of the motion picture that lent themselves well to the miracles performed by the gods of Hindu mythology. They became his lifelong interest. He was the Hindu Méliès, determined to promote his religion through the special effects he kept inventing. All of the 100 films he made were mythological, right up to 1937, when he made his second talkie, *Gangavataran* (The Descent of the Ganga). The cinema's power, based on the principle of 'seeing is believing', was thus put to use to reinforce the anthropomorphic polytheism of Puranic (mythical) Hindu faith at a time when a scientific temper, rationalism and social reform had begun to take root and to lay the foundations of modern India. A product of science was harnessed, in effect, to blunt the edge of growing criticism of tradition that reform movements brought into play.

In course of time, the mythological turned into the mainstream of popular cinema and the realistic film into the less popular strand. As the divide widened, myth-making turned from the past to the present, creating types, absolutist categories like the rich man and the poor man, the modern and the traditional, the docile (good) wife and the independent-minded (bad), the obedient son and the defiant one, and so on. Behind every type, there lurked the doings of a god endorsing the doings of man.

Maharashtra dominated the early decades of cinema and brought to it its revivalist pride in Hinduism, inspired no doubt by the image of the heroic Shivaji, a Hindu king who had bravely fought Aurangzeb's Muslim empire. At this stage, the urge to turn cinema into an Indian industry was modern; but the content loaded into it was predominantly traditional. The avoidance of contemporary reality was one of the aspects of the revivalist credo that dominated this period. D.G. Phalke worked for Hindu patriot Bal Gangadhar Tilak's newspaper *Kesari*, and Raja Ravi Varma painted and printed oleographs of gods of the Hindu pantheon in British naturalistic style blissfully unaware of the rise of Impressionism in Europe. Phalke saw a foreign film on the life of Christ and was inspired to do for the Hindus what it had done for the Christians. No less was his determination to prove that what the westerners had done with the new technology of cinema the Indians could do just as well. Phalke was the fountainhead of the urge towards self-sufficiency in cinema—something that managed to hold Hollywood expansionism at bay for a hundred years. But he was at the same time the fountainhead of not just the mythological genre but the myth-making strand which was to overflow from the stories of the past into the realities of the present, imparting to everything a perpetual sepia tone.

On the other hand, cinema critical of the xenophobia of a closed society mired in superstitions was seen in the battle of two Shakuntala films, both based on the play by fifth-century Sanskrit dramatist Kalidasa. One was made by Suchet Singh with American participation, including an actress. The other was made by Patanker Friends whose publicity said it was 'Neither Jew nor Gentile—an Aryan drama in Aryan drapery and actors—Real *Swadeshi* (indigenous) from start to finish'. Suchet Singh claimed for his film a quality far above that of 'the general run of films in India', which he could well have done, with the film's mix of Indian and American expertise. The controversy seems to have prefigured the opposition we were to see later between B.R. Chopra's *Mahabharat* and Peter Brook's in the 1980s. It has remained as a persistent divide between the liberal and the conservative, the woman hostile and the woman friendly, the xenophobic and the pluralist, the realistic and the mythical, these categories combining in various ways.

II

In the context of mythology and the bent towards mythologizing generated by it, the occasional forays into realism, any concern with the here and now, became a form of dissidence. The spell of mythology cast upon Indian fictional film-making by its intrepid pioneer was broken by Dhiren Ganguly with *Bilet Pherat*, a satire on the mores of the 'foreign returned', in 1921. This was quickly followed by Madan's portrait of Parsi society in *Tehmuras and Tehmulji* in 1925. Chandulal Shah in Bombay made *Gunasundari*, a story of a modern wife's struggle against traditional male domination. Then came a similar yarn in *Typist Girl*. Baburao Painter, one of the early icons of Indian cinema, who had filmed the historic session of the Indian National Congress in 1918, made the classic *Sahukari Pash* (1926), a tirade against the moneylenders' exploitation of the poor. Although many of these films can no longer be seen, the accounts one can read would suggest that these films paved the way for a cinema of social criticism, which was later to manifest itself in no uncertain manner.

In 1925, Indian cinema was given an international dimension by Himanshu Rai in Bombay with *Light of Asia*, based on the Edwin Arnold classic on the Buddha. Rai gave up a career in law in London and journeyed to Munich with the passionate vision of a film on the Buddha. But his success with this project did not deter him from turning to a film of social criticism. *Achhut Kanya* (1936), produced by Bombay Talkies, the company he founded, spoke out against the evil of untouchability in traditional

Hindu society. Thus Rai's efforts were directed at the important objective of achieving modernity that revered tradition but was critical of superstition; they sought to promote pluralism and tolerance, and laid the foundations of the progressive, rationalist and pluralist strand in Indian cinema.

India's first talkie, *Alam Ara* (1931), had a plethora of songs in it and promptly set a model that the bulk of Indian cinema has followed ever since. The popular ('commercial') cinema puts the film song at the very centre of film-making. To this day, the song expresses the innermost aspirations of the characters in the story, even more than dialogue, which is often too stereotyped to aid in either the logic of narrative or the connected unfolding of events and character. The variety show model was firmly imprinted on the bulk of Indian cinema and was to provoke an overreaction from the parallel cinema when it arrived decades later.

Meanwhile, the number and significance of films concerned with social and political freedoms continued to grow through the 1920s and 1930s. V. Shantaram and Vinayak were celebrating the modern woman in *Duniya Na Maane* (The World Does not Care, 1937) and *Brahmachari* (The Celibate, 1937). Both films vigorously advocated women's liberation. In the first, a woman given in marriage to a man old enough to be her father, refuses to consummate her marriage and finally wins her point with the help of her stepdaughter, herself a social worker. The second satirized all icons and celebrated the modern woman, vigorously endorsing her rights in a unique form of comedy.

With these films the divide began to open up between the popular film which marshalled all possible myth-making guiles to reinforce tradition and the less popular social film which challenged this adherence to the past. Basically, the commercial cinema must confirm the prejudices and stereotypes of a traditional society because it requires a large, homogenized audience with common tastes cutting across classes and regions to give it the economy of scale required by all large industries. Conformity to popular attitudes is thus central to the objectives of the film industry. Consequently, the proposition that the commercial film advocates tradition and the art film espouses progress remains true to this day. Despite occasional exceptions, especially in the 1990s, it has survived the many upheavals that Indian cinema has weathered.

But the divide was to take a firm shape over several decades, culminating in the late 1950s. Meanwhile, realism asserted its need in the 1940s. The period was buffeted by World War II and its enormous outcomes. It brought India's freedom movement to a point of crisis the British were unable to solve. Successive waves of political unrest rocked the foundations of Britain's Indian empire, the 'jewel in the crown'. In 1943, the British war effort visited a terrible man-made famine upon Bengal by taking away the grain to feed soldiers in the eastern theatre. About five million people perished. Then came the Japanese bombing of Calcutta and the Great Calcutta Killing and finally the partition of India, which created Pakistan.

Predictably, cinema reacted to the events in a few realistic, socially sensitive films by activist directors. An immediate outcome was Khwaja Ahmed Abbas's *Dharti Ke Lal* (Children of the Earth, 1946). It was based on a landmark play, an Indian Peoples' Theatre Association (IPTA) production in Calcutta, on the Bengal famine of 1943. Inevitably, the thrust of this product of the cultural front of the Communist Party was towards a graphic realism. It also had shades of Eisenstein and bore the marks of its theatrical origins. Yet it constituted the first of the many attempts at cinematic realism during the period. Another in the same vein was Chetan Anand's *Neecha Nagar* (Low Life, 1946) with its rich–poor contrasts. Abbas's film was the first to be released in theatres in the USSR, while Anand's participated in competition at the Cannes Film Festival in 1947. Both were worthy attempts somewhat flawed by a penchant for operatic and theatrical stylization, which prevented the cinematic realism their directors sought, from emerging fully. A third film that calls for mention in this context is Nemai Ghosh's *Chhinnamool* (The Uprooted, 1951) which was relatively free from theatricality and in fact had sequences of candid shooting of refugees arriving at Calcutta's railway station. One of the actors in the film was Ritwik Ghatak who was later to emerge as a much-acclaimed film-maker with a marked lack of popularity. However, *Chhinnamool* failed to develop a sufficient unity and remains interesting mainly in its pioneering fragments of realism. Abbas's film had a catalytic effect on Shantaram (whose *Kotnis* was based on Abbas's book), and on Raj Kapoor, some of whose most successful films in the 1950s were written by Abbas.

III

A notable film was to celebrate India's growing new internationality: *Dr Kotnis Ki Amar Kahani* (The Journey of Dr Kotnis, 1946), made by one of India's most celebrated film-makers, V. Shantaram, who had already made a mark before the war with his socially courageous reformist films and his innovative techniques. *Kotnis* was based on the true story of a young doctor who went to China with an Indian medical team, sponsored by national leader Jawaharlal Nehru, to work among the Chinese war victims, and died there. Shantaram himself played Kotnis and shot the film in Hindi and English in the hope of finding a market for it in the United States. The story had Dr Kotnis working with a young Chinese doctor, Ching-Lan, who turned out to be a woman and with whom he fell in love. They had to part after some time but by then Ching-Lan was pregnant. They were reunited but only to find Kotnis dying. All the parts were played by Indians, and China was recreated in a Bombay studio in a markedly Hollywood style. Seen today, the film is not a tribute to realism, but the internationalism of spirit remains notable in a very enclosed film industry.

Another seminal film reflecting a resurgent India's new consciousness of tradition was the famous dancer Uday Shankar's *Kalpana* (Imagination, 1948). It was an all-dance film with a thin storyline but its techniques showed a rare grasp of cinematic form, discarding practices then current in India in the filming of dances. Shankar's emphasis was not on the continuity of dance but on cinematic continuity and a fast pace ensured by a plethora of quick cuts and camera movements. The dances were derived from classical forms that had fallen into disrepute through their association with courtesans and temple prostitutes. The film gave a fillip to the revival of classical dance in a new, socially acceptable context. Almost overnight, it made dancing respectable. It ran successfully only in Calcutta; elsewhere it was unpopular cinema.

Historical films, which were to go into steep decline in later decades, had their heyday in the 1940s and 1950s. A memorable example thrown up by Prabhat Films of Pune in the twilight of its glorious era was Gajanan Jagirdar's *Ram Shastri* (1944). Jagirdar played the eponymous hero with aplomb, and the film impressively evoked a period and a personality without recourse to melodrama. It was the first Indian film to be screened at the Calcutta Film Society (CFS) founded in 1947 by Satyajit Ray and others.

IV

During the early years of World War II, German U-boats made it increasingly difficult for British ships to maintain the routine of taking raw material from India and bringing finished goods. As the shortages grew acute, the British were forced to develop industries within the country, triggering the rapid growth of an industrial working class which gained momentum with the country's independence and its accent on industrial development. A similar curve was followed by the growth of unaccounted wealth or black money, whose owners, like the new working class, were low in education and culture. Migration from the villages to the cities received a fillip and urban destitution began to grow. These were the factors that determined the character of the makers and consumers of popular cinema and combined to set the scene for a rapid change in the style and content of the film in the decades that followed the Second World War and Independence.

From a predominantly middle-class orientation, cinema moved towards a new working class growing by leaps and bounds. As industry expanded, this working class did too; only its education did not keep pace with its prosperity. The stage had been set for a divide between two cinemas—one for the growing proletariat, the other for the educated middle class. Spreading unemployment and urban destitution only emphasized a trend that had surfaced gradually over the years. The educated middle class began to feel the need for a cinema more suited to its mores.

But before the chasm widened enough to set up a more consciously oppositional set of values, the 1940s and early 1950s, often dubbed the

'Golden Age of Indian Cinema', threw up the last memorable group of film-makers who were able to leave a personal stamp and displayed a marked social concern in their work within the ambit of the box office. The cinema of Bimal Roy, Raj Kapoor, Guru Dutt and Mehboob provided a unity of art and commerce seldom to be seen in later decades. If remade today in the mainstream cinema, the films would probably turn Guru Dutt's delicate personal feeling into a rambunctious public spectacle. Basically, they were concerned with the realities that affected humans rather than mythology and mythologizing, that is, with the shadows of gods forever cradling the activities of man.

Certain pluralist and liberal trends coexisted with the rise of black money and the increasing illiteracy of the new audiences. Altogether, the 1950s remained true to the spirit of the times and shared in the modernist, progressive outlook of a new India. As with later generations of sensitive film-makers, its only regret was over the yet unredeemed promises of the leaders of contemporary Indian society. The personalities thrown up by the times were to carry this spirit forward in the afterglow of Independence when there was faith in the future and disillusion had not yet set in. This upbeat mood dominated the 1950s as well as a part of the 1960s in the films of Raj Kapoor, Bimal Roy, Guru Dutt and Mehboob, making a glorious chapter in Indian film history in which the divide between the commercial cinema and the art film had not yet arrived.

Foremost among the precursors of personal cinema was one of the names to reckon with in the mainstream. Guru Dutt conveyed an individual passion, a statement of his personal reaction to a world that suppressed individuality. His was the unique distinction of creating a very personal cinema within the parameters of the box office with films like *Pyaasa* (1957), *Kaagaz Ke Phool* (1959), *Chaudhvin Ka Chand* (1960) and *Sahib Bibi Aur Ghulam* (1962). Emotionally rich, laden with haunting melodies, these films fired the imagination of the public and have stood the test of time as well.

In *Pyaasa*, he cried out against society's unjust rejection of the poet because he would not conform. In *Chaudhvin Ka Chand*, the anguish of love is very personal; it is not a stereotype repeated according to a formula invented by others. This is even more true of *Sahib Bibi Aur Ghulam* whose unusual story added to the sense of the individual and whose fluid camera movements and delicate lighting heightened the sense of seeing something uniquely the film-maker's. Guru Dutt used the standard language of transcendence through song but did not stereotype character or dismiss causality in narrative or the logic of development of character. *Sahib Bibi Aur Ghulam*'s story stays close to the logic, the finely integrated chain of events, built up by the novel on which it is based. Yet the restrained passion, the gentle nostalgia that informs it is Guru Dutt's own, not that of Bimal Mitra, the author of the book. The Bengali film made by Kartick Chattopadhyay never measured up to Guru Dutt's delicacy, his quiet intensity, or the very personal nature of his observation.

Raj Kapoor welded a form of his own out of the new social context. He reacted in a romantic yet real way to the life of the vagrant in a period of the expansion of the working class and the beginnings of urban destitution. Migrant workers, often unemployed, rushed to the large cities, becoming victims and often slaves of antisocial forces. The agonies and the hopes of these people were reflected in a romantic kind of realism in films like *Awara* (1951), *Shri 420* (1955) and others. It is not surprising that audiences warmed to his films not only in India but even as far afield as the USSR and China.

Among others who shared in this post-Independence zeal for social reform was Bimal Roy, who had migrated from Calcutta during the declining years of New Theatres, the foremost studio of eastern India. Roy brought a Bengali style of film-making to Bombay—gentle, relatively slow, free of crudities, concentrating on story development and other literary qualities without losing grip over film technique. His *Do Bigha Zamin* (Two Acres of Land, 1953) was the outcome of exposure to Italian neo-realism at India's first International Film Festival in 1952. Under the threat of confiscation of his land for the non-payment of a loan, a farmer goes to Calcutta to become a rickshaw-puller for the three months the court has granted him to pay back the loan and retain his land. The realism of the film holds out till the end; the farmer is unable to make the money and loses his land on which a factory is being built. In its absence of make-up and glamour and song-and-dance formulas, the film broke many conventions and heralded the new language of cinema that Satyajit

Ray was to fashion from *Pather Panchali* onwards. In fact, it took these qualities somewhat further than Satyajit Ray's later work would, betraying Bimal Roy's impulsive reaction to the sudden exposure to Italian neo-realism rather than lasting traits in his film-making. Thus *Sujata*, another landmark films of his, made in the same year (1959) as Satyajit Ray's *Apur Sansar*, found him backtracking into his more literary, Bengali style of mise-en-scène developed out of New Theatres' aesthetic. The film-making was less inventive or vigorous; it fell back on a standard vocabulary. However, the inhumanity of the caste system touched a chord in every heart and the film was an instant success. It was fully in tune with the optimist–reformist mood of the 1950s. Roy never quite gave up this course, despite changes in the country's situation, and never played to the rising new gallery of the urban lumpen.

V

Almost immediately after Independence, the Government of India had displayed a keen awareness of the influence of cinema and the need to coax a new kind of cinema into existence. In 1951, a high-powered Film Enquiry Committee headed by Cabinet Minister S.K. Patil recommended a series of infrastructural growth centres. Its recommendations were, in the main, accepted by Parliament. By 1961, the Film Institute of India, the Film Finance Corporation (FFC), the Children's Film Society and the National Film Archive of India (NFAI) came into being. Over the years, the Film Institute and the FFC's efforts produced a whole generation of new and talented film-makers and their works. There was a felt need for money to cease to be the sole motivation. The foundation of the FFC turned out to be a landmark in the growth of the alternative cinema. It produced, over the years, a large number of low-budget films many of which won, with almost monotonous regularity, the President of India's annual awards. These awards gave much-needed recognition to many of these talents, some of whom, while firmly remaining within the confines of unpopular cinema, won international acclaim as well. Some state governments followed the example of the centre and financed such films themselves. Nationally and internationally, these films gave Indian cinema a high profile, ridding it of much of the malodorous association of cinema with sin that had prevailed in Indian society for a long time. Altogether it must have been one of the most ambitious pieces of cultural engineering in the world of cinema after the USSR, without curtailing the freedom of the artist.

VI

No less significant was the Film Enquiry Committee's decision to support the work of film societies. Two of them had been in existence in Bombay—the Amateur Cine Society of India (founded as early as 1937) and the Bombay Film Society (founded in 1942). They included pioneer documentary film-makers like Dr P.V. Pathy, Paul Zils, V.M. Vijaykar and Clement Baptista. There had been other, somewhat short-lived, efforts to promote film appreciation. Dhruba Gupta has drawn attention to outstanding film criticism in the 1930s in Bengal and Debaprosad Ghosh to The Cinema Library and the Art Institute of Film Technique, also in Bengal in the 1930s. Yet these societies were not able to do much more than getting together to see good films or making sporadically inspired attempts to create an infrastructure for the enhancement of film culture. There were too many obstacles in British India to the growth of stable institutions with wide interactions within the country and abroad. The time for the idea had not come.

It did with Independence. In October 1947, Satyajit Ray and a group of like-minded film enthusiasts, anxious to open a window on world cinema, so tightly shut during British rule, started the Calcutta Film Society. In no time it turned into a movement that was to spread all over the country, providing a new impetus to film viewing, film criticism and, eventually, to film-making. Among the film-makers directly or indirectly thrown up by the movement, there were, apart from Satyajit Ray himself, Ritwik Ghatak, Mrinal Sen, Shyam Benegal, Adoor Gopalakrishnan and many others. The movement had an impact far in excess of its size. It prepared the ground for international film festivals and built an audience for the new cinema. At its peak in the late 1960s and early 1970s, the Federation of Film Societies of India had about 300 film societies affiliated to it. Many societies had as many as 2000 members. At one stage it was estimated that Bengal alone had a total membership of over 30,000 individuals belonging to these societies.

The movement was recognized and supported by the government at the centre and some state governments, resulting in the exemption of film club shows from entertainment tax and censorship. The movement also helped to create new standards in film criticism through its many publications and to form an audience for the new cinema that came about in its wake.

India's doors and windows had started to fly open. In 1948, the CFS imported a copy of *Battleship Potemkin* and showed it, dodging police restrictions, to stunning effect on its viewers. Hard on the heels of this event came Jean Renoir's visit for a recce in 1948 and for the shooting of *The River* in 1949. There was intensive and continual interaction between film society members and Jean Renoir whose great reputation as a French film-maker the film industry did not know about but the CFS aficionados did, having read about him in international books and journals on cinema. The shooting of *The River* was observed by many who were later to turn famous practitioners such as cinematographer Subrata Mitra, art director Bansi Chandragupta, documentarist Harisadhan Das Gupta and so on. Roberto Rossellini came a few years later and so did John Huston, Frank Capra, V. Pudovkin and Nikolai Cherkassov—all names to reckon with in cinema, popular or unpopular.

Among well-known critics there was Marie Seton who gave a series of lectures that inspired the revival of the CFS, which had been dazed into inactivity by the impact of the 1952 International Film Festival. The inauguration of the new CFS was attended, among others, by Arne Sucksdorff, the Swedish film-maker whose short film on Stockholm inspired the CFS to make *Portrait of a City* about Calcutta, the first of four films produced by the CFS.

VII

The coming of sound in the early 1930s had already dealt the uniformity of the cinema experience a body blow. Most of the regional cinemas in India—Bengali, Oriya, Assamese, Marathi, Gujarati, Tamil, Malayalam,

Kannada—arose at around this period. Many foreign-language-speaking actors and actresses disappeared almost overnight. Independence gave a further fillip to the growth of regional identities in cinema because states were organized on a linguistic basis somewhat in the style of the Soviet Union. Regional film-making centres took time to proliferate. Films in all languages continued to be produced for decades in all-India film-making centres in Bombay, Calcutta and Madras. But the practice gradually yielded ground to the exclusive production of regional films in many state centres such as Cuttack in Orissa and Guwahati in Assam.

There was the seed of realism in the very nature of regional cinema. It was proud of its cultural identity and, unlike the all-India film, accentuated rather than concealing its specificities in names, costumes and linguistic idiosyncrasies. Despite the inbuilt advantage of Hindi, the growth of regional cinemas in a variety of languages became inevitable. Many of these, such as Bengali, Oriya, Assamese, continue to proclaim the separate identity of the cultures centring on the language of each region. The ever-widening acceptability of the Hindi film made in Bombay has largely owed itself to the success of the lavishly mounted song and dance numbers, impossible for regional resources to match. On the other hand, the regional film expresses the cultural specificities important to the highly pluralistic mindset of the country as well as the particular anxieties and ambitions of the regions.

Not unnaturally, the regional centres became the playground of the parallel cinema. It gathered momentum from the film society movement and took off with the release of *Pather Panchali* in Bengal. It then spread to film-making centres in Karnataka, Kerala and Maharashtra in the 1970s, reaching Assam and Manipur in the north-east in no time.

Although regional films often glorified their own cultures, their film-making idiom was largely derived from the all-India cinema. The big-time Hindi film was, is, ever-present before them as a model. The divide between the art film and the popular film was clear in the regional cinemas. So were the frontiers between the mythical and the realistic, the 'artistic' and the 'commercial'. Polarity between commercial and artistic motivations has been as marked in the regional film as in the all-India product. The tendency that prevailed in the critical literature of the 1960s and 1970s to equate the regional film with the artistic was thus a somewhat persistent fallacy. Nowhere has this been more true than in south India with the enormous size of its film industries. The parallel cinema had to fight for every inch of the space it eventually acquired. Even then, it remained negligible in number, albeit far-reaching in influence.

VIII

In 1952, India's first International Film Festival was held (later to become an annual event). Outside the confines of film clubs, this was the first large-scale exposure of Indian audiences to some of the best products of world cinema. Its immediate effect was seen in Bimal Roy's *Do Bigha Zamin*, Raj Kapoor's *Boot Polish* (1954) and many other lesser attempts at creating an Indian equivalent to Italian neo-realism.

This trend was monumentalized in a small film. Satyajit Ray's *Pather Panchali* not only broke all the rules reigning in current Indian cinema but established a model which numerous serious film-makers followed. Low budgets, absence of make-up and of song and dance numbers, realistic lighting, the use of non-professionals, the director's complete control of his work and similar new modes set up a new credo of film-making which has remained generally unchanged in art-predominant cinema. Numerically few—perhaps no more than five per cent of India's total film production—these films had an impact disproportionate to their size of business. They caught the attention of the intelligentsia and the bureaucracy, the ministries, the Parliament and, in general, the opinion builders of the country. They helped to make the educated audiences aware of how the other half lives and how little has changed despite momentous claims. Many of the films went to international film festivals abroad, won prizes and were shown on small circuits and on television, creating a new recognition of Indian cinema on a scale that had never been achieved, especially in Western countries. It is said that not a day passes when *Pather Panchali* is not shown somewhere or the other in the world, nearly half a century after it was made. The film may also be said to have divided Indian cinema, by its tremendous impact, into the somewhat suspect categories of Art and Commerce, categories that had never been so separated before, and which persisted through the decades that followed.

The 1950s were thus notable, on the one hand, for the marriage of art and box-office considerations that Raj Kapoor, Guru Dutt, Mehboob and Bimal Roy achieved in their best work which was hardly ever repeated; on the other, the art of film climbed new heights in the psychological development of narrative and character with a conviction never before seen in Indian cinema. In films like *Apur Sansar*, formal perfection and personal poetry joined hands to create a series of masterpieces of world cinema. Ray's striking example inspired generations of film-makers who built up a body of work of abiding value within a minority culture. Neo-realism provided the starting point, but with *Jalsaghar* (The Music Room, 1958), Ray, working in one of India's most primitive studios, created a picture of aristocratic decadence and obsession with perfect artistry, departing from neo-realism like Visconti. *Kanchanjungha* (1962), his first colour film, was shot in twenty-eight days and captured the mercurial atmosphere of the background and the drama of a family up in a hill resort with deftness of touch and exquisite humour. Ray thus quickly showed his mettle in a number of directions, reaching perfection in each. He set up an extraordinary model of tightly controlled low-budget film-making appropriate for the limited resources and markets of the regional cinemas, emphasizing the integrity of the director's personal vision rather that the richness of spectacular melodrama. This model, marked by a complete control of all aspects of the medium by the director, became the standard pattern for those who came in his wake.

Pather Panchali's example had a phenomenal impact on film-makers first in Bengal and later in Karnataka, Kerala and Maharashtra. A whole new generation of film-makers came along to turn out films they felt were both artistically valid and socially relevant. In Bengal, Ritwik Ghatak made an immediate mark and was later to be regarded as an author of seminal works sharply different from Ray's. In Bombay, there arrived Shyam Benegal, M.S. Sathyu, Ketan Mehta, Saeed Mirza and others; in Kerala, Adoor Gopalakrishnan and G. Aravindan; in Assam, Jahnu Barua; and in Karnataka, Pattabhi Rama Reddy, Girish Kasaravalli, Girish Karnad, Prema

Karanth, to name only a few. The establishment of an infrastructure for a better cinema, the growth of film societies, the spread of serious writing on cinema, the national and international recognition of the new cinema, state government support for the new thrust—all of these came together to heighten the feel-good factor of the new cinema. In the 1970s it seemed as though the real golden age of cinema had arrived.

This trend coincided with the rapid rise of the educated middle class after Independence and resulted from the inner drives of its intellectually most advanced segment. Throughout the country, regional-language cinemas were strongly influenced by this impulse and gave occasional glimpses of power. While the Hindi commercial film continued and expanded its all-India empire, art in the regional cinemas stood up against the current much as French or German or Italian cinema does against Hollywood.

Governmental intervention also helped the rising prestige of cinema. The remarkable aspect of this patronage was that it built the infrastructure for a socially responsible, artistically superior cinema, but did not seek to control it. Unlike the USSR or China, it did not tell the film-maker what kind of films to make or pronounce on the results. The convention has been for the film director to submit a script for examination by an independent committee and, once approved, to be funded without further ado. Indeed, non-interference has been so taken for granted that its value can be seen only in the context of the totalitarianism that afflicted Eisenstein or Tarkovsky. This is particularly worth a mention in the case of India, where a 'socialistic' bias could easily have mandated a closer approximation to the Soviet model.

However, a certain degree of self-censorship may have prevailed among the film-makers themselves, prompted by their awareness of what attracts acclaim or opprobrium. In a way there was no need for Soviet- or Chinese-style governmental interference. The film-makers, far from opposing, were out to support the declared objectives of the government. They were not critical of most of the policies. What roused their anger was the lack of implementation of progressive laws. The age-old patterns of oppression of the poor, of women, of what governmental prose calls 'the weaker sections of society', the superstitions that held sway despite legislation, the injustices towards minorities—these became the cause for anger. The concerns were what many diplomats abroad, bureaucrats at home, film magnates in their dream world wanted to keep as well hidden as possible. The new breed of film-makers wanted to expose the reality, to shake people out of their indifference.

A governmental enterprise which lent some indirect support to the new minority culture in the cinema was the documentary. The wartime Information Films of India was converted in independent India into the Films Division of the Ministry of Information and Broadcasting in 1948. Curiously enough, the big impetus for a large-scale diffusion of short educational and newsreel films came from the commercial cinema. In a resolution adopted at a convention of the Motion Picture Society of India, the government was urged to make the exhibition of such short films compulsory for every film theatre in the country. The recommendation was promptly put into effect by the government, and overnight, there sprang up an audience of well over ten million per day. Production was financed by the fee mandatorily paid by the theatres. So every week some 10,000 theatres showed one documentary (of not more than twenty-two minutes) and one newsreel film in fifteen languages before the main feature in every show.

The word 'documentary' was not entirely honestly employed, for the films were, for the most part, commissioned by various ministries to publicize their achievements in specified fields. Nonetheless, a giant piece of machinery, for the production and distribution of documentaries unlike anything in the non-Soviet world, had been created. The twenty-two-minute format and the haranguing style of commentary came to be the recognized features of documentary so much so that anything else tended to be rejected outright. Within these constraints, however, a number of outstanding films were also made, mostly by independent film-makers commissioned by the Films Division to supplement its somewhat dull departmental output. A signal role was played by Burmah Shell which had its own films department and made a number of documentaries of fairly high quality under the leadership of James Beveridge from the National Film Board of Canada. Paul Zils, a German national, made a number of these films (*Martial Dancers of Malabar*, for instance) and so did Harisadhan

Das Gupta (*Weavers of Maindargi, Panchthupi*). Despite the stiff joints of bureaucracy in the Films Division, the 1950s on the whole seemed full of promise for the documentary. Some outstanding work appeared on the scene, especially those coming from Sukhdev and during the overseership of J. Bhownagary. A certain tradition of commitment to fact, outdoor shooting and realism was being created and audiences exposed to these values—not without some effect on feature film-making. A tenuous but significant alliance grew up between the many infrastructural institutions of the government, the film societies, the documentary and the New Cinema.

A passageway was thus established for new film-makers to graduate from the short film to the feature which some were to make use of in the coming decades. Notable among them was Shyam Benegal who served an apprenticeship in advertising and documentary films before emerging as a major figure in feature cinema in the 1970s.

The Nehru government's policy of reforming the film industry, however, continued with his 'dynasty', right up to Rajiv Gandhi as prime minister. The vice-president of the Federation of Film Societies for many years was Mrs Indira Gandhi who became the Union government's Minister for Information and Broadcasting in 1965. Film society activists were inducted into many government committees and had a great deal of influence over India's Third International Film Festival in 1965 (the second having taken place in 1961, nine years after the first in 1952). The fourth festival came in 1969 and thereafter, under Mrs Gandhi's prime ministership, a Directorate of Film Festivals was established under the Ministry of Information and Broadcasting in 1974 to hold an annual international film festival as well as an annual national film festival at which the President's awards were distributed. The 1960s thus laid the foundation for a government-supported serious cinema (or the 'art' film) which continued to develop throughout the 1970s.

IX

The FFC had been formed with too small a capital base to realize its objective of cleaning up the Augean stables of film finance and to drive out the wicked influence of 'black money'. When experience showed up this inadequacy, the FFC (later to be renamed National Film Development Corporation or NFDC) turned to low-budget films by young new directors, for which its resources were more suited. The success of Mrinal Sen's *Bhuvan Shome*, financed by the FFC without any security, consolidated this trend.

However, the majority of the films sponsored by the FFC were box-office failures. The corporation had concentrated on the making of the films, leaving their distribution and exhibition to take care of themselves—something they were, predictably, unable to do. The films faced some amount of hostility from the diehards of the industry who resented the new-found prestige of these low-budget films for what was to them an esoteric, perhaps non-existent audience. No wonder such films found the gateways to distribution and exhibition, designed for mass-scale catering, closed to them. However, the talent of these young directors was hailed by the media and the elite and, in some cases, obtained international recognition which made it difficult to dismiss them out of hand.

X

The popular product was on the other hand left to the tender mercies of the black-marketeer and the smuggler and others in need of a subterranean growth of their incomes outside the reach of the tax department and in the glamorous pursuit of a game of fortune in which the winner takes all and the loser disappears into the night. The character of fictional film-making as an industry had not yet fully emerged and had to wait till almost the 1990s to begin to take some shape.

In the early-1980s, the enormous success of some pro-development soap operas made television a new force. *Hum Log*, followed by a number of other serials, suddenly showed that popularity was possible even without the sex and violence ingredients claimed as essential by the film industry. Television has since then expanded its frontier to admit a certain degree of both and yet retains the character of a home apparatus, to be patronized by the family and necessarily somewhat sanitized. Popular serials demonstrate the difference between what the traffic will bear for the cinema and what is made for television. The distinction between the two continues to show that audience taste is not immutable.

In the 1980s started a decline in the support system for alternative cinema. The governmental will to maintain the infrastructure in prime condition wavered. It relapsed into the common illusion of culture as a decoration to be worn on one's sleeve rather than an essential ingredient of national development, expendable whenever there was any pressure on resources. In the decades immediately following Independence, the government was sure of its continuity and therefore of its responsibility for the future, however distant. Later governments, especially those dependent on fragile coalitions, were caught in the throes of constant manipulation to save the powerboat from sinking. The International Film Festival of India, the National Film Development Corporation, the President's awards, the National Film Archive of India increasingly found their raison d'être coming into question. If they have not been altogether abolished it has partly been due to inertia and partly the fear of alienating powerful sections of the intelligentsia. They have therefore been allowed to continue listlessly, without positive faith in their necessity. This lackadaisical attitude has been further undermined by religious orthodoxies with their xenophobic compulsions.

The general run of the film industry, always hostile to the idea of an alternative cinema running parallel to it, has not come forward to energize the infrastructure. Perhaps some of its hostility has been prompted by the fear of a large, educated and expanding middle class opting for the alternative. The fact that the industry has benefited enormously from the technical virtuosity brought to the quality of its sound and visuals by the graduates of the Film and Television Institute of India (FTII) has not tempered its impatience with notions of training in film-making or film appreciation.

However, it will not do to lose sight of other factors that have contributed to the decline in care for the infrastructure. The FTII became heir to the many ills educational institutions in general have suffered. Student unrest, undoubtedly due to authorities' failure to understand student needs, has caused much bitterness and endangered the future of the institution. The

NFDC's productions have failed consistently at the box office, party due to the nature of the films themselves and partly because of the failure to present the right mix of products plus the lack of professionalism in governmental marketing.

Much of the alternative cinema owes its existence to the initiatives of Satyajit Ray. But few of them have inherited Ray's concern for the viability of his projects and his occasional successes at the box office. In 1964, *Charulata*, despite its subtleties, was the second biggest hit of the year in Bengal. Later, *Goopy Gyne Bagha Byne* (1968) became an all-time hit. His other films fared differently at different times, but more often than not their combined sales in India and abroad justified their investment.

There is substance in the case for supporting the growth of higher artistic and social standards in cinema, at times regardless of immediate returns, but it is not too much to expect them to create their audience and become viable over a length of time. Parallel cinema cannot expect to live forever on governmental oxygen in intensive care protected from predators in the real world outside. Some film-makers have graduated from this condition but this cannot be said of all, and not all of them have extended the frontiers of cinema far enough to justify special nourishment.

In tracing the development of the parallel cinema, it is important to note that there has been a slow but sure weaning from governmental patronage. Some have fallen by the wayside but the majority of film-makers in this category have survived the ups and downs over the decades and today enlist the support of private entrepreneurs because their films have been able to find an audience. Governmental oxygen is no longer required. Among those who have managed to interest producers/financiers regularly one might name Shyam Benegal in Bombay, Adoor Gopalakrishnan in Kerala, Buddhadev Dasgupta, Goutam Ghose, Rituparno Ghosh and Aparna Sen among others in Calcutta.

Opposition to the Ray model with its Hollywood narrative tempered by a contemplative undertone came from Mani Kaul and Kumar Shahani, pupils of Ghatak at the FTII and leaders of a group owing allegiance to Marxism in politics and Bertolt Brecht in its interpretation of art. They regarded the cinema of illusion with disfavour and argued for Brechtian alienation to create a thinking cinema. Hardly any film of the group was ever released in the theatres; their ideology made nought of the need to communicate. Like Brecht's own plays written for the people, their Marxist films never reached the people. Since this predicament has been common to the large majority of parallel cinema, Kaul and Shahani may be regarded as the outer limit of the margi cinema, meant solely for the aficionado.

XI

The lessons of all the positive developments—the impact of technical and artistic growth centres, the success of many serious films in the regions, their winning of prestigious prizes in India and abroad, the emergence of the documentary and of television, the increasing emphasis on realism—cannot have been altogether lost on the mainstream film industry despite the hostile noises it often made about these trends. Signs of a rapprochement between the art film and commercial cinema began to appear with the approach of the 1990s. New producers and directors went into overtly serious social concerns within the idiom of the box office. Notable among these was Mani Ratnam with his *Roja* (1992) and *Bombay* (1995), the second of which launched into hitherto forbidden territory like marriage between Hindus and Muslims.

Another example was of actor–director Kamal Hasan's *Hey Ram* (2000), a film re-examining the role of Gandhi in the context of rioting between Hindus and Muslims on the eve of the partition of India and the creation of Pakistan. Divesting Gandhi of his charismatic leadership did not win the film many friends, but one had to admire the aplomb with which events of the period were realistically recreated in a manner not customarily seen in the mainstream cinema.

Similarly, Aamir Khan's *Lagaan* (2001) and Shah Rukh Khan's *Asoka* (2001) signalled a meaningful urge to grapple with serious social concerns within the melodramatic. *Lagaan*'s conflict with the British was old hat rousing little ire; but the subtext of the unity of all caste and religious loyalties in the village accounted for much of the warmth with which the film was received. Its success at home and abroad heralded a new appraisal of outstanding Bollywood films by the international community.

Notwithstanding *Asoka*'s thundering failure, it must be regarded as one of the signposts in the same direction because of the very willingness to turn to the treatment of large social and historical issues. The great thing about the film is that it was made; it could not have been without a personal concern with non-violence and religious tolerance as essential qualities of Indian civilization. Its failure is also interesting because its weaknesses are congenital to popular cinema's lack of research and realism in historical films. What *Asoka* needed was the creation of characters and events at once living and true to period. On both counts, its melodrama failed because it merely paraded familiar contemporary figures in a fancy dress party. It was never able to create the sense of distance in time in events supposed to have taken place more than 2000 years ago. The film clearly needed some of the typical virtues of unpopular cinema in order to become popular. It showed, like never before, that melodrama also needs a dose of realism, particularly in dealing with history.

At the same time, there was a new realism in films like *Satya* (1998) and *Company* (2002). Although both films looked to the critical eye like the poor man's combination of *Godfather* (Francis Ford Coppola, 1972) and *Pulp Fiction* (Quentin Tarantino, 1994), it has to be said that Bollywood has never looked more like Hollywood since the day of *Sholay*. The stranglehold of the mafia over the cinema is well known, and films like *Satya* and *Company* reflect that. Yet they also make it seem possible that one day Bollywood will be able to range more freely, like Hollywood, from one end to the other of cinema's spectrum, its varying blends of melodrama and realism, its ability to turn the unpopular into the popular and to create space for both strands of cinema. At least in technique, both mechanical and creative, India's mainstream cinema has become capable of that versatility, thanks to the infrastructure in training India had created and nurtured soon after Independence.

Popular cinema also seems to be emerging from the variety show mode stamped on it by the Parsi theatre from which it had taken its birth. Films like *Satya* and *Company*, even *Lagaan* which is otherwise different from the two, make songs a more integral part of the narrative, often turning them into a form of background music rather than the outpourings of a character or as chorus-like commentary on a personal situation.

Is it conceivable that the smugglers and murderers, the dons of the underworld of Mumbai and Dubai have no hand in what goes into the films they so often finance, directly or indirectly; that, regardless of where the money comes from, the products remain pristine expressions of the will of simple people with their simple faiths; that the dons' own idea of morality (honour among thieves?), their sense of right and wrong, tradition and modernity, do not permeate or insinuate into their celluloid products by inevitable osmosis? Perhaps the answer lies in the complex workings of Bollywood's innards that increasingly allow the reactionary and the progressive to coexist.

There are signs of an assertion of dissident points of view in films like *Bombay*. Such films are no longer intimidated by the traditional need to endorse the prejudices of the majority and are more prepared today to wean orthodox audiences away from their preformed ideas. The new century may thus see a change of values in at least an influential section of mass entertainment. It might take us back to the time before the divide, the golden age of Indian cinema. To make that possible, a force must arise, as it appears to be doing at this point in time, from within the mainstream, to counter the power of the underworld over the style and content of our cinema.

If the gap between art and commerce is closing today, it is because the art cinema impregnated the commercial in the period since India's independence, empowering it in terms of concepts and technique and qualifying it for international acceptance at world forums like international film festivals. These festivals had already recognized the artistic prowess of Indian cinema; they only had to see the marriage of art and commerce on a grand scale such as Hollywood has been in the habit of bringing off from time to time and such as Bollywood has of late shown signs of doing. The coexistence of margi and desi within the ambit of the film industry may also become more peaceful.

7

A WORD ON AWARDS

Living with awards is, predictably, as difficult as living without them. India's cult icon Ritwik Ghatak never got one; nor did Guru Dutt, perhaps the first film-maker in India to carve out a personal cinema within the precincts of the box office. In the year of Andrei Tarkovsky's *Sacrifice* (1986), the film that got the Grand Prix at the Cannes Film Festival was Ronald Joffé's *The Mission.* Time and again, despite the best efforts of festival directors, the audience has booed the awards. Rumours always abound about behind-the-scenes doings, political arithmetic on which award would bring more advantage to the festival, or who got an award the year before and could therefore be left out this time, and other such important irrelevancies. Desperate to escape this syndrome, one national system of awards in Italy picks only foreign critics for its jury and still cannot overcome all the problems.

India is no more free of such machinations, aberrations, solemn exercises in purification, than other countries; yet, a tally of the Best Film awards over the decades gives some indication of the high points of unpopular cinema. Given this cinema's success with awards more than with the box office, an overview of the highest national awards may be of worth in getting to know this margi face of the cinematic coin.

The utility of competitions is somewhat more obvious than their futility. Encouragement for the arts can be deemed praiseworthy by itself: in a country where patronage is perforce limited, it may be essential. It is still more so in a medium in which art fights a constant, and mostly losing, battle with the apparent commercial necessity for non-art. Without state patronage, many of the best films in the country since Independence would not have been made. The cash prizes of the national awards, not considerable especially for regional films, add substance to the honour, which itself has some convertibility to cash in terms of extra box-office receipts. Many a financier, loaded with more money than honour, is lured into supporting offbeat film-makers by the prospect of a prize.

What makes competitions futile in the arena of films is often the illusion that there exists some absolute standard for judging them. The fact, of course, is that such judgements must vary with the individuals nominated to make them. Every year, different individuals are chosen; even if the same were to stay, the constancy of their standards of judgement would come into doubt. Snap judgements are hardly the most reliable guide to excellence in art. Every work cannot be understood in the first encounter with it. In films, as in books, recognition must sometimes come late, and is not less valid for it. Jean Renoir was hounded by critics and audiences alike for his *La Règle du Jeu* at the time of its release in 1939; today, it is considered a masterpiece. It took an Andre Bazin and a whole school of critics at *Cahiers du Cinema* to give the film its due. Indeed, from a purist point of view, the very need to pick 'the best' is questionable, to be tolerated only for its incidental benefits. Besides, India is not noted for its film critics. Of our hundreds of film magazines, and film pages of newspapers, few publish any meaningful criticism. We do not have our *Sight and Sound* or *Cahier.* In the early years of independence, there was, at least in the film societies and their little magazines, a certain 'divine discontent' with Indian cinema which kept it abreast of the standards of film-making and held up a challenge to it; today, serious cinema is far ahead of serious film criticism. There is little written about the works of our best directors which can seem meaningful to them. This is undoubtedly because good film-making has received more incentive than good criticism. Newspapers have banished serious film criticism from their pages. It is not even the unavoidable adjunct it was for many years.

Even the few worthwhile critics we have are yet to earn their rightful place as judges of national or international cinema in the country's competitive events. Why, there was a time not so long ago, when the favourite pronouncement of the chairman of a national awards committee would be: 'I hardly ever see films.' However, this never prevented him, or others who shared his innocence, from passing judgement on what they saw, often riding roughshod over the more knowledgeable members, invariably in a hopeless minority.

What else would explain the award of the highest prize for 1953 to *Shyamchi Aai* in the year of *Do Bigha Zamin*, or to *Dada Thakur* in the year of Guru Dutt's *Sahib Bibi Aur Ghulam*? Guru Dutt never got the top national award. Nor did Ritwik Ghatak. In the year of Ghatak's *Ajantrik*, the highest national honour went to Debaki Bose's *Sagar Sangame* (1958); in the year of *Meghe Dhake Tara*, to Hrishikesh Mukherjee's *Anuradha* (1960). The 1961 prize went to *Bhagini Nivedita* in preference to Ghatak's *Komal Gandhar* and Guru Dutt's *Chaudhvin Ka Chand*. To see *Shyamchi Aai, Dada Thakur or Bhagini Nivedita* again today is to suffer untold agony.

Obviously, the committee which judged them had little understanding of cinema, and more respect for the subject matter and the literary original than for creativity in the film medium. The early years of the national awards hardly covered themselves with glory.

Cinematically, the surviving fragments of Phalke's films from the second decade of the twentieth century are more interesting than *Shyamchi Aai*, made one year after India's first international film festival. The film is conceived so theatrically that even the two or three shots taken out of doors, except the seascapes towards the end, appear to be inside the studio. Frontality dominates the choreography of the actors' movements, interspersed with profiles. Turning one's back to the camera is inconceivable. Exits and entries are almost always horizontal. Characters are one-dimensional. The acting, with the partial exception of that of the boy Shyam, is undistinguished. In contrast, Bimal Roy's *Do Bigha Zamin*, especially in its first half, is like a breath of fresh air, and heralds the lyrical realism of Ray's *Pather Panchali* and the beginnings of new Indian cinema.

Although made in the next decade, the cinematic values of Bijoy Basu's *Bhagini Nivedita* and Sudhir Mukherjee's *Dada Thakur* belong to the *Shyamchi Aai* period. The altogether different qualities recognized in the intervening years, which saw the national and international triumph of Ray's Apu trilogy, made no impact on the prize-winning films of 1961 and 1962 or those who sat in judgement on them. Apart from Ray, even the standards recognized in films like Sohrab Modi's *Mirza Ghalib* (1954) and Debaki Bose's *Sagar Sangame* are distinctly higher. Both Modi and Bose belonged to earlier styles of film-making which they themselves had helped to create; yet their work had a consistency of internal logic and dramatic construction. Debaki Bose was particularly able, in spite of the unabashed sentimentality of his material, to generate a true feeling through the restraint of his style. Some of the passages show an excellent blending of documentary and studio shots. The greatest distinction, however, belongs to the subtle tensions Bharati Devi brings to bear on her role as the God-fearing high-caste woman thrown together with a dancing girl's daughter due to a boat wreck on the way to pilgrimage at Sagar Island. Her superb performance is well matched by that of Manju Adhikari as the little girl. In spite of the conventional opening and ending, the film, seen today, still has a compelling narrative ability. Sohrab Modi's *Mirza Ghalib*, on the other hand, is little more than a competent work by a professional film-maker of that period, and has no trace of personal feeling about it. Of similar character are two other films by famous directors—Shantaram's *Do Aankhen Barah Haath* and Hrishikesh Mukherjee's *Anuradha*, the first of which won the award for 1957 (plus one in Berlin) and the second for 1960. Both appear to have scored more by the appeal of their subject matter than their creative excellence. Mrinal Sen's *Baishey Sravan*, made in the same year as Hrishikesh's film, reveals a far maturer talent and finer perception of cinema. Khwaja Ahmed Abbas's *Shehar Aur Sapna*, one of the less schematic of his films but nevertheless too poster-like and polemical to achieve any depth, won the award in 1963. It was the year of Ray's *Mahanagar* and young Partha Pratim Chowdhury's brilliant first film *Chhaya Surya*, little known outside Bengal.

So neither vertically in the time sequence nor horizontally did the award until this time show any consistent sense of standard even within the variations that are inevitable to all such jousts.

Around 1964 a better standard appears to have emerged. Perhaps this was because of a certain rise in the basic quality of the new cinema. Perhaps neither the film-makers nor the judges were any longer content with the glories of subject matter. A greater awareness of the overall quality of the cinematic statement seems to inform the judgements of the mid-1960s and the 1970s. Perhaps the problem of awarding Satyajit Ray (or Bengal) year after year was also resolved by the emergence of good cinema along a wider front. The Bengali cinema's peak was reached with Ray's masterpiece, *Charulata* (1964). Seeing it for the seventh time the other day was an experience for which I was not fully prepared. It made one recall the words of those who had described it all the time as a perfect example of craftsmanship and little else. One realized that the number and influence of intellectuals without sensibility in our country is frightening. For, the film not only has the stylistic delicacy of a miniature painting, but great depth of underlying tension, its expression achieved in the manner of a perfect musical statement. 'All arts,' one is tempted to quote Schopenhauer, 'strive towards the condition of music.' *Charulata* is a rare example of that kind of success.

Perhaps *Charulata* represented the peak of Bengali cinema and of Ray's genius at the same time. He won awards with *Goopy Gyne Bagha Byne* (1968) and *Seemabaddha* (1971), but neither the charm of the first nor the new, harder realism of the second brings a sense of experience of his earlier quality. Fresh winds began to blow from many directions, not all of the same force, but mostly of a certain new impulse unified in the cinematic quality of their expression. Ramu Kariat's *Chemmeen* (1966), made from a classic novel, was not a great film, but it brought with it a salty-real taste of the sea. The thrill of experiencing a new reality from another part of the country gave the film its compelling power. In 1966, Basu Bhattacharjee transported Bengal's realistic narrative style into Hindi cinema, with *Teesri Kasam*. Two great performers, Raj Kapoor and Waheeda Rehman, surrendered their stardom to some genuine acting, even though Kapoor could not completely shake off his instinctive showmanship. Subrata Mitra's photography brought to Hindi cinema a new clarity of which *Do Bigha Zamin* had barely given a foretaste in its village outdoor sequences. The subject of Nautanki also brought some freshness to a familiar plot. Tapan Sinha's *Haatey Bazarey* (1967) was a more complex presentation than the unidirectional dramatic propensity he had exhibited in his

Kabuliwala (top prize winner, 1956), where the delicately woven magic of Tagore's short story had come in for some heavy-handed traditional dramatics, overstretching its credibility in spite of Chhabi Biswas's great presence. Sinha's lack of appreciation of photographic values, and generally of a cinematic vision, was better compensated in the construction of his later prize winner than his earlier. The year 1969 brought first wide recognition to Mrinal Sen with *Bhuvan Shome.* Although its treatment somewhat overwhelms its subject, Sen's delight in the film medium is infectious, and even his ability to make the audience believe that something is happening when nothing actually is (for example, the scene of man chasing buffalo which he turns into buffalo chasing man), excites admiration. Suhasini Mulay's charm helps the film enormously, but is by no means the only attraction of the film as some would have us believe. Breaking away from Ray's slow rhythm, accepted by most of the new film-makers including Sen in his earlier films, *Bhuvan Shome* refreshed the senses with its fast cutting and its aggressive use of sound.

The 1970s began with a bang. Pattabhi Rama Reddy's *Samskara* (1970), with Girish Karnad in the lead, startled one with its strong sense of confrontation, its remarkable close-ups, and its perception of tradition in a way totally different from Ray's. It heralded the rise of a new cinema in the south more clearly than *Chemmeen*, which had lacked an original point of view. Tom Cowan, *Samskara*'s Australian cameraman, at times betrays a penchant for the exotic, and some of the groupings are almost self-consciously borrowed from Japanese period cinema. The cutting is at times too abrupt, giving one the sense of a Western tempo suddenly ruffling an Indian calm. Snehalata Reddy, as the fallen woman, is too stilted and unconvincing, perhaps more due to miscasting than an acting failure. But the relationship of the Brahmins is brought out powerfully in perfectly chosen faces. Lakshmi Krishnamurty turns in a striking performance. However, it is Girish Karnad who epitomizes Ray's classic description of Eastern expression: 'Calm without; fire within'. The scene of the seduction is superbly achieved, the intercutting between the lovemaking and the Yakshagana performance powerful, the walk through the forest with the extrovert traveller reminiscent of Bergman and Kurosawa in its depth of philosophic suggestion: a powerful film, albeit far from perfect. In the history of awards over the next few years, the southern cavalcade is briefly interrupted by Ray's *Seemabaddha* (1971) and Mrinal Sen's *Chorus* (1974) and *Mrigaya* (1976). Adoor Gopalakrishnan's *Swayamvaram* (1972) derives much from Ray's narrative rhythm, his use of silences in suggesting feeling and relationship, but takes a step towards a harder realism. An adroit use of camera and cutting distinguishes it from M.T. Vasudevan Nair's more dramatic *Nirmalayam* (1973). Adoor came up through film societies and the FTII; M.T. through literature and journalism. The difference shows. *Nirmalayam* attacks its action sequences with power and Anthony's acting is charged with tension; but the film's dialogue sequences tend to be theatrical. Altogether, it seems to have a better sense of drama than of cinema. It must have been a hard choice that year, for M.S. Sathyu's *Garam Hawa* (1973) was, both in the force of its subject and its combination of delicacy and power in treatment, a strong contender, arguably the better of the two.

Chorus and *Mrigaya* are both expertly crafted films with a political stance veiled by an avant-garde exterior (or is it an avant-garde cinematic interest clothed in political gesturing?) but neither has the sincerity and simple power of B.V. Karanth's *Chomana Dudi* (1975), again from the south. After *Samskara*, it was the first film from Karnataka to claim national attention, followed in 1978 by Girish Kasaravalli's *Ghatashraddha*. This remarkable first film by a young film graduate is a little simplistic in character development and the weaving of relationships, but powerful in its dramatic structure. There is a sureness in its rhythm and the unfolding of its narrative.

Although unequal in their excellence, the winners of the 1970s fluctuate less widely than in the previous two decades. There is no sudden harking back to bygone styles of film-making. Nor is there a glorification of subject matter at the expense of style without some appreciation of the unity of the two. The films of the period have a more sustained social awareness; they entertain through the participation of their audience and not through a spoon-feeding process. The cinema bears more of a personal stamp. The relatively uniform quality of the films awarded prizes reflects not only a maturing of the new cinema, but of its judging by the juries appointed. It is significant that the more meretricious and self-conscious wave brought about in the Hindi cinema by the sponsorship of the Film Finance Corporation is hardly represented—the films of Mani Kaul, for instance, which made a lot of noise at the time, were bypassed (regrettably along with Shyam Benegal's *Ankur* and Sathyu's *Garam Hawa*).

To this relative maturing of the judgement, the removal of the regional–central committee hierarchy may have contributed by taking off a pressure system. The freedom resulting from this appears to have been well utilized. And what more aggressive gesture of firm judgement could there be than the withholding of the top award in 1979, the year of Benegal's *Junoon* and Karnad's *Ondanondu Kaladalli* (are they worse than some of the winners of that period?).

Many new voices were heard in the 1980s and old ones made themselves heard anew. Indeed, one witnessed an explosion of talent such that only a constant expansion of prize categories did some justice to the claimants for them. In 1980, the first prize went to one of the best-ever films on the film-within-a-film format. Mrinal Sen's *Akaler Sandhanay* (In Search of Famine) drew attention, at once sharp and poignant, to the impact of art on reality and reality on art which has rarely been explored so vividly. But the same year saw the emergence of a new talent in Ketan Mehta, whose *Bhavni Bhavai* made singular use of traditional art to carry a modern message. Besides, its black humour introduced a much-needed new note into Indian cinema. Its musical satire on the institution of the untouchable in Hindu society is uniquely Brechtian and Indian at the same time. G. Aravindan's *Pokkuveyil* (Twilight, 1981), a remarkably sensitive study of adolescent insanity marked by Aravindan's characteristic respect for the human being and his person, was awarded the second best place to a somewhat tepid piece of Marxism, *Dakhal*, by no means among Goutam Ghose's best works. What could the jury do, faced with so many outstanding works, including *Imagi Ningthem*, a film from the tiny state of Manipur in the mountain fastnesses of north-eastern India?

The poignant study of filial love went on to win awards in foreign festivals despite its technical immaturities. Another contender for the first place was *36 Chowringhee Lane* by actress-turned-director, Aparna Sen. This very mature first film was given three awards, in compensation, as it were, for denying it the label of 'The Best'.

Awards will remain, one fears, as necessary and as frustrating as they have always been.

8

FILM AS VISUAL ANTHROPOLOGY

In Mrinal Sen's *Akaler Sandhanay* (In Search of Famine, 1980), a film crew in Bengal goes to a village to re-enact the 1943 famine that had taken five million lives. The villagers get deeply involved with the film-making, which disrupts their lives, still lived in penury. Prices go up because the film crew is consuming whatever is left after the main produce of the village has gone to the city anyway. 'They came to take pictures of a famine,' says a villager, 'and sparked off another.'

A local woman is recruited to act the role of a wife who allows herself to be seduced by a contractor from the city, in exchange for some rice. When the scene is enacted, the father of the girl who had earlier agreed to the casting bursts into a rage and takes his daughter away. In another scene, an actor playing the husband, enraged by his wife's whoring for a handful of rice, lifts up his child and is about to dash it to the ground. The scene, played by professionals, goes perfectly for the director of the film until a local woman in the crowd, a wife and mother, screams and ruins the shot. Eventually, the local schoolmaster persuades the director to leave and to shoot their scenes in a city studio, and the crew packs up.

Seldom has the intervention of the observer in the life of the observed been so drastically construed and so graphically described. It took a fiction film to expose the realities of the relationship. As the schoolmaster says to the director, 'You belong to the privileged class . . . you have tried to impose yourself on them.' In your search for realism, he could have added. The fictional approach enables Mrinal Sen to push the observer–observed, self-and-other divide to its apotheosis, where its roots can be exposed in a way no documentary film or written ruminations of the anthropologist could have. It challenges the film-maker's pretence to objectivity and lays it bare.

That, in a way, also brings us to the basic difference between ways of apprehending reality. One may be said, not altogether simplistically, to concern itself with the surfaces of reality and the other with the reality under the surface. It is questionable whether a documentary of the village shown in Sen's film could have brought out the real relationships and motivations of its representative inhabitants equally well.

For contrast, one can take an anthropological film, *Dadi's Family*, directed by Michael Camerini and Rina Gill (for the University of Wisconsin), which records the daily life of a peasant family in Haryana. In orthodox, thoroughgoing anthropological style, the film crew set up cameras and lights and observed the family for months, getting them used to the presence of the (minimal) crew and the equipment. The film is of two hours' duration, yet it reveals the observed only in what might be called a-scene-and-a-half. One is a long, remarkably real quarrel between mother-in-law and daughter-in-law, and the other a scene of a wife bringing food to her husband in the field and talking to him of their problems and hopes. The second does not come off altogether, although it offers some glimpses of the relationship (hence I call it 'half'). For the rest, all we see are the surfaces of daily life that tell us little about the people they observe so meticulously over such a length of time. Clearly, the family is never totally unaware of the camera and the real moments arrive only when they unwittingly lower their guard. They reveal something of themselves when they are agitated or when they think their real selves can't be seen in what they are doing. If one were to consider the issue of voyeurism, *Dadi's Family* would prove to be more voyeuristic than *Akaler Sandhanay*. The fictional film is open and direct in its intervention: it makes no pretence to objectivity. The documentary, by staying long with the family, by keeping the apparatuses set up and ready everywhere, all the time, seeks to be the voyeur, to lull the observed gradually into an unawareness of the observer.

For an in-between situation, one can take a well-known, albeit old, film—Jean Rouch's *Chronique d'un été* (Chronicle of a Summer, 1961) made with sociologist Edgar Morin. Rouch is a good example because he began as an ethnographer in the classic mould and, using the camera as a hobby, began to realize its ability to record more than what written tomes could tell us about people. His beginnings in film-making were typical too; *Les Maîtres Fous* (The Manic Priests, 1955) showed possessed Hauka adepts, their mouth foaming, slaughter and eat a dog, reflecting the colonial anthropologist's penchant for recording the strange practices of the colonized and attracting strong criticism for it from the country of the observed. *Chronique d'un été*'s scene is Paris; it was, for a change, home-ground anthropology. Rouch had developed a way of bringing people of different backgrounds together before his camera. He and Morin first go about asking Parisian participants, 'Are you happy?' with themselves on-camera; then a number of people are interviewed in detail about their work and their private fears and anxieties. Afterwards, they are introduced to each other before the camera and encouraged to interact. Finally, some of the people filmed are shown the footage in a screening room and their discussions filmed.

'People, perhaps because there is a camera there,' said Rouch, 'create something quite different and create it spontaneously.' He never pretended that the camera was a mere observer; he filmed improvised sequences that set amateur players in fictional situations not dissimilar to those of their own lives. The result was predictable; only where the amateur was a good communicator did the film come to life as in the woman Marilou, who, had she cared, could have gone on to be an actress of note. In other words, the revelations of character and relationship were accidental, meagre in the context of the twenty solid hours' film that he had shot with synchronized sound, which was then a new technique.

Compared to what fiction achieved by way of revelation of individuals, relationships, habits and ways of life in Satyajit Ray's Apu trilogy (1955–59), Rouch's achievement was sketchy, even though his experiment was interesting, even essential. What Rouch attempted to do by placing amateurs in improvised fictional situations close to their own was, in essence, not all that different from Ray's films, also acted mostly by amateurs and based on Bibhutibhusan Bandopadhyay's highly perceptive and basically realistic fiction. The fact that Ray had a rambling, meandering semblance of a plot and a scenario, mostly sketched in pictures rather than written, seemed to have done little to prevent the emergence of a sense of real people in real places and situations acting in ways in which they would have acted in real life. The trilogy is nothing short of a profound revelation of the changing lifestyles, thinking patterns, evolving relationships of the impoverished middle class of traditional rural India emerging into the urban world of today. There is no pretence over the truth of representation, even though it is imbued with lyricism and compassion not entirely unlike Robert Flaherty's in his documentary, *Louisiana Story* (1948). And the dialogue would not, by any stretch of the imagination, attract Flaherty's comment after the first screening of *Louisiana Story* (recounted by his cinematographer Richard Leacock), 'Jesus Christ, did I write that crap!'

'I think *Pather Panchali* is a masterpiece, but I know the young girl didn't really die,' Richard Leacock says, 'and although granny looked like she was ready to, I don't believe she really did!' Actually she did, only a few months after the release of the film. The thought that the girl did not really die arises in the mind because there is a touch—the only one, I think—of contrivance in the death sequence; it is a shade too dramatic in its construction. For the rest, where would we get a better picture of 'life in a Bengal village' than in *Pather Panchali* or 'the ghats of Varanasi' than in *Aparajito*? As for strange marriage customs, what could be more strange, and more natural, than Apu's marriage to Aparna in *Apur Sansar* where he becomes the accidental bridegroom, replacing the one who had come for the wedding but turned out to be insane, threatening eternal celibacy to the bride-to-be if she missed the auspicious hour of marriage?

If anthropologists are the 'miniaturists of the social sciences', as Clifford Geertz famously said, so are many of the realistic feature film-makers. Except in some instances of simplistic Marxism, there are no grand conclusions announced in them; they are content to acquaint us with characters and relationships within a community, with sympathy and even participatively, but without prescription. There are many examples of this outside of Ray, who is noted for his non-partisan view of social change in which there are no heroes or villains, and characters and events are part of a continuing process. Let us consider Prema Karanth's *Phaniyamma*.

Regardless of what the director may have said about the principal character in her work, the film itself does view both the widows—the old and the young with their different predicaments and perceptions—with equal interest. T.G. Vaidyanathan makes an interesting point about the older widow's misogyny arising from psychological trauma. But the director's view need not be seen as partisan. The very fact that she seems to endorse both the older widow's horror of sex (as TGV seems to think) and the younger's enjoyment of it goes to show a non-partisan view of two streams within the Indian tradition—the ascetic and the life-embracing. The second needs no contemporary rediscovery; of the first there is a living example that has intrigued anthropologists in the community of the Brahmakumaris.[1] This contemporary religious movement with a fairly high visibility advocates celibacy in women. Like *Phaniyamma* it expresses a horror of what Vaidyanathan terms the 'instinctive side of life' consisting of the gore, grime and sheer earthiness of the process of sexual intercourse, conception and birth. The Brahmakumaris believe that in the first half of the 5000-year cycle of creation, human reproduction took place by yogic powers; the second spelt the fall of woman as a result of sex, lust and preoccupation with the body including the act of intercourse and childbirth that they, like Phaniyamma, find so revolting in their sheer physicality. Thus, the *Phaniyamma* experience is a recounting of an ascetic horror of the human reproductive process that persists to this day and runs parallel to the zest for it so evident at all social levels in India.

Women have provided the focus of the realistic feature film in India's 'new' or 'parallel' cinema to a large extent. The status of women has often been taken as the index of social change or the country's progress. Aspects of the man–woman relationship have in any case been central to the preoccupations of the fictional film practically all over the world. The conjunction of these two interests has therefore provided a strong impetus to the treatment of the feminine condition in the New Cinema. In this the widow often figures as at once a victim and a symbol of the persistence of traditional superstition and social oppression. Besides *Phaniyamma*, an important example of this is Girish Kasaravalli's film (also made in Kannada) *Ghatashraddha*. Throughout the 1970s, the new forces in the Kannada film were obsessed with the problem of oppressive religious institutions in rural areas. Indeed, this aspect has formed an important part of the New Cinema's largely realistic explorations of the tensions of tradition and modernity that Indian society at most levels struggles to resolve within a continued identity.

The socially marginalized widow of *Ghatashraddha* gets drawn into the processes of 'the instinctive side of life' without deliberation, driven by forces too big for her to comprehend. Nature is in conflict with society that does not forgive transgressions. Unlike *Phaniyamma*, this film does not play up different aspects and attitudes of woman and her bodily processes; it draws a stark picture of one village, one woman, one transgression and its inexorable consequence: expulsion from society. It is a less complex but more relentless film than Karanth's. As such what it reflects is the uncompromising antagonism of its maker to the subjugation and oppression of widowed women, and through them, of all women in the grip of tradition. The understatement of the style only underlines the criticism of the traditional treatment of widowhood. The young Brahmin boy's silent sympathy for the predicament of the woman hints at the inevitability of attitudinal change in the younger generation. Both *Phaniyamma* and *Ghatashraddha* underscore the polarity between the 'commercial' and the 'new' cinema. Stylistically and in terms of content and treatment, the commercial cinema could not have thrown up such products in the period since Independence. Even though it is equally obsessed with the problem of tradition and modernity beneath the tinsel of its entertainment, its resolution of such a situation as *Phaniyamma*'s or *Ghatashraddha*'s would have come out firmly in favour of the traditional view through some *deus ex machina*—if it treated such a subject at all. Thus the realistic film, despite such sympathies as it may directly harbour, holds up something of a mirror to actual social practices, in spite of its fictional form.

Indeed, its fictionality can be seen as a means of creating, almost like a re-enacted documentary, a simulation of reality in which the camera is accepted as an important factor. The problem of polarity between the observer and the observed is solved by making them equal partners in a single process. In the Frits Staal and Richard Schechner controversy over the filming of *Agnicayana* in Kerala, Schechner points out what is missing in this tremendous exercise in recording and commentary: '. . . respect for the contingency of ritual performances and a full discussion of the very powerful contingent circumstances surrounding and profoundly changing the 1975 Agnicayana . . . a genre of anthropological game is being played.' The Vedic ritual was performed after twenty years, and because of widespread protest an essential element, the sacrifice of fourteen goats, had to be dropped. Barely hours before the performance of the ritual, rice cakes wrapped in banana leaves were substituted for the goats. As Staal himself remarked: '. . . it is not easy to kill rice cakes by strangulation and cut them open to take out particular organs.'[2] To Schechner, the film (by noted visual anthropologist Robert Gardner)—and Staal's two-volume book *Agni* backed up by tape recordings of the twelve-day event—were vitiated by the input of money: $127,207, the cost of the yagna, was paid in dollars and rupees by sources outside India. Money, says Schechner 'is a clear indication of where the power is . . . the patrons of the ritual (the Vedic *Yajamana*, who takes part in the event) were not Indians but foundation officials . . . the 1975 Agnicayana existed because it was to be filmed and scholared.' The only person in the film crew allowed near the bird-shaped altar, it seems, was Kunju Vasudevan, a Brahmin with a Bolex. In other words, the intervention of the film-maker and the scholar in the event changed the event itself and this aspect was glossed over by Staal and Gardner in the book and the film.[3]

The 'observational' model of visual anthropology finds an occasional, if rare, reflection in the fictional film. A unique film-maker like G. Aravindan turns its lack of statement into a form of eloquence: he is able to create resonances and metaphors that expand within the mental space of his audiences even though what we see is a series of unimportant, undramatized events. An itinerant rural circus troupe, with a few ordinary acts, moving from place to place, is observed in detail, with a rare reverence. Aravindan's work is imbued with a sense of the sacredness of life; every face is as a portrait of evanescence, every action, no matter how minute, becomes a sacrament. There is a well-known actor, Gopi, in the film, but he merges into the troupe. What Aravindan requires of his actors is, in his own words, 'behaviour not action'. The observation of behaviour as a flowing rhythm obscures the deliberate elements of film-making—the camerawork, the organization of material, the editing. The film is neither dramatic in its transitions, nor is it the observation of bacteria under a microscope. It does not, according to Jhala, 'reduce human societies and their environments to human laboratories in which change and progress are to be controlled by the observers and the dominant culture'. Indeed, Aravindan's most remarkable trait is that his own high culture never intrudes into the observed, much less dominates them. A film like *Thampu* may in some ways, at least in terms of style, be considered the best kind of visual anthropology—the kind we seldom see in the more official, academically approved versions of it. By comparison, Akos Ostar's film on the Charak festival in Bishnupur (West Bengal) is, for instance, a highly impersonal, 'scientific record' in which the feelings, motivations and attitudes of the observed are obscured by the observer's emphasis on the accurate presentation of surface events, that is, by the very lack of artifice.

The advocacy approach has been in evidence in the segment of Indian cinema we are concerned with here, as frequently as the observational. In fact, the advocacy often borders on the inflammatory, sometimes the demagogic. A successful, restrained and yet angry example of it is in Govind Nihalani's *Aakrosh* (Cry of the Wounded, 1980). A young Brahmin lawyer takes up the case of a tribal accused of killing his wife but is unable to make headway; although innocent of the crime, his client maintains a stubborn silence throughout the film. At first this seems stupid, but as the film progresses we discover its reason. Speech will cost him even more than silence; it will bring retribution on his aged father and his young sister from the very combine of power and money that had raped and murdered his wife. The film is a searing indictment of the system and the society it sustains. The indictment is made quietly, lucidly, systematically and, mostly, non-ideologically, without rhetoric, without sloganeering and without table-thumping propaganda, as Anil Dharker asserts.

The subject of the Muslim minority's problems in India has always been a sensitive area but never more so than immediately after Partition, for those who had chosen to remain. M.S. Sathyu's *Garam Hawa* (Hot

Winds, 1973) is to this day the only film that touches this raw nerve. Other films sanitize the Muslim community, showing only the decorative aspects and isolating individuals from their context to turn them into saints. Sathyu concentrates on one family's predicament and its conflict with Hindus as also the pulls towards Pakistan which it finally resists. Structurally removed from the documentary, it nevertheless portrays a community's anguish in very real terms.

Almost all of Shyam Benegal's films are concerned with particular communities, and succeed in revealing something about them. From *Ankur* (The Seedling, 1974) to *Trikaal* (Past, Present, Future, 1985) it is a series of studies of relationships within and between communities. Two of them, *Manthan* (The Churning, 1976) and *Susman* (The Essence, 1986), were participatory to the extent that the community paid for them: a milk cooperative in the case of the first and a community of weavers in the second. Both show a singular ability to make fiction out of documentary material without compromising the complexity and basic truth of the material. Technical fluency plus an extraordinary penchant for good casting and for the structuring of material make the films dramatic without being too fictional to be true. A remarkable sureness of feeling for people and places in this prolific film-maker enables him to overcome some elements of contrivance in the mix of drama and documentary. With Benegal we reach the frontiers of documentary and fiction and get the feeling that beyond this point, the portrayal would cease to be recognizable.

The question that arises in my mind after this brief examination is: visual anthropology (to quote Jhala) broadly speaking, 'is the study of mankind, employing as its principal instrument of investigation the camera'; what is left of it as a discipline after we have seen the realistic fictional film and the documentary film and the skills of major photographers? In India, the body of work of high quality done in these three media, mainly since Independence, is quite considerable. The fact that the authors of this voluminous material have not seen it as 'visual anthropology' seems to be of little importance.

In developing visual anthropology in India as a discipline in itself, one must recognize the fact that there is not a very great deal that the serious, realistic Indian film-maker, feature or documentary, has to learn today from the West in terms of technique or style. As far as the content goes, he is intensely interested in bringing out the conditions of being of his fellow Indians, even in small, neglected communities. The Indian mind today is—one is not speaking of the mindless here—deeply involved in self-exploration, identification with its own people, and the betterment of their lives in their many incarnations and manifestations, large and small. In this respect India's New Cinema (mostly realistic) is sharply different from the consumerist existentialism of cinema in the West and of India's own popular films. It causes a separation of the study of mankind through the camera from the constant concocting of sensations—aesthetic or visceral, voyeuristic or participatory—based upon the material of human actions and emotions. As soon as such a separation takes place, we have a crying need for visual anthropology, because then the fictional film avoids reality and the documentary is marginalized. When Pare Lorenz's films became popular and Roosevelt wanted his government directly to support such film-making, the American film industry was up in arms and Congress cut off this governmental bid to enter the preserve of private enterprises. This is not to deny that private enterprise in America has produced outstanding feature films with a fine sense of reality in dealing with the underworld, with war and many other areas. Later, the 'Direct Cinema' movement in the USA remained mainly peripheral both to the film industry and the corridors of power.

In India, on the other hand, the serious and realistic New Cinema, although inconsequential in all-India box-office reckonings (despite a fair amount of success within regional–linguistic limits), has a very high profile. It is largely sponsored by government; although it frequently bites the hand that feeds it, it is showered with honours. With its high national and international visibility, it retains an ability to influence opinion-leaders and decision-makers in spite of its low box-office takings.

From this point of view, Indian cinema has done better than Italian neo-realism which was influential but very short-lived or the French cinéma-vérité which never gathered much steam and nouvelle vague which offered sharp observation of the French middle class in many films but never compared with the influence of India's social critiques on the country's decision-making classes.

9

THE CRISIS IN FILM STUDIES

'In the beginning was the word. And the word was with God, and the word was God.' The only fault we can find with this proclamation of the Gospel According to St Matthew today is the use of the past tense; for the word remains God. Otherwise why should anyone look at a picture and call it a 'text' to be 'read', not 'seen'?

Cinema came in when it did, among other things, as a revolt against the tyranny of words. In the print civilization, reality is described, analysed, assembled, built upon, in myriad ways. For the discipline of words, it is necessary to translate all direct sensory experience into word-symbols, store them in the memory, compare them with other such translations and put them to a vast range of uses from poetry to philosophy, nuclear physics to advertising slogans. But words are not direct experience as music or cinema is. And there is a limit to language's ability to translate sensory experience into words; without that limit, there would have been no need to invent music or painting or cinema. There is a whole world of experience in reality or in dream that lies beyond the realm of words. It lies in the area of the ineffable and the inscrutably ambiguous: *Yato vacho nivartantay aprapya manasa saha*:[1] From where words return, unable to comprehend (the reality) with the intellect.

By turning what is basically a picture into a 'text', a beginning is made towards appropriating cinema back into the domain of the print civilization, divesting it of its directness, its non-verbal being, both in the making and the seeing of films. This is so that the keepers of the print civilization can stand guard over non-verbal communication, police and control it in aid of the state or the corporate world or academia. The entire apparatus of education throughout the world puts overwhelming emphasis on the development of the intellect. It marginalizes the training of the sensibility, inhibits and corrupts the capacity for the direct experience of art. And the more criticism inhabits the realm of abstraction, the further away it gets from the world of direct experience. The word-image of the sensory experience is never the sensory experience itself, for which there is no substitute. What is more, the habit of arranging and rearranging logical abstractions built out of these word-images tends to dehydrate the sensory experience, draining it of its lifeblood, its context of emotional, visceral response and filtering it constantly through the verbal–cerebral process. The difference between a professorial dissertation and a piece of imaginative, non-academic writing on cinema is that the latter enhances instead of diminishing the quality of the sensory experience. Besides, its focus on the non-verbal is sharper.

'"Text" conveys,' according to Bill Nichols in his introduction to two hefty volumes rather lamely titled *Movies and Methods*, 'a greater sense of methodological exactitude than the term "movie" or "film".' Why? 'Partly because it implies that films are manifestations of certain characteristics found across a range of words that many non-film-specific methods are adept at analysing.'[2] In other words, it delivers film into the hands of professors of literature (who today form the large majority of academic film critics) and helps to underplay the most important part of cinema—the non-verbal.

What is there to be gained by marginalizing the distinctiveness of film form by emphasizing the aspects that it might share with non-film? Surely we understand film better by emphasizing its differences from non-film?

The growing co-option of cinema by the universities is encouraging in some ways but fearful in others. 'The number of PhDs in film in the United States,' we are told in Bill Nichols's introduction to Part II of *Movies and Methods*, a massive collection of ninety-nine essays, 'rose from approximately two hundred in 1964 to more than two thousand today.'[3]

There is only one essay, in these tomes of 'political correctness', that deals with non-Western cinema. It takes Gillo Pontecorvo's *Battle of Algiers* as its central 'text' and holds it up as a model of politically correct film-making. It is ironical that the whole of Asian cinema should be left out of the discourse in what must be a prime example of the marginalization of the 'subaltern' that the book's ideology denounces so loudly. There is a quiet but rather grand assumption that whatever is true of Western cinema is ipso facto applicable to the non-Western as well, or worse, that it is not worth considering at all, never mind Kurosawa or Ozu, Ray or Ghatak.

There is a still more careless yet utterly fundamental assumption at the back of all these theories: that intellect and sensibility are interchangeable categories, that, in fact, they are one and the same thing. The arrogance of the assumption is such that one of the ninety-nine essays in this 1500-page collection says, and many others imply, that a film is no more than the sum of its parts; the parts are eminently analysable and each ingredient that goes into the making of it is identifiable. If that were indeed so any competent professor would be able to make arresting films that moved the minds of millions of men and women. Yet most of them would hesitate to underwrite that proposition. Why? Is there some peculiar absence that would hold them back? Jean Renoir solved that problem perfectly when he said, 'Give everybody the same story and ask them to make a film from it; you will soon find out who is an artist and who is not.'[4] Ideologically correct cinema does not necessarily move the minds of men and women. Of course there are those who will say that it is not important to move minds; to be correct is enough. But you will invariably find that film scholars concern themselves with the most successful films either in terms of the box office or in widespread critical esteem or both, that is, films that have moved minds.

Actually it is infinitely more difficult to create a living character than to depict a politically correct one; for the latter all you have to do is to assemble the right traits to construct what may be no more like a living character than a scarecrow. It is a problem very like painting a still life or *A Man with a Hat in His Hand*. In cinema, it takes nothing to write that line in a film script but it is infinitely difficult to make him come alive on screen. This is what frustrates the unintuitive intellectual, the intellectual without sensibility, makes him feel inferior and is responsible for much of his perverse desire to act the sovietique policeman of the arts dealing out decrees on political correctness, creating a hostile relationship between the critic and the artist, making criticism incapable of interacting with the creative. Indeed, one Indian film scholar told me: 'Why should I want to interact with the creative person?' There is no regard here for the dynamics of the relationship between the two which is of considerable importance to the spiritual sustenance of both. If creative artists don't give a damn about what the academics write, it is largely because of the policemanly attitude of the critics of the PhD variety. The intellectual wants to take the sensory experience for granted and to build superstructures of meaning on it and thereafter to inhabit a world of meanings alone.

To which Susan Sontag's rejoinder: 'Like the fumes of the automobile and of heavy industry which befoul the urban atmosphere, the effusions of interpretation of art today poison our sensibilities. In a culture whose already classic dilemma is the hypertrophy of the intellect at the expense of energy and sensual capability, interpretation is the revenge of the intellect upon the art. Even more, it is the intellect's revenge on the world. To interpret is to impoverish, deplete the world—in order to set up a shadow world of meanings .... In most modern instances, interpretation amounts to a philistine refusal to leave the work of art alone.'[5]

What Susan Sontag said in the late 1960s, is many times more true today, with the proliferation of PhDs. One cannot help being left with the feeling that the present-day advocates of so-called 'scientific criticism' and enemies of 'liberal–humanist' writing are strikingly similar to the medieval scholastics whose 'philosophy of beauty was often a purely verbal matter. Whereas the Greeks had examined our immediate experiences of concrete beauty, the medieval often deployed Greek theory within the framework of metaphysics.'[6]

II

Fortunately, of late there has been a renewed attempt, even among the ranks of the Marxists, to recognize the autonomy of the work of art and the primacy of the sensory experience; it is no longer idealist or liberal–humanist to talk about these definitions of the status of art. 'The Body' is being rehabilitated by those who once espoused the 'Vulgar Marxism' of the Christopher Caudwell variety, which had once inspired the unspeakable torment of the artist in soviet socialist states. This is now being decried in favour of a more balanced interpretation of the artist's responsibility towards society and his responsibility towards his own vision. The effort is to accommodate the autonomy, indivisibility and magicality of the creative process without altogether relinquishing the right to ethical control. Thus Terry Eagleton in 1990 virtually echoes Susan Sontag in 1966 when he says: 'With the birth of the aesthetic, then, the sphere of art itself begins to suffer something of the abstraction and formalisation characteristic of modern theory in general . . . Aesthetics is born as a discourse of the body.' He refers pointedly to 'the body's long inarticulate rebellion against the tyranny of the theoretical'. Demolishing the professorial claim that in art 'the total is no more than the sum of its parts', he declares that 'The mystery of the aesthetic object is that each of its sensuous parts while appearing wholly autonomous, incarnates the law of totality'.[7] Most of the concepts here were anathema to an earlier generation of New Left commentators who, unfortunately, continue to influence academic Indian film scholars. Adorno had said: 'Only art is capable of providing an immanent critique of instrumental reason.'[8] Now, Andrew Bowie sees in music, more than in any other artistic activity, 'The impossibility of understanding subjectivity through theoretical articulation' and talks of 'Prereflexive subjectivity'.[9] The much-maligned T.S. Eliot had, generations ago, said it in more limpid prose: 'Poetry is communicated before it is understood.' Today, Bernstein asserts that 'art's rewards are not reducible to Knowledge' and discredits Adorno's social theory as his 'Vulgar sociologism'.[10] How fast these positions on art have changed, and how disastrous it would have been if the artists had paid any attention to them! T.J. Clarke once accused Michael Fried of the sins of formalism and ahistoricism, calling him 'the spokesperson of the bourgeoisie's detachment of art from the pressures and deformities of history'.[11] In the early 1990s, however, Clarke adopted Fried's principle that 'looking at art is already ethical and needs no supplementary ethical support to justify it'.[12] Historical materialism (and the social theories of art that it spawned for generations) have virtually capitulated to the idealism of Kant. Is Fried's above statement very different from the Kantian dictum that 'works of art are purposeful in themselves while lacking any positive, practical (moral) end over and above their internal complexion'?[13] Needless to say, this equation turns the writings of George Lukacs and his allies into instruments of the suppression of individuality and supporters of the 'Gulag mentality' which many Indian acolytes of the New Left are still desperately clinging on to, even though, for all practical purposes, the materialist social theories of art have been relegated to the dustbins of history.

As at the end of the battle of Kurukshetra, one might ask: What has been gained by the mighty battle, after death has undone so many? How many more masterpieces would Eisenstein or Dovzhenko or Tarkovsky, and many others born and stifled or aborted talents have produced if they had not been hounded by leftist social theories of art? Translated into political terms, what is the difference in the outcome from Pol Pot's massacre of some five million ending in Sihanouk's liberal democratic regime in Cambodia?

Despite all the ifs and buts and backtracking and renewed search for compromises granting art a 'rational autonomy' in order to break out of the manifestly counterproductive prisons of 'Vulgar Marxism' (themselves inevitable after the resounding fall of sovietism in praxis), it is impossible to overcome the impression that these late Marxist rearguard exercises are directed towards salvaging as much as possible of the domination of ethical theory over cultural production. It is as though saving the remains of Marxism is more important than saving humanity or what best enshrines the humanity of the human being, that is, art.

III

If there is a case for freeing art from the grip of social and ethical theory in order to establish its autonomy and subjectivity, there is a doubly valid one for freeing film criticism from the same constraints. Recognition of the subjectivity of art also opens the door for subjectivity in criticism. Invalidation of the cry for 'scientific criticism' becomes inevitable.

Not that this would make the discussion of social issues in criticism unacceptable. Only it would admit subjectivities of many kinds and propensities, freely using different methods. For decades critics have connected films to events and trends in society using Marxist methods, deconstructed their elements, analysed their structures, gone into psychoanalytic explanations, sometimes all within the same article, without ballyhoo, without signing structuralist, post-structuralist or deconstructionist manifestoes and getting straitjacketed into a theory bearing a label. Indeed, free criticism represents a revolt against the tyranny of the academic labelling industry which has of late been working overtime. Very often the grand announcement of a new label means no more than old wine in new bottles.

Outside the purely Marxist discourse in the West, the denial of the magic of creativity and of establishing 'political correctness' above all considerations of the autonomy of art may have its roots in consumerism. The call for 'scientific criticism' may have taken its birth in the very modernism the postmodernists so strenuously denigrate. Otherwise why should 'scientific criticism' be so unconcerned with emotional, visceral responses to art and so obsessed with the explicable as opposed to the ineffable? Why should it need to separate aesthetic excellence from the truth of character and event instead of seeing an inseparable link between the two? There is no doubt that the relentless pursuit of higher consumption of goods promoted by the corporate world's imperative of economies of scale, itself essential to mass production and therefore calling for maximal homogenization, had led to a desertification of the spirit in highly industrialized societies, making their intellectuals decry the transcendental aspects of art.

Thus, English poetry in Britain and America pursues a sort of minimalist concreteness, considering the transcendental an anachronism, an embarrassment in this age of cynicism. It derides poets like T.S. Eliot who were acutely concerned with problems of spiritual development of the individual. Having marginalized the myths of Christianity and made the cynical pursuit of instant gratification at the cost of the well-being of others into a political, social and economic dogma, these societies have left themselves no area of transcendence, of connecting the self to something greater than itself.

IV

'Modernity is the separation of spheres, the becoming autonomous of truth, beauty and goodness from one another, and their developing into self-sufficient forms of practice: Modern science and technology, private morality and modern legal forms, modern art. This categorical separation of domains represents the dissolution of the metaphysical totalities of the present age.'[14]

One of the outcomes of this fragmentation in post-medieval Europe is the factor of specialization, now driven to an extreme and further vitiated by the growth of a cabalistic shorthand of 'technical' terms (fruitlessly imitating more exact physical sciences) understandable only to participants within a closed circle. The jargon in which the discourses are clothed sets up a wall around, sealing them off from other disciplines and obviating the possibility of holistic thought. Even where some self-conscious 'interdisciplinary' linguistic expansion has taken place, the obstacles against interaction between the critical and the creative are very much in situ.

Not for nothing did Umberto Eco in his 1988 Introduction lament the style of his 1954 classic *The Aesthetics of Thomas Aquinas* in which 'youthful work . . . (and its) convoluted style (had) a tendency to equate the readable and the unscientific, the headstrong insistence of a young scholar upon technical-sounding phrases instead of plain language and an overblown apparatus whose purpose . . . was merely to show that the writer had read everything he could find on the subject'. In film studies such language obviously turns the concrete constantly into the abstract, denying thereby the value of the concrete terms in which the sensory experience of art is clothed. It sets up an unnecessary, confusing contradiction. In fact, it becomes incumbent upon those who discuss art to do so by staying as close to the concrete as possible, supporting every argument with linguistically vivid examples.

The aesthetic alienation of art resulting from this separation of spheres, breaking up the medieval European unity of art with truth (how the world is), morality (how we should act), is an essentially Western problem. This *loss* or *Bereavement* as Bernstein calls it did not take place in Indian thought, ancient or modern.[15] In the philosophical assumptions and assertions of almost all modern Indian thinkers, including those closest to the framing of principles of action such as Tagore, Gandhi and Nehru, the traditionally unified field of *Satyam*, *Shivam*, *Sundaram* (truth, goodness and beauty) was never given up; in fact, it contributed to India's isolation from the world in some ways, making it seem strangely self-righteous in the context of the cynical pursuits of self-aggrandizement in today's nation states. In almost all philosophies of action formulated by the leadership of modern India, of course including the sphere of the arts, holism has tended to prevail over compartmentalization as the wellspring of thought. Brahmoism, the Tagorean world view, even the Bengal brand of Marxism which dominated early independent India's concepts of art and in cinema was represented dominantly by Satyajit Ray, never allowed for an alienation of art from truth and morality. The concept of art's loss or bereavement (from medieval European art's constant and compulsive representation of Christian truth) is irrelevant to India.[16]

This among other things makes it ironical that India's film scholars today should argue mostly from the European position of alienation and should internalize categories and systems of thought mostly derived from this loss or bereavement of art, creating grave misunderstandings and investing their thoughts with incomprehensibility to readers bred in the Indian tradition. In many of their writings, there is hardly a mention of ancient or medieval Indian sources of tradition, not to speak of Indian texts on aesthetics or on specific arts or on principles and facts related in the epics and Puranas.

Let us take the case of 'Humanism'. It has been understood in the West as the credo of an anthropocentric universe. Descartes's Man is in the centre of things and is designated the master of all: *Maître et propriétaire de la nature.* Baconian inductive logic supplied the first scientific base to this belief. The Enlightenment, followed by the Industrial Revolution, strengthened this doctrine of the supremacy of man who, having conquered nature upon earth, has now set out to conquer space.

'Humanism' in the Indian context has always meant the exact opposite. The *Rig Veda* and particularly the Upanishads view man as an infinitesimal speck on the cosmic vastnesses of time and space. It is only by perceiving oneself as a minute fragment of the universal consciousness which permeates all that the individual begins to realize his/her destiny. In the *Devisukta*, man begs the earth's forgiveness for treading upon her. The sense of infinite space and time is reflected in numerous verses like this: *Na tatra suryo bhati na chandratarakam / Nema vidyuto bhati kutovayam agnih / Tameva bhantam anubhati sarvam / Tasya bhasa sarvamidam vibhati* (There neither the sun shines nor the moon; nor is there fire or lighting; it is by reflecting the light of that universal being [force] that all these shine).[17]

It is not a personalized God that the Upanishads discover; through step by step enquiry, they try to understand the order of the universe, the power that regulates it. Michelangelo's bearded, muscular Caucasian God stretching his hand across the ceiling of the Sistine Chapel is anathema to Vedantic thought. What Vedanta finds from its contemplation is a universal, invisible, nameless, formless consciousness permeating existence and non-existence in and out of time and space. Even in Puranic Hinduism, the universe lives within Vishnu's dream. All of this represents a cosmocentric way of thinking as far removed as anything could be from the anthropocentricity of the European Renaissance or the Enlightenment. Indeed, Indian humanism arises from the sense of the unimportance of man and the evanescence of life (the latter it holds in common with medieval European scholasticism). Among the philosophic currents that flow from this are the accent on karuna or compassion and the doctrine of ahimsa or non-violence dominantly articulated in Buddhism, both of which have had an abiding influence on the arts in India. The Indian sense of the sadness of evanescence is untouched by medieval Christianity's dark shadow of original sin; its particular value in art comes from the enchantment with which the present moment is invested. Because the moment will vanish, it invokes compassion for those who are shining in its light (a feeling so fundamental to Satyajit Ray's work). There is thus no scope for confusing Indian humanism with the Western concept.

The word *myth* too has come to acquire distorted values and a false halo under Western tutelage. Having lost their own myths to a cynical society, many Western scholars are now building our Indian myths into a kind of panacea for all spiritual ills. The way myth is invoked by some Indian New Left film critics, it sounds almost like some prescribed drug to be injected into every film, regardless of the particular malady of the patient. Their Western mentors have bred in themselves and their acolytes a perverse desire to see the Third World live by myth instead of fact, without a meaningful interaction between the two in the behaviour of society and the individual—while the West itself steadily makes away with the non-renewable resources of the earth.

V

That the unmediated glorification of myth can result in the events of 6 December 1992 (the decimation of the Babri Masjid *believed* to have been built on the site of a Hindu temple some 500 years ago, a site *believed* to have been the birthplace of Rama whose historicity itself cannot be proved), does not dampen the enthusiasm of the myth merchants, most of whom stay safely away from the consequences of their actions. Unwittingly, some of our scholars of this persuasion play into the hands of religious fundamentalists by their self-conscious espousal of myth as the Holy Grail of all life and all art. Parading this aggressively, they accuse religious reformist and rationalist movements like the Bengal renaissance or the Brahmo movement of some naïve, unthinking modernism hurtling us towards a cultural disaster in which the subalterns and the 'little traditions' by which they live will be bulldozed out of existence and replaced by a mindless Western elitist–scientist project of some sort.

To examine such a proposition let us take the case of Rabindranath Tagore, one of the most important figures in the late nineteenth and early twentieth centuries whose long shadow still extends over large groups of the intelligentsia.

The fact is that knowledge of Sanskrit and especially the Upanishads was central to Brahmoism from Raja Rammohun Roy to Pandit Shivnath Shastri to Tagore. What they did was to adapt Hinduism to the needs of the age by eliminating the encrustations of superstitious obstacles to progress without giving up their essential Hindutva. At a time of extreme decadence they used both persuasion and confrontation to make the country evade mass conversion to Christianity and to wake up to the rational side of the mind, reducing the power of unmediated tradition. Rammohun Roy stimulated thoughts on comparative religion in modern India using a number of languages, pioneered Bengali prose, and was instrumental in having the institution of Sati banned. Ishwarchandra Vidyasagar, a Sanskrit pundit with a strong streak of Western democratism in him, wrote important works in Bengali and virtually forced sections of society to accept widow remarriage. All of them combined to abolish polygamy. It is their acts of logical positivism which created an intellectual elite that forms the leadership of the opposition to Hindu national fascism today. Without their labours of the time the Indian left or New Left would not have come into being. And it is not as if their work is over; one look at the mighty infrastructure of superstition that survives in society, reinforced by the rise of religious fundamentalism, convinces one of the overwhelming need to reassert the mediating power of rational thought, and, in some respects, to re-invoke modernism. Indeed, the gradual erosion of the reformist movement within religious discourse has been one of the tragedies of modern India, directly leading to the rise of fundamentalism.

Those like, say, Rabindranath Tagore, who were among the pioneers of the reformist world view, were not thereby alienated from their tradition or from the myths that have provided spiritual support to large masses of people for thousands of years. Indeed, much of Rabindranath's poetry or his songs are impossible to understand without identifying with his deeply Vaishnava roots and his basis in classical learning. Take the well-known Tagore song '*Kyano jamini na jetay jagalena nath / Bela holo mari laajay*' (Lord, why did you not wake me before the night was over / Now that it is day, I will die of shame). If you did not have the Radha–Krishna myth in your bloodstream and could not instinctively invoke the nightly tryst of a young married woman with an adolescent, both of whom are human and divine at the same time, if you had not in fact ceased to be conscious of that knowledge, it would be impossible for you to get the full emotive value of the words, or, for that matter, the music wedded to it. Thousands of such examples can be given from Tagore's works. Indeed, in the entire Tagorean tradition there is no question of reading and learning about or self-consciously cultivating myth; it is in one's bloodstream, an integral part of one's consciousness, of even the dream world that lives within one. Myths do not remain thereby unchanged forever; they naturally keep in step with every reorientation of the self to changing realities and to all desire for change. Tagore's literature is replete with this constant, dynamic, reinvention of the equation of tradition and change.

VI

Among other buzzwords that need re-examination are *Brechtian alienation*, *the epic theatre* as opposed to *illusionism* and *Aristotelian catharsis*. Almost the entire Indian theatre and narrative tradition has been one of alienation for more than 2000 years. Our epics have stories within stories, our plays have sutradharas or presenters who break into the narrative; both serve to keep their audiences completely aware of the fact that they are watching a play or listening to a story and prevent them from surrendering themselves to an illusion of reality. This is also true of the folk theatre. Obviously the total influence of these forms in India for some 3000 years has been immensely greater than that of Brecht.

It would be idle to suggest that those who adopted the illusionism of the novel as a fictional form for modern India were not aware of the epic or the alienation features of Indian traditional theatre. They did what they did because they felt the new form would have a greater impact and in this, over a period of more than 150 years, they have been proved right. The Indian novel in a dozen languages has come to embody the quintessentially Indian experience of the entire modern period on a mind-boggling scale. Neither their illusionism nor the shades of Aristotelian catharsis in them have anything intrinsically invalid about them; more than anything else, the question of the novel has been, and remains, a question of the social and ethical value of a particular form in a given society at a given point of time. It is obvious that through the immersion of oneself in the experiences of the other, readers/audiences come closest to transcendence from self-love and are changed in however small a manner from what they were before the experience. The fact that they may not be 'intellectually' conscious of that fact makes little difference to the mutation through experience.

The problem on the other hand is that at the heart of India's film studies, there is no urge to redefine categories in the light of the country's own tradition and its modern experience. Indeed, the capacity to do so is not even considered central to the issue. There has been a wholesale importation of premises, assumptions, categories and definitions from the West, which has a well-organized, relatively free academic structure that readily rewards talent, allows the individual enough support and enough freedom to develop himself/herself. It is not surprising that some of the best minds from the Third World should rush to this intellectual haven and flee—physically or spiritually—the mindless roadblocks to creativity that Third World structures set up in order to inflict the power of the average on the talented. In one way or another, countries like India regard talent as an obstacle to the vested interest of the untalented and dub the pursuit of excellence as elitism. 'Vulgar Marxism' is still a powerful force and, along with rightist philistinism, lends muscle power to all forms of opposition to intellectual growth.

Nor is it surprising that the West's combination of freedom and discipline should throw up systems of knowledge and a network of theoretical structures which represent the cutting edge of progress in understanding society and the arts, among other things. These understandably influence the avant-garde of Indian scholarship and impose themselves upon the disarray by which the Indian scholar is constantly surrounded.

This in turn prevents the growth of theoretical and speculative structures from within the Indian soil, firmly connected to Indian history, tradition, languages, literatures and arts, yet open to ideas from elsewhere which they can accept on merit by their own standards of judgement. The illusion of belonging to an international fraternity obscures the Indian scholar's awareness of the absence of firm indigenous foundations to his/her thinking. Many of the influential critics/scholars do not even have Indian language skills of a respectable order. All discourses and judgements tend to follow patterns emanating from the contemporary West and are mostly conducted in English. The need to study Panini's unique grammar or the narrative strategies of ancient Indian epics, works of fiction and theatre, murals, and bas-reliefs, the edicts of Indian *shilpashastras* and to bring them to bear on the study of cinema through joint manoeuvres with other specializations and holistic studies along with them has not even been realized. Without this, Indian film studies will never have an independent foundation or acquire the capacity to fuse or reorder thought streams from all directions to give them a new universality.

10

HOW INDIAN IS INDIAN CINEMA?

The international accessibility of India's 'New Cinema' often gives rise to the perverse thought that it is not Indian, or not Indian enough. The contention seems to be that any fully indigenous product must be so culture specific that perforce it would be a closed book to the outsider.

On the other side of the coin, there is the proposition, graven in the minds of some foreign votaries of pop culture and their Indian acolytes, that the big commercial cinema, the formula film, is the essentially *Indian* product that adheres to the canons of the *Natyashastra* and carries on a tradition of two millennia. Thus, Lothar Lutze says: 'Seen without highbrow prejudice, the Hindi film may well appear like a tree rooted deeply in Indian tradition and reaching out, fumblingly perhaps, into the space age.'[1] Exactly how the space age is assayed in this cinema Lutze does not specify; but he easily succumbs to the seduction of finding an enclosed, separate space for a cinema of Indianness and indeed of 'Asianness'.

Anthropologist Akos Ostar draws a direct line from the *Natyashastra* to the Indian 'pop' film, as did art critic Herman Goetze. Goetze stated firmly that, by contrast, Indian films 'of the very highest quality, such as those made by Satyajit Ray . . . are essentially international'.[2] Perhaps Goetze understood more of India's past than her present. Are 'Indian' and 'international' mutually exclusive categories? Take classical Indian painting and sculpture that Goetze admires and explains so well. They are Indian and at the same time international.

There seems to be a firm conviction behind such theories that Indian (and Asian) forms must be seen as distinct from the Western at the grassroots, free from the highbrow prejudices of the 'westernized' elites of Asian countries. Many of these redoubtable scholars have the idea that Satyajit Ray became a success in India only after he became famous in the West. They do not appear to know that *Pather Panchali* was an instant box-office hit in Bengal long before it became famous abroad, and that Ray has been one of the most successful directors at the box office within the Bengali cinema; *Charulata*, for instance, was the second-biggest box-office hit of 1964. Used to thinking in terms of single-language homogeneous society, they are surprised that Ray's films are not seen outside Bengal as often as McDonald's hamburgers are eaten in any part of the United States. So used to are they to the pervasive soap opera of television and Hollywood that they think it has to be a world phenomenon. Some Americans are therefore appalled when they hear us discuss serious cinema in contradistinction to the commercial product, oblivious of the fact that the distinction often holds true in Europe as well.

That this approach must preclude a universal significance for international audiences of India's pop cinema is obvious from the fact that neither the art circuit of film festivals nor the large audiences of commercial Western cinema are known to have displayed any fondness for it. Britain had at one stage more than fifty theatres completely dedicated to big Hindi formula films, but the audiences were overwhelmingly Indian and Pakistani with Africans and other Asians at the fringes. The natives of Britain have, with marginal exceptions, given these latter-day Kalidasas the go-by. The same is true of Indian enclaves in other Western cities, including the video availability in Indian spice shops almost everywhere abroad. Exclusive expositions of Indian cinema have occurred in places like Paris, New York and Pesaro among others and have included a few examples of popular cinema in their programmes. But nowhere have they created any noteworthy response, except partly the films of Guru Dutt and the early Raj Kapoor ones among cult-seeking groups. For the most part, they have been found, like films based on Peking Operas, merely curious. Their culture specificity has been proven beyond doubt by both the elite and the groundling in Western countries.

Yet it cannot be held that the art of one civilization will not be understood in another because its idiom of expression is different. Facts do not bear out such a proposition. A good deal of modern Western music has been influenced by the Indian musical system, both at the level of high art and pop music—ranging from Philip Glass to the Beatles. The rather unusual marriage of the latter to Ravi Shankar inevitably did not last long; but the sitar and the tabla have remained a part of British pop music and have found their way into other pop groups. No such osmosis has taken place between Indian and Western cinema. Given the coexistence of the two over several decades in Britain and America, it could have occurred—if the potential had in fact been there.

II

Most of the scholars who see Bharata's *Natyashastra* as the fountainhead of Indian pop cinema base their theories on superficial similarities between the two and an inadequate understanding of the Indian dramatic tradition. All variety shows are not *Natyashastra* merely because they include song, dance and drama. Is it their contention that Bhasa (fourth century BC) or Kalidasa (fifth century AD) are aberrations from the models Bharata codified because their works are considered masterpieces in the West? *Shakuntala* has been translated into, and successfully performed, in many languages. Obviously the fact that it does not observe the Aristotelian unities of time, space and action has not locked it into an exclusively Indian cultural space. Bhasa's plays, made up of a mix of song, drama and dance, have been repeatedly staged in Kerala and elsewhere in India. Their form has come through as a thoroughly integrated whole. Their humour and their theatrical unity and rhythm have captivated audiences. If they are performed in Western countries, they are certain to find ready acceptance as masterpieces of world theatre, despite certain culture-specific characteristics that distinguish them. It is well known that the Japanese did not send Yasujiro Ozu's films even to European film festivals because they thought he would be too Japanese to be understood outside his own culture. The fact proved to be the opposite; he was immensely liked *because* he was so Japanese and brought to international audiences an altogether new approach to cinema. That, alas, has not happened in the case of India's pop cinema. It has, in the case of Satyajit

Ray; his Indianness is as indisputable as that of Nehru or Tagore, and is inseparable from his universality.

If pop cinema has found favour in other Asian countries, the reason is altogether different from what Lutze and others have advanced in their excitement of the anthropological 'discovery'. The fact is that Indian pop cinema has been exported for decades to non-Indian audiences of Southeast Asia, West Asia and certain African countries. Significantly, it does not go to highly industrialized Japan; in China, where it has been seen occasionally, only its songs have found some acceptance with a few. In other words, its acceptance is confined to pre-industrial, mainly agricultural societies that have thrown up large urban lumpens in the process of industrialization and urbanization, generating marginalized migrants to the cities whose adaptation to a technological society has yet to begin or is at its earliest stages. Yet it is this audience that gets catapulted into the consumerist dream factories of the cinema theatres. Indeed, the forward section of these countries, the so-called 'elite', detests the Indian product, in Thailand or in Mali. As their indigenous cinema develops its own identity, the popularity of the Indian cinema dwindles. The entire phenomenon can be viewed only as the result of the grafting of a technological medium developed in the industrialized countries on to the body of a pre-industrial, agricultural tradition, producing unusual forms in only the culture of societies similarly placed at a particular historical junction. In Pfleiderer and Lutze's book on the Hindi film, it is only Anil Saari who recognizes this socio-economic fact when he observes that in India 'modern technological society is interlocked with a largely feudal pastoral reality'.

It can be predicted with some confidence that as India is more completely industrialized and its people adapt themselves to technological transformations and their effects such as fast communication, high social and geographic mobility and homogenization of tribal (in the sense of an enclosed group) identities, the popular cinema in which they find satisfaction will also change. Its indigenous character will no longer preclude universality of expression or understanding. I have shown elsewhere that almost all of Indian popular cinema, particularly since its bifurcation into high art and pop in the late 1950s, has been a continuation of the mythological film in different garbs. Western popular cinema of Superman and other comic-strip characters mythologizes the future; Indian pop used to mythologize the past and now does so with the present. It is by nature a preoccupation destined to disappear as the socio-economic scene is transformed into that of an industrially developed, socially and geographically mobile society. In saying this I am in no way precluding the possibility, preferred by most Indians, that the country's development will not follow Western models but shape its own directions, absorbing the industrial phenomenon and its fallout into its remarkable continuity over the millennia.

III

An ingrained idea in the minds of Western scholars is that any Western borrowings must be equated with a loss of identity. Indeed, it is predicated upon a sort of general theory of Indian development loaded with Western clichés about modern India. It draws heavily on the fashionable Western view that Indian intellectuals, Jawaharlal Nehru included, are elitist, ape the West and have no sense of the truly Indian. Implied in this is also the thought that the West must tell us how to be true Indians. None of these westerners or expatriate Indians, it is clear, have seen the vast rural concourses that assembled to hear Nehru and have no idea of the degree of his rapport with them. In discussing economic planning, they lose sight of India's goal of real independence, free from manipulation and economic imperialism, to be found only in a substantial industrial–agricultural self-sufficiency. They set up a dramatic opposition between Gandhi and Nehru, painting one Indian and the other Western, forgetting the Western influence on the former and the Indianness of the latter—both of which ran equally deep. What is also forgotten is that despite their differences Gandhi did nominate Nehru as his successor. The Nehruvian policy of non-alignment is an extension of non-violence and the doctrine of import substitution an extension of the charkha (spinning wheel), the Gandhian symbol of individual self-sufficiency in the pre-Independence period.

There is a lack of understanding here about the reversal process that so-called 'Westernization' brings in at the creative, intellectual level in an ancient civilization. Macaulay's educational policy sought to generate a tribe of 'brown Englishmen' and partly succeeded in doing so, but he never foresaw that they would in fact turn into a great force to liberate Indians from the British and to engage in a discovery of India. Indeed, it can be shown from the history of the nineteenth and early twentieth centuries that in virtually all fields of creative endeavour, it is the so-called westernized segment which led a great movement for Indianization. It is they who turned from a European philosophy, literature and art to a rediscovery of their roots in Indian tradition. It can also be shown that those who did not go through the process of reversal became victims of cheap Western mores and are today celebrating a macabre marriage of consumerism and fundamentalism that is threatening the very integrity and unity of India, creating a new divisiveness on religious, linguistic and regional axes. Few Western scholars understand the vital need in developing countries for a successful synthesis of tradition and modernity that would trigger progress without loss of identity. An unchanged, unmediated continuity would destroy itself by its very unawareness and its consequent imitation of the most superficial aspects of Western society.

It needs to be argued that such an unmediated continuity in an ancient country rapidly industrializing itself is fraught with the dangers of fundamentalism, signs of which are evident among some sections of the urban public—sections most devoted to the popular cinema. Transition from the ancient to the modern needs within it a dynamic process of reinterpretation and contemporarization of tradition. Unless an ancient tradition is infused from time to time with fresh blood from outside, it becomes anaemic and sterile. Its constant inbreeding makes it recoil upon itself, and renders it incapable of inner change. As its vitality dwindles, it can only adopt the superficies of changing contemporary reality without understanding their underlying forces or being able to absorb and subordinate such forces with the metabolic vitality of which Indian tradition has given ample proof through five millennia.

If inspiration from the West were to be taken as the fountainhead of 'un-Indian' internationalism, much of the vast creative output of developing countries in the modern era would have to be rejected outright. Prose literature in many Indian languages began with foreign missionary translations of the Bible; the novel as a form was developed in eighteenth-century England and has been adopted in countries like India. Should the entire prose literature in at least ten languages and the modern Indian novel of the last 200 years be therefore dubbed un-Indian? Unfortunately, Western scholars who are troubled by this issue of Indianness of our cinema are virtually unacquainted with the richness and variety of modern India's literature and the depth with which it has examined the country's problems of tradition and modernity.

For this reason it is possible to see, in the exclusivity of Indian cinema formulated by the apologists of the present popular form of the Indian film, a desire to deny it all international communication and a sense of belonging to a world community. The fog that is gathering around the whole discourse on the worth of India's popular cinema can be dispelled by reading 'scientific–industrial' for 'Western'. The transition of pre-industrial societies towards an industrial revolution is unnecessarily seen as westernization. Similarly, the creative works that function as engines of social change are dubbed un-Indian. It has been the misfortune of the formerly colonial countries to have first been thought of as the 'white man's burden' and then as the targets of a mummification drive which is merely the other side of the same colonial coin. Two of Asia's most advanced countries today—Japan and China—were never colonized by the West; yet they both consciously sought technologies developed in the West in the last century in order to modernize their economies. Japan's entire history is one of cultural importation which, however, always made it more Japanese instead of less. Among these imports were, inter alia, a script, an administrative system and a religion from China. To varying extents, this has happened in India, China and the South-east Asian countries which, for nearly a millennium-and-a-half, imported culture from both India and China. Until Western pundits realize that the borrowings are not from the West per se, but merely an import of inputs necessary for development at a given historical juncture, their misunderstanding of the problem of tradition and continuity will persist. Besides, borrowings, indeed scene-by-scene imitations, are rampant in pop cinema, which do not prevent it from exploring Indian problems constantly in its products.

IV

Apart from the *Natyashastra* stereotype, another line of argument sometimes advanced is that popular Indian cinema is based on folk forms (folk variants of the *Natyashastra* model) in its sharp division of good and evil, its happy endings and its song–dance–drama combination. It is good because it exists. It is great because it sells: that seems to be the refrain of the song in praise of our soap operas from some of our foreign commentators. The apparent success of the big commercial cinema dazzles the eyes of even some notable intellectuals who then celebrate their discovery of the greatness of what has been traditionally described by Indian commentators as the prime expression of the lowest common denominator in entertainment.

There is a disconcerting note of populism in the newly awakened interest in popular culture. Its motivation appears to spring from the awe with which consumerist societies regard anything that sells. What is more, there is latent in its concerns and the nature of their manifestations, an anxiety to persuade developing economies to adopt this awestruck view towards the high-selling commodity, more particularly when that commodity is some form of art. At best, it is a part of existentialism that must accept, without demur, anything that goes; at worst, it is an active consumerist crusade; developing societies must somehow be persuaded to exclude the pursuit of social goals and to learn to accept what are considered the inevitable outcomes of the free market process. Economics, like politics, must be freed of any ethical bias. Very often the interpretations of what is popular read like rationalizations of what may otherwise appear ethically questionable to societies that want to direct their development towards a humanist plan of performance.

It is necessary to observe here that populism in the discussion of popular culture is intrinsically different from the traditional Indian distinction between margi and desi.[3] Between the episode of Kichakavadham in Vyasa's Mahabharata and its performance in Yakshagana the difference is not one of world view but styles; what makes a gulf between Valmiki's Ramayana and Ramanand Sagar's presentation of it is the humanism of one and the fundamentalism of the other. Similarly, popular cinema in India can be contrasted to serious 'New' cinema in terms of the opposition to the secular–democratic values of the Indian Constitution in the first and their espousal in the second.

The inability or unwillingness to differentiate popular and high culture in terms of values, particularly in cinema, arises from the unawareness, or disregard, of the vast manipulative forces at work in mass-produced cultural commodities. One vital difference between folk and pop is that one is produced by the people themselves and is predicated upon their participation in it in a two-way process, the other is entertainment manufactured by corporate bodies in metro cities and injected into the mass consciousness in a one-way hypodermic model of communication. The advocates of existential acceptance of popularity thus act on behalf of its manipulators in consolidating and extending their empire.

Besides, cinema is by nature incapable of achieving an instant give-and-take rapport between entertainer and audience. The film on the screen is complete in itself, autonomous; nothing can be added to it along the way. The audience reacts, but the screen does not. It may, with the next film, but certainly not with the present one. By and large, it is one-way traffic. Folk entertainment presents no such fixed formulae. It demands, quite like Indian classical music, a constant participation of its audience and its interaction with the performer. Much of folk entertainment is improvisation within known boundaries.

Discussing the Ramlila in Benares, Richard Schechner talks of 'the constant erasings and superimpositions' that go on in the performance in relation to its particular audience. The event becomes environmental theatre, the basic form of folk entertainment.[4]

Nor are film actors like folk performers, the fellow next door who plays Rama on Ramlila day. Like the manufacturers of any mass-produced articles, they are inaccessible to the consumer. They lie hidden behind the brilliance of the screen, living lives utterly different from those of their audience. This relationship between performer and audience is basically uncharacteristic of folk tradition. Again, folk performance is, traditionally, not tightly time-bound. It can go on for a whole day and night or longer. The scope such an open form offers for adaptation, for the interpretation of local events and their incorporation into traditional stories in many subtle, ever-changing ways, is almost infinite. Put on a stage for a one-and-a-half-hour span, folk theatre becomes canned cabaret for the city bred. It begins to look filmi.

In the area of music, folk melodies have been a source and an inspiration for 'high art', both in India and the West. The pentatonic raga Shivaranjani was fashioned out of the songs of Abyssinian slaves singing at night in the loneliness of their captivity in Mughal palaces. One authority has it that Dhrupad was created by Haridas Swami from the songs of the Dhadhi community in Oudh. One can find hardly any trace of such a traffic of ideas from soap opera to high art in cinema.

The intensely regional peculiarities of folk music were universalized by classical composer-musicians at a high level of courtly or spiritual sophistication and spread across the elite over wide areas. The process in cinema is deceptively similar; it rejects the local features of regional forms and tries to mould them into a nationally acceptable model. In doing so, it places the rural and traditional elements of its content before a basically urban audience, not at the level of the highest common denominator, but at the lowest. Then there is the concept of cinema as a collective fantasy which is supposed to have a healing effect on large audiences caught in serious stresses in their lives. It is a dream; therefore, it is good therapy. Some writers display this attitude to an extent that suggests an indulgent, condescending attitude towards cinema as by nature an inferior medium. Their attitude is totally amoral, non-judgemental; the question of social good or aesthetic value does not enter their consideration. It is almost like the scientific enquiry of, say, an ornithologist. Thus, in an otherwise very perceptive article, psychoanalyst Sudhir Kakar said sometime ago:

'Unlike the novel, the portrayal of characters in film is neither intended to enhance our understanding of the individual complexities of men and women nor to assist our contemplation of the human condition.'

It is obvious that he equates the novel with its best and the cinema with its worst products. But what can one say about the mass of sentimental novelettes and pulp fiction that forms the bulk of best-selling literature? Do they not portray stereotypes of character and situation in fantasy in almost exactly the same way as popular cinema? On the other hand, has all cinema—including the work of Bergman, Antonioni, Kurosawa et al.—proved itself incapable of enhancing our understanding of individual human beings or of the human condition?

V

There is another dimension of denial to this glorification of what sells. Consumerist Western societies to which these commentators belong will not permit India a moral view of art because they themselves have promoted a hedonistic aesthetic to which a stock exchange valuation of art is wedded. Thinking Indians are deeply concerned that their pop cinema mostly opposes social change in conflicts between tradition and modernity. In the battle of equality guaranteed to women by the Constitution of India, and the traditionalist view of woman as chattel to be valued only as a reproductive agent and nursemaid for children, popular cinema will, almost invariably, side with the latter. Because it felt the need for a cinema that would act as a catalyst for change, the social leadership, the so-called 'elite' of India, as represented by Jawaharlal Nehru, promoted the harnessing of new talent in that direction. The Film Enquiry Committee Report of 1951 led to the establishment of growth centres such as the Film and Television Institute of India, the Film Finance Corporation, the National Film Archive, national awards for the best work in cinema and so on.

By the 1960s the process of creating a new cinema to re-examine tradition and support the forces of change was in full swing. A whole new generation of talented film-makers came into being. But in the all-India field, it found its way into cinema theatres barred by the vested interest.

In their own language regions, many of these film-makers have had considerable success. The Neenasam society in Karnataka found in its trials that rural audiences first exposed to film were much more open to the best of cinema than had ever been supposed. In fact what has been called the 'Heggodu (name of the village) experiment' found the same audiences relatively hostile to the 'commercial' product as immoral. K.A. Abbas, writer of many of Raj Kapoor's films, called all his life for the nationalization of cinema theatres. But this the Indian government, committed to a mixed economy that leaves the consumer product to private enterprise, could not do. And there is no doubt that audiences fed for generations on the lowest common denominators of entertainment refuse to be converted to the highest.

In all fairness to foreign critics advocating the *Natyashastra*-style legitimacy of the Indian pop cinema, it must be said that they come from 'arrived' societies, where the basics of life are already available to all and there is therefore no moral imperative arising from the chasm that divides the elite from the common man in India. One-quarter of the population of India lives in cities; this, in absolute terms, means more than 200 million people. The educated and better-off sections of the rural areas and the number of Indians who have stepped into modernity and are part of rapid social and economic progress, would be equal to the combined population of Great Britain, France and Italy or to the entire population of the United States. It is easy for this privileged sector of the Indian economy to forget the nearly three-fourths of the population or some 750 million people who remain behind. That generates the moral need to rouse the conscience of this sector and to keep reminding it of how the rest lives. It is not easy for the sensitive artist in cinema to ignore the human condition and to drift within the consumerist dream.

If the worst interpretation were to be put on it, the advocacy of escapist entertainment could be seen as an anxiety to sell laissez-faire economics to India and to stay the hands of those who seek alternative modes of development. It could also be suspected of continuing the thinly disguised imperialist doctrine of keeping the other half below, where it belongs, because of its intrinsic inferiority.

The fact is that as consumerism grows, success is measured in harder material terms, and the intellectual is increasingly under pressure to accept that criterion. The traditional respect for learning and wisdom begins to go under and the intellectual feels cornered, isolated; the only escape he can find from that predicament is through a subtle exercise in self-deception, dressing up this acceptance in justification and rationalization, perhaps glorification, of the popular culture of the moment, no matter what its values. A whole process of homogenization is set in motion when society's traditional ideological brakes on it are eased. Mediocrity becomes the norm, and deviations from it have to be disguised. In super-industrial cultures this process is almost complete; in the developing countries, it is becoming increasingly evident. Yet they are in no position to make a surrender to existentialism and give up all effort to bring about better conditions in the life of the mind.

11

CINEMA TAKES OVER THE STATE

'In the next ten years, there is going to be a big increase in the semi-literate population. I shall be their leader. My determination will be to keep them semi-literate.'

—*C.N. Annadurai*, 1967[1]

Few events have revealed the nexus between culture and politics as dramatically as the coming to power of film stars in two of India's most populous states—Tamil Nadu and Andhra Pradesh.

Both were the most popular stars of their different language areas; both were at the peak of their popularity at the time they became chief executives of their states. Even when they stopped acting, their films continued to be screened with revivals orchestrated by themselves. One had made 262 and the other 292 films at the time they became chief ministers. In both cases, it is clear that their political victory was the direct outcome of their screen *image*. Neither of them was a chief minister who happened to be an actor in the past and was merely using that experience to enhance his public performance as a politician, unlike President Ronald Reagan of the United States, who was never a superstar anyway. The Indian actor–chief ministers became political leaders *because* they were the superstars of their cinema. Their political personae are extensions of their cinematic selves. This fact must also be considered in the context of the number of cinema theatres in the south (6830 out of the country's total of 12,284 in 1984), which is twice the national average. The bulk of the touring cinemas, which have a higher penetration into the rural areas than the permanent theatres, are also located in the south. The highest number of cinemas is in Tamil Nadu (2136), followed by Andhra Pradesh (2131). 'No village in Tamil Nadu is so isolated as to be beyond the reach of film.'[2]

Both chief ministers restructured the entertainment tax in their states in such a way that reruns of their films would be more profitable than new films—in most cases. The quantum of tax levied is no longer based on the sales of a film; it is now dependent on the population of the town in which the cinema theatre is situated. This slab system based on population provides an edge to films with big stars. The dissident film with new actors and values must pay the same tax as the big star 'vehicles', and thus has no means of making itself economically viable in relation to the particular audience for which it might have an appeal. M.G. Ramachandran's reruns were besieged on opening nights by his fans all through his life. N.T. Rama Rao's last film, made before he became chief minister, was released after his assumption of office on his birthday. The film was titled *Chanda Sasanudu* (The Dictator). As the two chief ministers sat in their offices deliberating matters of state, their painted faces and caparisoned bodies flickered on the screen, reinforcing their images. With more than 250 films to each chief minister's credit, these reruns have had a useful inexhaustibility.

'You will forgive me if I am overcome by emotion when I talk of cinema,' said N.T. Rama Rao, the chief minister of Andhra Pradesh, at an international film festival in the capital of his state. 'It nurtured, promoted and made me what I am today.' M.G. Ramachandran, chief minister of adjacent Tamil Nadu, could have said the same thing, with equal truth.

Tamil Nadu presents a unique case study in the history of cinema as well as of politics. In 1967, when the Dravida Munnetra Kazhagam (DMK) defeated India's ruling political party, the Indian National Congress, the cabinet of ten formed by Chief Minister C.N. Annadurai (1908–69) had nine members from the film industry, including himself. A scriptwriter at a time when his tribe was billed above the director in the titles, Annadurai was the engineer of the cinematic force that laid low the mighty Congress party. 'How can actors run a government?' scoffed Kamaraj, Tamil Nadu's highly capable (and by caste, untouchable) chief minister before the 1967 elections. But the DMK had the last laugh. The cinema had taken over the state. As if to underscore this, M.G. Ramachandran, a Keralite of Sri Lankan origin who through 292 films had been the matinee idol of the

Tamils for years, became the chief minister in 1977, and, but for a brief interlude, remained so till his death in 1987.

II

To understand how this came about and how the intricate, usually unconscious, link between culture and power was deliberately forged by the DMK, one must briefly outline the history of the movement that catapulted cinema into the centre stage of politics.

Traditionally there are four castes among the Hindus—the Brahmins, or the intellectuals; the Kshatriyas, or the warriors; the Vaisyas, business people; and the Sudras, or labourers. The Brahmin is said to have been born out of the mouth of God Brahma, the Kshatriya out of his arms, the Vaisya from his thighs and the Sudra from his feet. Over a period of some 2000 years the occupational division stratified into an unshakeable hierarchical status accepted by the bulk of Hindu society. There is a fifth class—the untouchables, like the *Eta* (later called the *Burakomin*) in Japan. But in south India, there are no Kshatriyas or Vaisyas; all castes are either Brahmin, Sudra or untouchable.

Over the centuries the Brahmins, a tiny minority of three per cent in the state and less in the rural areas, had to work out a power-sharing relationship, a modus vivendi, with landowners of a Sudra caste—Khammas, Reddiars and Vellalas.

For Brahmins, position and status were independent of their residence in any given local area; for non-Brahmins, rank was directly dependent on village economic and ritual dominance transactionally corroborated.[3] The conflict was therefore primarily between Brahmins and non-Brahmins of high status. Suddenly, transition from village to town meant, for the non-Brahmins, drinking water out of a separate pot, not from the same as with Brahmins back in the village. As forward segments of the non-Brahmins became urbanized, this disenfranchisement caused a severe reaction among their ranks and quickly found its focus in a 'Dravidian', anti-Brahmin, anti-north, anti-Aryan crusade.[4]

The concept of Dravidian-ness was, unsurprisingly, one that had been developed by European scholars, some of them British, and all of them excellent Tamil scholars. The Reverend Robert Caldwell (1819–91) developed the theory of Aryan domination of the south through the Brahmins (three per cent of the population). Some British officials agreed with this formulation and felt that the word Sudra had been forced upon the south by Brahmins from the north. 'It was these Sanskrit speakers, not Europeans,' said Grant-Duff, Governor of Madras, in an address to the graduates of the University of Madras in 1866, 'who lumped up the southern races as *Rakshusas*—demons [*sic*]. It was they who deliberately grounded all social distinction on *Varna*, or colour.' The words must have fallen on avid ears.

It was not the first time, nor the last, that the British had fuelled the fires of division among their Indian subjects. Educated non-Brahmins were quick to point out that the Brahmins (being descendants of Aryan invaders) were also foreigners to India, like the British. When the Indus Valley civilization was discovered and posited by many as a pre-Aryan Tamil manifestation, the Brahmin–non-Brahmin, north–south, Sanskrit–Tamil divide became sharper than ever. In 1916, the Justice Party was founded with the idea of securing justice for the non-Brahmins. It constantly submitted petitions to the British government seeking increased non-Brahmin representation in the administration. Socially and culturally, the thrust of the movement was towards establishing the Brahmin as the negative symbol and the non-Brahmin as a positive one. In the new modes of self-definition, non-Brahmin became synonymous with Dravidian, with the rejection of Sudra status, that is, of *Varnashrama Dharma*. The past greatness of the Tamils and their language mooted by European scholars was promptly internalized and idealized into a utopian vision of a casteless pre-Aryan society. The religious basis of the superiority of the Brahmin was steadily undermined among the urban non-Brahmins; it was necessary to harness the vast masses of the underprivileged by infusing them with a pride in the cultural distinctiveness that had become the motive force in fighting the north and Sanskrit-deprived Brahmin supremacy for the elite non-Brahmin of Tamil Nadu.

The philosophy was radicalized and elaborated into a doctrine by E.V. Ramaswami Naicker (widely known as EVR) with the publication of his book *Kudi Arasu* and the formation of the Self-Respect League in 1925. EVR had been a staunch supporter of the Congress, but resigned in 1924 over an incident in which Brahmin and non-Brahmin eating facilities were segregated in a school run under Congress auspices. EVR represented the radical section of the Self-Respect Movement which sought, not the reform, but the overthrow of Hinduism. EVR publicly criticized the central mythologies of the Hindu religion and advocated the burning of the *Manu Samhita* and the Ramayana. One of EVR's famous statements was: 'If you see a Brahmin and a snake, kill the Brahmin first.' Periyar (as he came to be called) broke images of Ganapati, paraded floats on the street showing Sita in the embrace of her husband's brother Lakshmana, and lionized Ravana, the traditional symbol of evil whose effigy is burnt during the Ramlila in large parts of north India to this day.

Many scholars dispute the north–south, Aryan-Brahmin vs. non-Brahmin Dravidian concepts as simplistic or untrue. The whole idea of an Aryan invasion has indeed been challenged or bypassed by many scholars who see a possible continuity from the Indus civilization to later developments instead of a conflict between the two.[5] According to some scholars, the Brahui language in the north-west of the Indian subcontinent is proof that the Dravidians, once upon a time, inhabited parts of the country other than the south.[6]

Sanskrit and Tamil were closely related even 2000 years ago. *Silappadikaran*, the great Tamil epic composed in Kerala between the second and fifth centuries AD, describes a festival in honour of the great Aryan God Indra held at Pumpuhar. 'In the din created by politicians, the Tamil people have become deaf to the voices of their own past.'[7] However, the call for self-respect was a stronger manifestation of the attempt, not only to secure political 'justice', but to achieve structural change in south Indian society. Self-respect meant self-respect for the Dravidians (culturally and politically downtrodden) and freedom from the 'slavery of the mind'.

III

For a while the Justice Party and the Self-Respect League functioned side by side in a pattern of increasing cooperation. While the Congress party was dominated by the Brahmins (their three per cent of the population provided 20 per cent of the prisoners in the 1942 Quit India movement), support for the Justice Party and the Self-Respect League came from 'Tamil, forward, non-Brahmin, caste Hindus'. To enlarge this base, Indian-language newspapers were developed. But a mass movement was yet to be born. Politics belonged to high culture and was still petitional, not agitational.

The introduction of compulsory Hindustani in schools in 1938 triggered the first explosion of the gathering force. This was when C.N. Annadurai, later to become a leading author and screenplay writer before taking over as chief minister, first gained his reputation as a skilful agitator, propagandist and organizer. The demand arose for a separate Dravida state. The language issue was portrayed as a superficial manifestation of the sinister infiltration of Aryan ideas into Tamil culture through the political control of the Brahmin. It made the separation of the land of Dravidians from the rest seem essential. EVR supported the British war effort, and his paper was subsidized by the British government during the war years. He met Sir Stafford Cripps, then Jinnah and Ambedkar, to press upon them his plan for a separate Dravida Nadu by partitioning India.

But the prospect of Congress ruling independent India loomed large, making it difficult for the Dravidian movement to enlist the support of the masses and even the backward non-Brahmins. Hence the birth of the Dravida Kazhagam (DK) party under the leadership of C.N. Annadurai ('Anna') at the Salem Conference of the Justice Party in 1944. Anna sought to mobilize mass support by removing the impression that the Justice Party was a rich man's self-interest group in league with the British and divorced from the main thrust of the independence movement. The name of the Justice Party was changed to Dravida Kazhagam at this conference as a result of a resolution moved by Anna. The demand for separation from India was dropped. When EVR declared 15 August, the day of India's independence, as a day of mourning, Anna publicly dissociated himself from that stand. At the 1948 DK Conference at Erode, Anna was chosen as EVR's successor.

But the seventy-one-year-old EVR named twenty-nine-year-old party worker Maniammal as his successor, also announcing his impending marriage to her. Many refused to accept Maniammal's leadership and came out in open criticism of EVR's despotism. In the rift that ensued, Anna found the opportunity to establish his Dravida Munnetra Kazhagam (DMK) or Tamil Improvement Party in 1949. Three-fourths of DK membership went over to the new party.

Annadurai invited intellectuals to join the movement, wrote radio dramas, presented party philosophy through travelling theatre groups, used songs to propagate his ideas, sponsored poetry contests on political subjects, combined political and literary conferences, and emphasized scholarly studies of Tamil, which led to a renaissance of Tamil literature.

Every party leader published a newspaper or a magazine. But all these became only the precursors and support structures for the main instrument he fashioned for converting the masses to DMK ideology: the cinema. It was not only eminently suited to reach the masses, but was owned largely by non-Brahmins, for example, large studios and producers such as AVM and Jupiter.

English had already ceased to be the main language of the DMK's political discourses; by elevating Tamil, it had expanded its frontiers and established an edge over the Congress. But the cinema was more significant because 'the Cinema Hall was the first performance centre in which all the Tamils sat under the same roof. The basis of the seating was not on the hierarchic position of the patron but essentially on his purchasing power . . .'[8]

Earlier Tamil tradition classified Kuttu performances (as in the early classic *Silappadikaran*) on the basis of the social status of the audience—the Vettiyal (of kingly nature) and the Potuviyal (of non-kingly or commoner nature). When the performing arts moved into the temple, the hierarchical division became ritualized because the lower castes were not allowed entry into the temple. Later, in the eighteenth and nineteenth centuries, Terukuttu was patronized by the higher castes, and the social hierarchy of the spectators was well reflected in the seating arrangement.[9]

IV

Much of this must have been clear in the mind of Annadurai when he decided to make the cinema his major instrument of wresting political power from the Congress. He instinctively realized what the Congress, too sure of its ground as the architect of Independence and the chosen leader of free India, did not: that the cinema was the leveller of classes, the only place where the lowliest felt equal to the mightiest because he had *bought* his right of entry. An unshaken Anna was prepared to bide his time when the Congress won a thunderous victory in the general elections after Independence. Congress Chief Minister C. Rajagopalachari, a Brahmin, compared cinema to alcohol and said that liquor also brought in tax money but still he campaigned for prohibition and had successfully implemented it. He went on to say that 'if the industry could stop producing films they would be doing a signal service to the community'.[10]

Considering that most of the actresses of the time were drawn from socially unacceptable groups such as devadasis (temple maidens often regarded as prostitutes) and that most of the entrepreneurs themselves were of lowly origin, such an attitude was not surprising. But the inability to see beyond its westernized–brahminical superstition was to cost the Congress dear. Kamaraj was merely echoing Rajaji's sentiments when he dismissed the DMK with his comment: 'How can actors run a government?' He went on to lose the 1967 elections.

In 1982, in the Andhra Pradesh elections, when Mrs Indira Gandhi was pitted against legendary film star N.T. Rama Rao, she may have had similar thoughts—even though she was the champion of the 'new cinema' and did not share the Victorian prudery of Rajaji or Kamaraj. She, too, lost.

The first film to make a clean break with the traditions of Tamil cinema was *Velaikkari* (Maidservant, 1948), scripted by Anna from his play. Its portrayal of the sufferings of Anandan, son of a poor peasant, showed how the traditional religious institutions were used to hold the peasants in ignorance and poverty. The arguments put forward in Anandan's rhetoric at the temple were so radical and heretical that they posed a threat to the very foundations of traditional rural Tamil society. DK's anti-Brahmin, atheistic, anti-Varnashrama rhetoric was woven into the personal lives of the dramatis personae. Anandan often directly addressed the audience, as in the scenes at the temple and the lawcourt. Anna was not taking a chance with the audience's understanding of visual subtleties.

Parashakti (1952) opens with a monologue bewailing the plight of Tamilians who have had to leave their native country because of poverty, and are now toiling and suffering in foreign lands or sleeping on the streets. Religious superstition and the corruption of temple priests are criticized, while the government is found to be indifferent. Even in 1968, a year after the DMK had come to power, there was applause in the theatre over these scenes and speeches. The film had been written by Karunanidhi, later to be chief minister and who would remain leader of the DMK for decades. The main actor was Sivaji Ganesan, who became famous through DMK plays and films but was later to join the Congress. In almost all the DMK films the characters at some point speak of the plight of the poor, of people living on the streets, of starvation, of political corruption, all linked to the ineptitude of the Congress government. What was internalized, however, was not always the radical ideas (such as atheism, DMK communism and so on), but the cultural definition of what it meant to be a Dravidian.

The irony of it was that the DMK's strategy in the cinema was made possible by the Congress party in two ways: first, the electrification programme helped the extension of the cinema into rural areas; second, cinema theatres were largely owned by Congress supporters, even legislators, and they, finding the DMK type of film popular, played these in their theatres, without realizing what the end result would be.

V

It is not as if earlier Tamil films had no social or political significance; even the silent cinema had clear political overtones. Thus, *Anadai Ponnu* (Orphan Daughter, 1930) dealt with injustice towards women, *Nandanar* (1930) dealt with the Hindi saint of that name who had belonged to a pariah caste but by dint of his great devotion to Shiva was able to obtain entry into the temple (a repeatedly remade story). K. Subramaniam's *Balyogini* (1936) showed the sad plight of child widows. Even titles like *Desamunetram* (Country's Progress, 1938) showed the urge to deal with social problems. The choice of these subjects was doubtless inspired by the Congress movement and the Gandhian effort to remove social evils such as untouchability, an essential part of the political struggle. If overtly political films could not be made, it was because of the vigilance of the British government. *Eknath* (1938) was banned because it supported Mahatma Gandhi's programme of the social uplift of Harijans, being a film about a sixteenth-century Marathi saint who preached against untouchability.[11]

In the films of comedian N.S. Krishnan, there was a distinct social and political thrust. To understand this, it is necessary to know the structure of the conventional Tamil film. 'Any average Tamil film would have its "serious" side in which the trials and tribulations of the hero and the heroine are portrayed but the comic side to provide relief was contributed by the comedian, a descendant of the traditional *Vidusaka* (buffoon) of Sanskrit drama, with his well-loved antics. N.S. Krishnan used this pattern to provide a parallel theme . . . a sub-plot within the major plot of the film—and the relevance it would have to the main theme would be minimal and nominal. Very often the comedian is a friend of the hero and would perhaps help the hero at some crucial moments.'[12]

Ramalinga Swamigal has a dig at the caste system and argues that there are only two kinds of human beings, the good and the bad. In *Anandashramam*, any rich man who exploits the poor is doomed to disaster. In *Salivahanan*, Krishnan argues in favour of inter-caste marriage. The anatomy of the comedy sequence is manifest in the very way it was developed. NSK composed the comic scenes and shot them himself with actors and actresses of his own choice; even the songs for them were written by a member of his troupe. N.S. Krishnan could rightly be regarded as a pioneer in exploiting film for political advantage. Though basically a Gandhian believer in non-violent non-cooperation, NSK began to support

Annadurai openly from the time the DMK was formed in 1949. In *Panam* (Money) he skilfully used a pun to mask, for the purpose of the censors, his glorification of the new party, *Ti-mu-ka*, explaining the word away as an abbreviation of Tirukkural Munnanik Kalagam. The DMK regarded the *Tirukkural*, an ancient Tamil didactic text, as a seminal work from which it derived many of its tenets.[13]

The opening up and exploitation of the various facets of Tamil films sustained political propaganda with a social overtone. It must be emphasized that their dialogues, noted for powerful rhetoric and profuse sentiments, were largely responsible for awakening among the masses in Tamil Nadu a close affinity for the ideals of the Self-Respect Movement and especially for the pro-Dravidian and anti-caste feeling of the DK and the DMK.

This phase of the DMK's orchestration of cinema as a means of political self-assertion was led by the writers Annadurai and Karunanidhi and was dominated by words—it was, in fact, in extending the use of political plays that the DMK discovered the power of cinema and began to accentuate it. The first phase began in 1948, and went on till about 1957, the year in which the DMK entered the arena of electoral politics. Two other factors contributed to the transition to the next phase: Annadurai and Karunanidhi's increasing investment in day-to-day politics as distinct from their philosophic–propagandist function (even though they did not give up film writing) and, more importantly, the rise of M.G. Ramachandran as an actor and a luminary of the DMK. One of the first films in which MGR played the lead was written by Karunanidhi in 1950 and called *Maruthanattu Ilavarasi*—a film about a princess who turned into a commoner in order to marry the poor man she loved because her status stood in the way of their union.

VI

If the first phase emphasized the word, the second provided its logical follow-up—action. The concepts broadcast by Annadurai and Karunanidhi were now embodied in the superhuman feats of a swashbuckling hero.

The switch to action helped to bring the cinema closer to the illiterate populace. Since M.G. Ramachandran chose to act only in the roles that showed him bringing succour to the needy in many walks of life, the identification of the actor with the character was quickly achieved. The hero had an immediate social relevance for the majority of Tamil filmgoers. He became the symbol of their wish fulfilment. Most of the time, he represented characters drawn from lower social groups, especially in the early part of his long career spanning 292 films. One by one, he covered the vocational groups of the underprivileged Tamils. He was projected as being always honest and hardworking, facing social opposition but overcoming it. By contrast, Sivaji Ganesan, the better actor, does not have the saviour image. 'In acting talent Sivaji is head and shoulders above MGR, but Sivaji had played a great variety of roles; he is often the tragic hero, people sympathize with him but do not idealize him. MGR is always portrayed as the saviour. As a result, Sivaji has never been a vote-getter.'[14]

The MGR image was constructed with finesse. Grid by grid the proletariat was systematically covered; there was a film about fishermen (*Padakotti*), another about rickshaw pullers (*Rickshawkaran*), about the peasant (*Vivasayi*), the carter (*Mattukara Velan*) and the domestic servant (*Neethikkuthalai Vananku*). In each, MGR plays the good man, the Robin Hood, the dispenser of justice, the saviour of the distressed. A maidservant came back home sobbing; she had just seen 'MGR killing a tiger to save his mother's life—in this day and age'.[15] He never entered the grey areas, not to speak of playing the villain or other unfavourable character. 'Between the mid-fifties and the early seventies, if MGR played in 100 films, not in one did he die.'[16] In real life, whenever he had a close brush with death, MGR's popularity increased on account of it—first after the incident in which actor M.R. Radha shot and injured him, and then after the illness that took him to Brooklyn Hospital, New York, for treatment in 1983.

Unlike his fellow Chief Minister N.T. Rama Rao in neighbouring Andhra Pradesh, MGR avoided playing gods or mythological characters, because the DMK began on an anti-Brahmin and anti-God platform. Entry into God's temples was guarded by the Brahmin. However, to bring

Christians into the DMK fold (the south has a long Christian tradition going back, it is said, to the fourth century, and to conversions by St Thomas himself), on 25 December 1969, MGR launched *The Life of Jesus Christ*. It was a great occasion that looked like 'a wedding of the DMK and the church presided over by Christ Himself. At the long table before the assembled guests, MGR, properly attired for the occasion, was joined on one side by the Archbishop of Madras and on the other by Chief Minister M. Karunanidhi, leader of the ruling Dravida Munnetra Kazhagam (DMK).'[17] The cunning with which this was done is plain in the eyes of MGR playing Christ; only he and his followers were typically unaware of the intimate vibrations given off by the cinematic image. All that the situation lacked was a Luis Bunuel to film this first supper.

MGR's production company sported the DMK flag, and very often he wore its red and black in his film costumes. His films frequently began with Annadurai's portrait and ended with the rising sun, which was the symbol of the DMK party. Within the film there would often be a portrait of Anna on the wall, alongside one of Mahatma Gandhi. An adaptation of *The Prisoner of Zenda* had MGR as the king issuing a decree which read like the DMK party manifesto. Screen populism was steadily supported by real-life paternalism; when there was incessant rain in Madras, MGR bought raincoats emblazoned with the DMK's rising sun for 600 rickshaw pullers. A film on the rickshaw pullers reinforced this charity and boosted the film's sales. He also consistently advocated temperance. His charity, his moral stance and his highly visible and intense party activity conveyed to his public the message that he was more than a film hero.

It has been said that MGR, being childless though he was married twice, gave most of what he earned to charity—a statement contested by his arch-rival M.R. Radha. To reinforce the image of his prowess, he was shown carrying K.R. Vijaya in a still photograph soon after her recovery from a broken leg.

Sivaji would act in any good role, but MGR would choose his film to make sure of his image. You never saw him smoking or drinking or chasing girls other than the one he was supposed to love. Even if there was a scene showing him drunk, there would be a twist to show that he was merely acting as a drunkard. In the film *Nadodi Mannan* (Vagabond King), when the vagabond becomes king, he orders his minister to give everybody a house in which to live and a bullock. The ordinary villager was encouraged to think that if MGR becomes a king, he will do all these things. Nearly ninety per cent of the villagers have these sentiments. Songs in the films praise MGR.

His circumstances are shown to be very ordinary—he belongs either to the working class, or the peasantry, or the impoverished middle class. No wonder, then, that MGR became the symbol of the audience's wish-fulfilment. He had been acting since 1936, but it was around 1950, with films like *Maruthanattu Ilavarasi* and *Marmayogi* that his clear links with the DMK were forged. In *Nadodi Mannan* (1958), he was the one to introduce the DMK symbol of the rising sun; from then on his place in the party was assured. He had attained a position of equal power with Karunanidhi.

As luck would have it, Sivaji Ganesan, hitherto the symbol of the DMK's social criticism in cinema, began to drift away, clearing the path for MGR with the DMK. Choosing his films carefully, MGR declared that he would act only in films consonant with his social and political views. The party came to be more and more dependent on him, especially for collecting crowds at its mass meetings and for votes in the elections. 'We need your image,' Anna said, and MGR gave it ungrudgingly. 'If he appears at a meeting, we get 40,000 votes; if he speaks, we get 400,000.'[18]

After Annadurai's death in 1969, there was the inevitable battle of succession, which was won initially by Karunanidhi. But Karunanidhi, with the entire party organization in his hands, yet needed MGR's support to become chief minister. The writer gradually lost ground to the actor.

In a rearguard action, Karunanidhi is said to have tried to build up his son as a superstar, presumably to produce a more manoeuvrable surrogate for MGR. The two leaders fell out soon thereafter. In 1972, MGR formed his own party, the All India Anna Dravida Munnetra Kazhagam (AIADMK). In 1977, he became chief minister, dislodging Karunanidhi. The actor had defeated the writer; action had taken over from words. In MGR's films, although rhetoric was retained, swashbuckling action was always more important. By this time the DMK's violent anti-Brahmin anti-God posture had weakened; MGR was able to preside benignly over a less divided electorate. Indeed, in order to heal the wounds of the traditionalists, he made highly visible journeys to various temples housing gods and guarded by Brahmins whom EVR, Anna and Karunanidhi had flayed for two generations. When *Parashakti* or *Velaikkari* were shot there was no puja at the opening. Now Karunanidhi attends all the pujas.

The wheel had come full circle. The early DMK films and plays had fulminated against religion and its guardians, the Brahmins; in the second stage, as it flowered into political domination through MGR, it beat a careful retreat from its atheistic doctrine. One reason for this may have been the countermove of the Establishment, which became popular: Sivaji Ganesan starred in a number of mythological films after his exit from the DMK. *Sampoorna Ramayanam* (1958), for instance, glorified the epic that was anathema to the DMK. Films were also made from what some scholars have called the 'Little Tradition', celebrating local cult gods and their prowess (as opposed to the Great Tradition of the Sanskritic gods). S.S. Vasan's *Avvaiyar* portrayed the life of the deeply religious Tamil poet of that name. These films were immensely popular. The Great Tradition had proved to be too powerful. There has, if anything, been a resurgence of religious ritual and festivity all over Tamil Nadu. The Aryans may have conquered the south, but it was so long ago that the people were not prepared to throw out their gods at the DMK's behest. The tirade against God had been an extension of the movement against Brahmin domination in the administration, in the universities and other power centres of urban expansion. Once the elite non-Brahmins had gained their place in the sun it became unnecessary, perhaps dangerous, to go against long-held religious beliefs. Has atheism ever been sustained outside the counsels of the intellectual? The DMK's return to religion (in real life; in films they have not actually re-emphasized the role of religion as such) has provoked little protest; it has perhaps provided welcome relief to the religiously minded majority temporarily disoriented by the atheistic rhetoric of leaders they otherwise admired.

Indeed, some erstwhile associates of the DMK affirm that it was when the party entered the elections that it dropped its strident atheism reflected in songs written by Kannadahasan, who wrote: 'An image cannot eat, why do you offer food to it?' or, 'When are you going to blast the images of Srirangam and Tirupati temples?' When Sivaji left the DMK, he too went to the Tirupati temple to underscore his change.

Manoeuvres and counter-manoeuvres like this are easier in the south than elsewhere. As we have noted earlier, film production was owned largely by non-Brahmins; many cinema theatre proprietors were Congress supporters oblivious of the havoc caused to their politics by the DMK films they played for profit; to crown this, the stars acquired control over the film industry and used it for political gain. Sivaji had his own cinema theatre, and MGR had his studio. It is reported that a contract for acting for either included control of distribution rights in Madras. Stars could make or break a producer, who therefore became pliant enough to carry the message of the master.[19]

VII

According to most observers, economic indications show a decline in Tamil Nadu. The spurt in industrial growth in the 1950s and early 1960s ran out of steam; power is in chronically short supply, and so is water. MGR's reign lasted many years but his populist actions yielded little concrete result. The per capita consumption of water in Madras has been one of the lowest—70 litres a day against Calcutta's 128 litres, Bombay's 178 and New Delhi's 218. Even these 70 litres had, by 1983, been cut to about 5 litres a day. Journalist S.V. Mani painted a lurid picture: 'Witness the rapidly expanding poverty scene: the thousands living like worms in the slums and pavements of Madras, the hundreds walking miles for a pot of drinking water in the villages or long water queues in the cities; human beings suddenly emerging from sewerage wells, shaking off the muck and slime . . . this is the reality, the outcome of the politics of illusion.'[20]

The power of that illusion can be measured by audience reaction to K. Balachander's film *Thaneer, Thaneer* (Water, Water), a film ostensibly out to indict the MGR government's failure to provide water. But the effect was the opposite. 'If only MGR had acted as the hero,' someone commented, 'it would have been a different story.'[21] MGR, with his supernatural strength, would have brought water to the village.

The economic policies of the MGR government tended towards unproductive, paternalistic patronage more than the generation of wealth and opportunity. Investments in modern India have often been of long gestation periods fraught with mass impatience with the slowness of governmental action; but many of them have paid off. They have relevance not only in terms of the country's achieving self-sufficiency but also in the mushrooming of ancillary private industries based on the heavy industries and the infrastructure developed by government. Not so in Tamil Nadu. After a brilliant start under the Congress in the 1950s and early 1960s, decline set in under the film Raj.[22] Madras has been heavily dependent for electric power on the Neyveli Lignite Corporation, a Government of India enterprise located in Tamil Nadu. Except for handlooms (Co-optex), there is hardly any other success story in the state's industry, the general picture being one of decline.

Dramatic attempts at rainmaking with imported technology or the much-touted canal link with the river Krishna in Andhra Pradesh produced little worthwhile result. MGR's propaganda secretary and erstwhile heroine Jayalalithaa claimed he should get the Nobel Prize for his pet scheme of providing free midday meals for children. 'The scheme had a tremendous impact on the enrolment of children in primary schools. An additional 2.63 lakh children in the 6–11 age group had been enrolled in standard I to V within 10 weeks of its inception . . . The scheme has, in addition, generated gainful employment for some 1,47,000 people—mostly widows and destitute women.'[23] Others point out that it is not an economic activity but a dole, like the distribution of raincoats to rickshaw pullers for the release of *Rickshawkaran*.

> The ill-conceived meals scheme is proving to be an albatross round MGR's neck . . . teachers spend more time at ration shops and groceries and kitchens than in classrooms . . . it has put immense pressure on food stocks, the public distribution system and the price line. What is worse, the scheme itself is said to have been the brainchild of

> Kamaraj, the Congress Chief Minister before the rise of DMK—something MGR is at pains to deny.[24]

MGR has been accused of many such attempts at rewriting history. Recalling the patriotism of P.T. Thyagarajan of the Justice Party, MGR recounted his exploits of 1932, whereas the man passed away in 1927. Similarly, he had Pattabhi Sitaramayya winning the Congress presidency against Subhas Chandra Bose whereas the actual results were the reverse. His age, too, commentators say, changed according to the event of the past whose glory he wanted to appropriate. He claimed that as a fifteen-year-old boy he had left the Congress in protest when Mahatma Gandhi had espoused Pattabhi Sitaramayya's candidature against Bose. Since his autobiography gives 1917 as his date of birth, he could not have been fifteen in 1939, when the Bose–Sitaramayya contest took place.[25]

The cavils of critics notwithstanding, MGR was conferred a doctorate in law (honoris causa) of the Madras University on the occasion of its 125th jubilee celebrations. Among others similarly honoured on the same occasion was world-famous astrophysicist S. Chandrasekhar of the University of Chicago. MGR announced the opening of departments to study Jainism, Saiva Siddhanta, Islam and Annaism. The last, he explained, was 'a blend of socialism, capitalism and humanism'.[26] The list of eleven names was ratified at a special meeting of the Senate 'convened under unprecedented haste'. Most of the members of the Senate and the Syndicate had not been informed of the meeting except by a newspaper advertisement published the previous day. 'Dr. Maradhur Gopalamenon Ramachandran, the Chief Minister of Tamil Nadu,' said *The Statesman*, 'has at last arrived. From playing bit roles in touring drama troupes to top star billing in Tamil films, from an ordinary worker of the DMK to founder leader of the AIADMK, he moved up the ladder of Tamil society till he reached the summit. But something was missing from his life which he eagerly craved—recognition as a man of learning and acceptance as an equal among intellectuals.' It should be mentioned here that Karunanidhi, writer and leader of the Opposition, had received a doctorate years earlier.

His 27,000 fan clubs with a membership of 1.5 million provided an important bridge between the actor and the politician. These fan clubs became the party units when MGR broke away from the DMK and formed the Anna Dravida Munnetra Kazhagam (ADMK). 'An analysis of the composition of the fan clubs showed that the bulk of the membership came from the non-professional classes and that Harijans and Vanniyas formed the largest section. 73.4 per cent earned less than Rs. 400 per month and 56.7 per cent less than Rs. 300. A large number among the latter were daily wage earners, and had a low literacy level—76.6 per cent of MGR fan club members had dropped out of education between the grades of 3 and 7.'[27]

Many would go without meals for days to buy a ticket on the black market for the opening day. A Youth Front launched by MGR in 1982 was likened by some journalists to storm troopers. Trained in combat skills, this 'private army' was composed of 'lumpen students and the unemployed and the marginally employed'. Half a million musclemen who formed the Youth Front would carry out the leader's orders without question. 'When three civil liberties organizations in Tamil Nadu jointly sponsored a national enquiry into the killing of 20 Harijans and agricultural workers in North Arcot and Dharampuri districts in 1980, a 300-strong mob attacked the lodge where they were staying. The mob banged open the doors, destroyed their baggage, beat them up and made sure they had no material to document.'[28] MGR is himself reported to have said at the launching of the Youth Front that if the officials tried to put obstacles in the way of the young, the party would not remain silent, sending a chill down the spines of even the police force.

In his efforts to tame the press with a draconian bill, MGR had to beat a retreat, but not before a protracted battle. Criticism of MGR in the press was as vociferous as his adulation by the populace. No wonder the creature of one medium, the cinema, set out to muzzle another, the press. His ordinance of 21 September 1981 came down heavily on 'grossly indecent or scurrilous matter' without defining the parameters of either offence. The police were empowered to take cognizance of such material, to arrest those suspected prima facie of being guilty and to keep them in custody. Ironically, the first petition under the law that came up at the Madras High Court was against obscenity in journals allegedly patronized by the chief minister's own partymen. MGR also issued orders prohibiting government officials from furnishing information to the press. The returning officer for a by-election refused to give the press details of nominations and withdrawals. The editor, managing director and two directors (who were not liable under the Press Regulation Act) of the Opposition paper *Ethiroli* were arrested on 6 January 1982 for reporting that the Central Bureau of Investigation would probe allegations of bribery and corruption against the then health minister in MGR's government. Similar action was taken against a newspaper for reporting that five children had vomited blood after eating a free meal provided by the government. 'The Tamil Nadu Chief Minister,' commented *The Statesman*, 'does indeed seem to have reason to be wary of an independent Press. With an estimated 300 deaths in police custody in recent years, the state is fast acquiring a particularly unflattering reputation.' It went on to say that Tamil Nadu was 'the only state which was called upon by the Supreme Court to answer charges of having tried to wreck the nervous system of Naxalite prisoners'. In the face of mounting criticism of his draconian law, and the resignation of the journalists from a committee to examine it, MGR first refused to repeal it but soon had to eat his words, pledging its annulment on 18 July 1983, nearly two years after its promulgation.

Repression extended beyond the press to all forms of dissent. Signatories to a petition complained of having been charged with sedition even for seeking permission to hold meetings or agitating for minimum wages. Anyone organizing the rural poor or talking about collective bargaining was a leftist in the Tamil Nadu government's vocabulary. A leftist was an extremist, and it followed that an extremist was a Naxalite to be dealt with suitably. The premises of Skills, a cultural organization, were searched without warrant and without the presence of two independent witnesses as required by law. The police were said to have misbehaved with one of its office bearers, Chandralekha, a well-known Bharatanatyam dancer. Skills sued the government in the high court and won.

But the godmen of the cinema, accustomed to adoring applause, are as impatient of the courts as they are of the press. On 27 April 1983, judges of the Madras High Court 'unanimously expressed concern over police surveillance of their movements and activities'. V.M. Tarkunde, an eminent jurist, had been ruthlessly beaten up a few months before as he led a peaceful procession of about forty members of the People's Union for Civil Liberties (PUCL) in Madurai in protest against police atrocities in the state. Justice V. Ramaswami caught a CID agent tailing him and his family; the agent confessed that he had been instructed to keep an eye on the judge. Justice Sadasivam, who had investigated charges of corruption against the government and was now probing the 'spirits scandal', received phone calls threatening his life. While government officials denied any link between judgments passed against them and the attack on the judiciary, the press thought otherwise. 'The current controversy does seem to have its roots in a series of recent judicial pronouncements by the Madras High Court which have embarrassed the State Government.'[29]

MGR himself gave the game away by making attacks on the judiciary. 'Courts in Tamil Nadu,' he moaned, 'are giving a stepmotherly treatment to the State Government . . . It is the law which speaks in the court and not conscience.' That last sentence befits a film star used to playing the do-gooder, the man of conscience who drew his gun at the drop of a hat to satisfy his conscience which was independent of the law. In virtually all of India's popular cinema—not only the Tamil—the heroes see the law as a hindrance to their superhuman ability to dispense instant justice. And true always to his fervent Tamil nationalism, MGR pronounced against the practice of appointing judges on an all-India basis: 'We are not in favour of a non-Tamil speaking judge to be appointed as Chief Justice of our High Court.'

That the MGR charisma lingered through his prolonged illness and survives his death underscores the power of the illusion he created. His ghost made its presence felt in the Tamil Nadu elections of 1989, with both his wife Janaki and his one-time heroine Jayalalithaa claiming his legacy and invoking his memory.[30]

VIII

A sixteenth-century astrologer in a hamlet in Andhra Pradesh is said to have made some startling predictions about the future of India in his book,

Kalagyanam (Knowledge of Time). Some examples for the twentieth century: 'A *bania* (merchant) will bring freedom to the country' and 'A widow will rule India'. Mahatma Gandhi did come from a merchant community. Indira Gandhi, India's prime minister (from 1966 to 1984 except for an interlude of three years) was indeed a widow.

Early in 1982, the superstar of Telugu films was asked to play the role of this astrologer, Veera Brahmendra Swami, in a film about him. He was given the book of predictions to read, in preparation to playing the role of its author. Poring over it, superstar N.T. Rama Rao came across a line predicting that, around that period, 'a man with a painted face will rule Andhra'. He sat up and exclaimed: But that's me! Within a few weeks, he had formed a party, Telugu Desam (Telugu Country), named after the language of the state, and after nine months of inspired campaigning, defeated Indira Gandhi's long-ensconced party in the state elections, becoming the second film star chief minister of a state in India.[31]

In deciding that the prediction was about him, N.T. Rama Rao was not being vain, but factual. At age fifty-nine, the foremost film actor of Andhra Pradesh carried a big load of paint on his face, transforming his dark skin into a glowing pink that contrasted vividly with jet black eyebrows and bright lipstick. Since he mainly played roles of gods or godlike men, the paint was a must, for all gods, with the exception of Krishna and (in the south) Rama, are supposed to have been Caucasian in the fairness of their skin. The Indian anthropomorphic pantheon came into being within some 1500 years or more of the coming of the Aryans and some 300 years after Alexander's invasion.

The time was ripe for a film actor with a god image to take over the affairs of state. Frequent changes of chief minister, dictated by New Delhi, had caused deep resentment, compounding the problems of corruption and maladministration, and highly incensing a proud people who had played an imperious role in ancient and medieval India. The abrupt dismissal of T. Anjaiah incensed all Andhra despite a lack of faith in his efficiency. According to many political commentators, the chief ministers were chosen, not for their regional following, but for their loyalty to Delhi.

As one local wag quipped, 'Mrs Gandhi changes Andhra's Chief Minister as frequently as her sari.'

The main NTR film playing in Andhra's theatres through 1982 was *Bobbili Puli* (The Tiger of Bobbili). The film's story is of a much-decorated Indian army officer who is turned into a deserter and an outlaw by the machinations of his villainous father. He escapes from prison, forms his own band of followers, rounds up the judge and the police officers in a cave, and treats them to a homily on the evils of modern society and on the nature of true justice. 'Whenever virtue is on the decline,' he tells them in stentorian tones, 'I appear on earth to rescue the good and punish the bad.' The words had been spoken by Krishna in the *Gita* when he was persuading the reluctant Arjuna to fight against his enemies. The film heralded NTR wherever he went, and played an important role in bringing about his victory in the elections.

The audience in the cinema not only cheered loudly but threw confetti on the screen. The ragged urchins in the front rows seemed to carry an inexhaustible supply in their pockets. The theatre I went to was so small, decrepit and tucked away in the heart of a slum miles from the nearest town that it took hours to find it. Once found, it proved to be empty inside and besieged by a crowd outside, waiting patiently all day for the power failure to end. Evening came, but the electricity did not. One had to go back the next day to contend with ticket holders of both days. Finally the manager arranged for us to see the film standing in the projection cabin. All around, the building bore the signs of the recent elections. The initials NTR still remained stencilled on urinal walls; torn 'Vote for NTR' posters flapped in the wind.

The film released on NTR's birthday after his accession to the chief ministership was, as mentioned before, *Chanda Sasanudu* (The Dictator). It opened in ninety theatres in fifty towns of Andhra Pradesh, spinning money for its makers and boosting the image of the just-elected leader. In the film, the dictatorial feudal lord drives out his sister for marrying a left-wing leader. Her son Raja, also played by NTR, joins the workers in their struggle against the dictatorial landlord. This film, said NTR, 'shows my true character as a strong-willed and just man'. It could well be said that playing the two roles, NTR's two selves, one dictatorial and oppressive, the other identifying with the common man and benignly anxious to relieve his lot, are shown locked in a struggle for ascendancy. His political actions as chief minister gave enough proof, as we shall presently see, of both these conflicting streaks in his character. In fact, at the time of the dubbing of the film, NTR was already chief minister and was thus actually living a brief double life.

IX

It became evident as soon as he assumed office that the chief minister had a simple and strong sense of mission. At this point his sincerity was never in doubt, even to his worst enemies. It was evident when he campaigned for nine months across his large state, often following or preceding Mrs Gandhi. People saw in him the God they had seen in 262 films. In most of these he had played supermen—the gods and their incarnations. For decades they had flocked to see him and bow to him, and now they were doing so again. Riding a 1940 Chevrolet turned into a caravan with a platform and a public address system on top, the god of cinema had criss-crossed his state's 275,000 square kilometres to be greeted with rousing receptions everywhere. The members of his 600 fan clubs served as his emissaries, and people came to his meetings in hordes. 'He would begin his day at 7 a.m. and end at 2 a.m. the next morning,' says his biographer Venkatanarayan. 'During the last nineteen days of the campaign, the travelling became a round-the-clock affair. He carried just two pairs of khaki trousers and full-sleeved bush shirts, bread, butter, honey, lemon juice and soda. Inside the van, he would sit in an aircraft-type seat, surrounded by garlands collected at the meetings and boxes containing cassettes of his speeches to be distributed to party workers.'

As soon as the driver alerted him to an approaching crowd, he would climb through a hatch on to the roof and speak to the thousands who ran towards the NTR 'chariot' as soon as they heard it coming. In the early hours of the morning, the caravan would stop wherever it was. After three hours of sleep, NTR would wake up, sit by the roadside or near a well, shave, bathe, wash his clothes, eat out of a leaf held in his hand and then carry on again. On the red-letter day, a record number of 21,496,754 voters exercised their franchise, of whom 9,623,361 voted for NTR's Telugu Desam Party, giving it 199 seats in the legislature of 286. And thus the cinema swept to power in one of India's largest and most backward states, weighted down with poverty and illiteracy. As the large, handsome chief minister sat straight on a big chair in his office at six in the morning, dressed in the saffron robes of a religious mendicant, an earring dangling from his left ear (as prescribed by his astrologer), it was impossible not to remember the lines from the *Gita* in his recent film, about God appearing on earth 'to rescue the good and punish the evil'.

Asked about his policies as chief minister in a 1983 interview, NTR said: 'You have seen the film (*Bobbili Puli*). There is a man who always sides with the wronged sections of the people. So naturally there is sympathy for the hero. That is the style of role I perform. So that people expect good things to come of my service to them.'

If any leader could ever be the total opposite of Jawaharlal Nehru, it is Nandamuri Taraka Rama Rao. He is the son of a farmer, born on 28 May 1923 in the small village of Nimakuru, then inhabited by less than 500 people. The village had no school of its own; a teacher would walk five kilometres to take classes in a shed. Few people in those days had money with which to pay the teacher. Says Rama Rao, 'If I close my eyes, I can see my master coming to our village, helping the villagers and teaching us the whole day and walking back to his place, with vegetables in one hand, a tumbler of buttermilk in the other and a sack or two of rice on his head.' His farmer father was determined that Rama Rao should be properly educated, unlike himself and other farmers of the day. If it rained, the father would carry his son to school on his shoulders along the muddy paths through the rice fields, and once there, wash his feet and wipe them and leave him in the care of the venerable teacher. Eventually, he sent the boy to college. Here Rama Rao caught the eye of his Telugu professor, who was a playwright. The handsome young man was cajoled into playing the role of the heroine, there being no question of girls acting with boys in those days. Rama Rao was ready to go on stage when the professor arrived in the green room and ordered him to shave his moustache. The future superstar of Telugu cinema politely but firmly declined to remove what he called 'the symbol of manhood'. In a frantic last-minute compromise, Rama Rao went on with his moustache hidden under a pile of make-up. He was an instant success and earned the nickname 'Meesala Nangamma' (moustachioed Nangamma).

At twenty, Rama Rao married Basavanna Taraka, who was to be the mother of his seven sons and four daughters. He recalls that marriage so absorbed him that he twice failed in his examinations. Finally he passed his BA and found a government job after a long wait, but gave it up to get into films.

On his first day's shooting Rama Rao played a police officer asked to punish a group of anti-government demonstrators. Like a bull in a china shop, Rama ran after the volunteers about 500 yards without a break and beyond the gates of the studio. His director's protestations that he was moving out of the camera, and that he shouldn't beat the poor extras so hard, fell on deaf ears. Later, he learnt to stay within camera range, but never to *pretend* to fight. The musclemen in fight scenes in his later films allege that he would pummel them with all his might. Asked why they did not hit back instead of taking it from him, one of them said: 'Sir, it's an honour to be beaten up by NTR.'

And no wonder, because he was not only strong and handsome as a God, but godlike in his wealth. Before turning to politics he is said to have charged a fee of Rs 20 lakh (two million) per film, acting in several films at the same time, in two or three shifts per day. In the five years preceding his chief ministership, most of his films yielded fantastic returns. Some of them—*Vetagada, Kondaveeti Simham, Bobbili Puli, Sardar Paparayudu* and *Justice Chowdhary*—were reported to have made crores (tens of millions) of rupees. K. Rameshwara Rao, director of several of NTR's films since 1953, said: 'Telugu films may never come across another artiste like NTR, so fully involved and dedicated to the role he portrayed . . . for example, in *Pandava Vanavasa*, a story from the Mahabharata, he had to play Bhima . . . he refused to use the light mace made for him. Instead, he made a real heavy mace for himself which was difficult to lift even with two hands. He struggled with the heavy mace, and in the process, he really appeared like Bhima. He identified with that role totally.'

Appropriately enough for his destined role, N.T. Rama Rao began his career in 1949 with the film *Mana Desam* (Our Country), the film in which he was to beat up the extras on the first day's shooting, as recounted earlier. His enthusiasm paid off. In the next film he was elevated from police sub-inspector to hero. Nagi Reddy and Chakrapani hired him for their newly founded Vikaya Productions. Here he worked in a series of hits such as *Shankar*, *Pelli Chesi Choodu* and others, of which *Patala Bhairavi*, a folk tale directed by K.V. Reddy, was the real blockbuster and catapulted N.T. Rama Rao to stardom, firmly establishing his image as the saviour of damsels in distress. As the gardener Ramudu, he saved the king's daughter and was of course eventually married to her. This image of the daring youth who crossed the shores and subdued the demons, obviously popular although lacking in serious drama, led to scores of Ramudu films.

It was in the mythological films that NTR found his métier. In 1957, he made *Maya Bazaar* under director K.V. Reddy and went on to act the main roles in *Bhishma* (from the Mahabharata), *Dakshaayagnam* (a Puranic tale of Shiva), *Lavakusa* (the story of Lav and Kusha, Rama's two sons in the Ramayana), *Krishnarjunayuddham* and others drawn from the epics and the Puranas. *Nartanshala* showed Arjuna, the Pandava warrior of the Mahabharata, in exile. During the year the Pandavas had to remain incognito at King Virata's court, the great warrior had to don a woman's garb and teach dancing to the princesses at court. In playing this double role, NTR summoned up all his acting prowess and made a success of it.

But it was in his own mythologicals that NTR began to introduce an ideological twist. He made sure of being seen as the saviour; even when he played a traditional villain such as Ravana (whose effigy is burnt as the image of evil during Ramlila celebrations in India's Hindi-speaking belt), the character took on a noble aspect. Most of these films demanded not only the grand gesture of folk melodrama but also its lungpower. 'Our films are more audible than visible,' said one commentator. '*Sardar*

Paparayudu has so much sound packed that [it] is enough for half-a-dozen films.'[32] In the story, the villain makes adulterated milk powder that kills schoolchildren, but his daughter falls for the good man—played, of course, by N.T. Rama Rao. Make-up on N.T. Rama Rao sometimes looks like the tattooing on some primitive tribes.[33] Whatever the make-up or the costume and whether the film was mythological or social or historical, NTR was invariably on the side of right. In real life, he maintained the image of Mr Clean, doing without cigarettes or drink or any other common vice. However, the ascent of the NTR image towards all-India leadership soon came to a halt and began, indeed, to decline. One incident after another showed him to be impulsive and lacking in foresight, fast eroding his credibility as a national leader.

X

A bull in a china shop: that is how some people think of NTR in politics. He tried hard to fulfil his campaign promises—fast. He never had the time for commissions and expert committees and even, according to some commentators, consultation with cabinet colleagues. From the beginning, he was impatient with the democratic process in the running, if not the election, of government. On a number of issues, he had to backtrack and whittle down impetuous promises, sometimes creating new problems in the process. Thus his free lunch programme for all schoolchildren had to be pruned continually until it was reduced to children from the low-caste and backward communities. The result was a peculiar caste- and community-based discrimination dividing the children in school. Impulsively, he reduced the retirement age for government employees from fifty-eight to fifty-five, without notice, two months before the end of the fiscal year, causing untold problems to those who had to retire without preparation, and to those who remained to prepare the government budget for presentation to the legislature. More than half the government's 600,000 employees went on strike.

'Wages of Populism' was a headline in comment when the Supreme Court of India directed the Andhra Pradesh government to reinstate hundreds of its retired employees.[34] Officers hurriedly promoted in the meantime had to be hurriedly demoted to their former positions. As in the case of the midday meal, somebody had forgotten to do his homework. Over the years, the chief minister's relationship with his administration soured so much that first his chief secretary, B.N. Raman, was thrown out for opposing some of the chief minister's repressive measures against the striking junior officers,[35] then a few senior administrators followed suit and by 1986, twenty of them were seeking transfer out of the state.[36]

Other evidence of the actor-politician's *Chanda Sasanudu* characteristics surfaced with widespread criticism of police brutality in his state. Like the hero of *Bobbili Puli*, the policemen were meting out instant justice. When the court ordered the exhumation of the grave of a tribal who was said to have died because of police torture, it could not be found; apparently it had been removed and the deceased's brother demanded the arraignment of the police for destroying evidence.[37] The list of complaints made by the Andhra Pradesh Civil Liberties Committee (APCLC) against NTR's attempt to curb people's rights is very long and included[38] alleged 'encounter killing' and twenty-four police lock-up deaths.[39]

Like his neighbouring actor-politician MGR, N.T. Rama Rao launched an attack on the press by legislating against it and, like MGR, had to withdraw the 'draconian' bill. He blamed on his aides his flagrant self-contradictions and his extravagant declarations of welfare measures, hastily withdrawn when they proved to be too grandiose. When the press reported these faithfully it attracted his ire. So did the Press Council for passing strictures against his ministry for its harsh treatment of reporters.[40] Besides, the press had widely reported illegal transactions in the attempted conversion of Rama Rao's Ramakrishna Studio in Hyderabad to two large cinema theatres,[41] as also his academic jihad for the replacement of university vice chancellors by men of his choice who were not always academically distinguished. With his flair for the dramatic on the other hand, he was always grist to the journalists' mill—his earring dangling from one ear, his saffron robes topped by religious leader Vivekananda's style of turban and his general air of flamboyance. 'He sits like a Duryodhana, walks like a Rama and talks like a Krishna,' said a journalist, well before NTR's elevation to chief ministership.

Faced with the need for funds for electioneering in local self-government polls, NTR announced his decision early in 1987 to act in films again to raise money. He would play, he said, the role of Vishwamitra, the mythological warrior-saint and teacher of Rama known as much for his bad temper as for his penances, in a film which he would himself direct. 'Significantly,' observed one newspaper, 'the Chief Minister has decided to delegate all party powers to his son-in-law and Secretary of the party during his prolonged absence from the state capital.'[42] 'NTR's decision to act in films,' said another, 'is only an exercise to refurbish his image and divert the attention of the people from the problems confronting the state.'[43]

XI

Indeed, catapulted to the apex of their state administrations, both chief ministers must have felt the loss of the lever that had landed them there. A nagging fear of what absence from the cinema would do to them may have played on their minds, for both MGR and NTR at nearly the same stage in their political leadership sought to get back into films. MGR's reason was his large backlog of income tax; he sought leave from his job to make a couple of films so as to earn enough to pay his taxes. The muhurat (auspicious opening of the shooting) was in fact held for the film *Vidamatten* (I Shall Not Leave You) in the presence of the entire Tamil Nadu cabinet with the exception of two ministers who were not in town, with the chief minister driving two kilometres of the approach to the studio appropriately festooned and overhung with banners. The subject of the film was said to be politically loaded against the Opposition, led by erstwhile screenwriter Karunanidhi. The girl to play against the sixty-four-year-old chief minister was Sangeeta, age twenty.[44]

In the event MGR did not follow up his intention. How he met his arrears, or to what extent, remains shrouded in mystery. But the reasoning was suspect anyway; new films would bring in money, but they would generate fresh income tax dues too. If the same logic had to be followed he would have to keep going back to film-making merely to postpone catching up finally with the taxman's demands. So a more real, behind-the-dark-glasses explanation would be the desire to swim with the sharks in the seas again, to feel the excitement and the refreshing sense of charismatic power renewing his vitality before returning to the toils of politics. Significantly, this was just before his fall from power.

N.T. Rama Rao expressed the same desire, for other reasons—'to divert the attention of the people from the problems confronting the state', according to a journalist;[45] but according to him, his object was to raise resources to meet his party's expenses in the local elections. The role he announced as his choice was intriguingly reminiscent of *Veerabrahmendra Swami*, in which he had appeared in the title role just before becoming chief minister, perhaps indicating a secret desire to take up where he had left off; the exhilaration of charisma, the savouring of another kind of power once more, in an arena where he was in absolute control. Finally, in 1988, unlike his peer in Tamil Nadu, NTR followed up on his announced intention and began the shooting of *Vishwamitra*. The sole difference with MGR was that he did not seek the permission of the state assembly. The film proved to be a big flop.

XII

Rajkumar is to Karnataka what MGR or NTR are to their own states. Hero of 187 films in thirty years, his record is not as impressive as that of Prem Nazir in Kerala with his Guinness Book record of over 600 films. But, as his fans tirelessly point out, he has acted only in films in his own language, Kannada, unlike his Keralite compatriot.

Rajkumar has all the characteristics of a southern superstar capable of taking over the state. Handsome despite a long nose (nicknamed nakasura or demon-nosed by some), his present-day fans have never seen him smoke or drink or 'do anything a pure man is not supposed to do'. The majority of the films in which he has played are mythologicals or films about famous saints like Kanakadasa, Kabir, Tukaram, Gora Kumbhara and Harishchandra and grand historical figures such as Krishnadevaraya and Kanteerava. His very first film was the mythological *Bedara Kannappa* (1954). Every punchline of dialogue delivered by him on the Kannada screen is accompanied by cheering and frenzied whistling that is almost unbelievable. Rajkumar can speak or do no wrong in the eyes of his fans. He has fan clubs and fan associations all over the state of Karnataka.

Rajkumar can also lay claim to a dictatorial status in and out of the film industry. He is producer, distributor, exhibitor and actor rolled into one, able to do what he likes; among the masses he has millions of fans organized into clubs that do his bidding or what they consider to be the duty of the followers of their guru. With the full knowledge of his power, he refuses to align himself with any existing political party.

One of the points of pride for his fans is that their mentor not only has not acted in a film in any language other than Kannada, but that he does not speak any other language. In Bangalore, capital city of Karnataka, the language issue is complicated by the fact that the majority of the population is Tamil. As always, the frustrations of the man on the street seek a scapegoat in the outsider; inevitably, too, the focus of this search for an object of hate lies here in language. As the nothing-but-Kannada star, Rajkumar is the natural hero of this hatred. He became the spearhead of the movement linked to the Gokak Committee Report that gave sole first-language status to Kannada. 'We will see that you step down,' thundered Rajkumar's close associate Dwarakesh, in a public warning to the then Chief Minister Gundu Rao, 'and Rajkumar becomes chief minister to implement the Report.' Rajkumar himself urged the huge meeting: 'Let our lives go, but let the language live.'

When his pronouncements, demanding that every inhabitant of Karnataka must learn Kannada regardless of their original home, sparked riots, Rajkumar realized to his horror that he could not control the violence, which had a life of its own. He hurriedly retracted and overtly withdrew from politics. Under the increasingly successful mediation of the then Chief Minister Ramakrishna Hegde, he had to lie low. But whether he has given up his political ambitions, and is waiting in the wings for his cue, is difficult to say. His best role, as he himself said, is yet to come; he may yet be 'chief minister by public demand'.[46]

But the situation in Karnataka is distinct from MGR and NTR land in certain ways. First, there is a strong awareness of the modern Western world that has entered the body of tradition in the novels of R.K. Narayan and U.R. Ananthamurthy, the theatre of B.V. Karanth and Girish Karnad—and, more significantly, in the 'New Cinema'. Criticism of the superstitious aspects of tradition is clearly voiced in Pattabhi Rama Reddy's *Samskara*, Girish Kasaravalli's *Ghatashraddha*, Prema Karanth's *Phaniyamma* and many other outstanding films honoured in India and abroad. For the forward sections of Karnataka's middle class, therefore, there exists a superior cultural leadership to what Rajkumar can offer. Like Kerala, Karnataka may for that reason fail to be a happy political hunting ground for the aspiring superstar. The propitious conditions for dictatorship that Annadurai so shrewdly recognized in Tamil Nadu are not as plentifully available in Karnataka as a star-politician would seem to require.

XIII

The fundamental difference between the two star chief ministers and other star politicians of India lies in the fact that in the case of the former, the films themselves created the politics and the politicians; the latter are merely film stars who decided to move into politics or were persuaded to do so as vote catchers. In the case of Amitabh Bachchan, for instance, the films which made his reputation, instead of helping him now, put him on the defensive. At the elections in Allahabad (his hometown) after the assassination of Indira Gandhi in 1984, Amitabh's astute opponent H.N. Bahuguna, a politician of many years' standing, put up posters showing Amitabh in violent action and asked: 'Is this the man you want to vote for?' The fact that Amitabh won the election may have been merely a part of the landslide victory of Rajiv Gandhi's party, riding on the double wave of sympathy for his dead mother and enthusiasm for her young son, the reluctant debutant. The fact that almost anyone the party chose won the elections makes the worth of the film star component highly suspect.

Dismissing the effect of his violent image in films, Amitabh said, 'People don't go out and be aggressive because they have seen an action film. They always distinguish between real life and what they see on the screen.'[47] We have seen in the case of MGR that they do not.

Whereas MGR and NTR were projecting the 'saviour' image from the film screen on to real life without disjunction, Amitabh, dressed in flowing white, signifying purity and simplicity and mouthing patriotic sentiments in favour of the Constitution and its upholders, presented an inescapable contradiction between his screen image derived from a long series of films, and the political image he was seeking to project through a newly acquired style of dress and content of speech. 'My own son expects me to fight tigers,' he observed, with a clearer understanding of the problem than his formal utterances indicated.[48] As a Congress (I) Member of Parliament he was on the side of the ministers and the law enforcers; but at the end of *Inquilab*, made after he was elected, he guns down a row of corrupt, inefficient ministers. Defending his violence in *Mard* to an interviewer ('People feel that as an MP you should not have indulged in such blatant acts of violence'), he said, 'I wasn't representing Amitabh Bachchan, Member of Parliament, in *Mard*. It was a typical Manmohan Desai film, not to be taken seriously.'[49]

Obviously, it is difficult for the hero and his audience to live with such a contradiction. After all, if Bachchan is taken seriously it is only because he is known through his films; otherwise he would not have been nominated for the elections. It is impossible to be known *through* one's films without being known *for* them. As the history of MGR and NTR shows, popular films have to be taken seriously. It is equally obvious from the MGR–NTR experience that people do not always distinguish 'between real life and what they see on the screen' (see Bachchan quote above). This is especially so when their films have a consistent pattern to them—the saviour image in the case of MGR and NTR, who managed to avoid being specifically known for their violence.

The contradiction between the Bachchan image in politics and in films proved hard to overcome. When Amitabh tried to improve the fortunes of his party in the elections in Assam (after the Assam Accord of 1985 signed by Rajiv Gandhi), he was hooted at and stoned. The fact that he was enormously popular in Assam as a film star did not help him as a politician—perhaps because he was posing an avuncular image totally contradictory to the embodiment of primeval violence his films had built up and therefore not credible for the political purpose.

The political debut of Hindi cinema's foremost all-India star was in some ways similar to the bandit Malkhan Singh's surrender to the police. Addressing a public meeting, the bandit claimed that he 'had never allowed injustice in his area and that he had taken up arms to serve society'.[50] Despite his success with character acting in Hrishikesh Mukherjee's *Anand* when he first attracted real attention, then with the romantic role in *Kabhi Kabhie*, and comedy in *Chupke Chupke*, Amitabh really came into his own with films like *Trishul*, *Deewar*, *Zanjeer*, *Adalat* and *Kaala Paththar*. In these he, like MGR and NTR, is the man who has no patience with the legal process and dispenses instant justice. In fact, where there is a possibility of the police redressing a wrong, he dodges the law enforcer in order to hand out justice himself. Thus, in *Kaala Paththar* he deliberately misguides the police at the time when they are about to arrest the villain. In *Zanjeer* he refuses to tell the police the identity of the man who had tried to kill him; in *Adalat* he will not tell them the name of the man who has raped his sister—in order to wreak his personal vengeance, which is to be preferred to the law's impersonal justice.

XIV

The comparison of Amitabh Bachchan with the two star chief ministers merits further pursuit, but before we do so, it is necessary to survey the extraordinary career of the nation's screen hero (popular even in MGR–NTR territory) and to know the nature of the image his films created over more than a decade.

The 1950s had belonged to Guru Dutt and Raj Kapoor. One was the direct inheritor of the *Devdas* tradition generated by P.C. Barua in films in Bengali and Hindi—of the hero unable to fight for his cause, taking refuge in drink under the wings of a golden-hearted prostitute and finally being withered by tuberculosis. The poet of *Pyaasa* is less passive than his mentor but shares his self-pity, the lyrical expression of which finally brings him the success he sulkingly despises.[51] Barua had always looked as though he had tuberculosis; Guru Dutt was built in more generous proportions and did not conform to the conventional portrait of the artist as a weak man. He was more of the ordinary man who was a poet but did not look like one. Saratchandra Chattopadhyay had written the novel *Devdas* at the age of seventeen; the artist's rejection of the world, in *Pyaasa* or *Kaagaz Ke Phool*, as an evil that disturbed his dreams, resembled, beyond Devdas, some of the early poetry of Jibanananda Das in lines such as these:

> I have seen the sun red in the morning sky
> Order me to stand up and meet the world face to face,
> And in response my heart has filled with sorrow, hatred and blind rage;
> Under the attack of that sun, the earth squeals
> With the voice of billions of skewered pigs;
> Some festivity!
> I have tried to drown the sun
> In the unrelenting darkness of my heart
> And to go to sleep again,
> To immerse myself eternally in the vaginal depths of darkness,
> To merge into it, like death itself.
> My soul yearns for this endless, dark sleep;
> Why awaken me?
>
> —The Darkness[52]

In other words, Guru Dutt, although closer in his naïveté to seventeen-year-old Saratchandra than to the more complex Jibanananda Das, was not what the popular cinema, despite the success of some of his films, would call a 'hero'. His rejection of the world was not a rejection of Indian society of the post-Independence period as such.

Raj Kapoor, the second great figure of the 1950s, also represented the ordinary man, in this case good-looking, naïve and attractive to the girls, who played the slightly Chaplinesque underdog with sincerity but also with ample flourish.

In the anti-heroic protest of both these heroes against the ways of society and the decline of values, there was hope that they would be heard by society and that something would be done. Newly independent India was lashed by problems but was buoyed by hope of deliverance through a kind of Fabian socialism that Raj Kapoor in particular reflected.

I am poor, so what? I have a song in my heart and a future ahead—this was the keynote of his carefree approach to life and love. It was a kind of street translation of Nehru's broadly humanist socialism. There was no trace of male macho in either Kapoor or Dutt.

The 1960s were the continuation of this hero in a more romantic if less socialistic mould in Rajesh Khanna, and male macho in Dharmendra. For Khanna, love was not a protest against poverty or injustice but basically an aesthetic passion for beauty untainted by musclemanship and never divorced from basic goodness of the heart. Dharmendra's macho, too, was without malevolence; he was 'a sort of male Zeenat Aman who only had to bare his hairy chest to have the women go gaga'.[53] His body was rugged but his face benign. His musculature did not distance him from the middle-class aura about him. Both Khanna and Dharmendra exuded a mood of hope that belonged to India of the Nehru period, of Lal Bahadur Shastri (which saw India's second victory over Pakistan in a war waged by the latter) and the early years of Indira Gandhi, climaxed by the liberation of Bangladesh.

The 1970s saw the emergence of cynicism on a large scale. The pre-Independence generation had grown old and with it, the idealism of the struggle against the British was dying. Even the patriots of old had grown corrupt; they had given a lot, now they wanted their share of the pie, and if possible a bit more. The country was richer but the people poorer. The mask had fallen off the slogan-mouthing politician. People had seen the face of greed in those who were to deliver them from their miseries. Consumer goods production had proliferated; shop windows were full of goods for the burgeoning rich. The majority of urban people, leave alone the rural, could not afford such goods by honest means. The thought arose that nobody was going to give you what you did not grab. To many, therefore, honesty began to seem the virtue of fools. The new times needed a cynical, violent hero, less bothered with love and romance and more with grabbing money and power with his bare hands. It found him in Amitabh Bachchan.

The 1970s no longer adored women, but asserted openly the right to treat them as chattels. In many parts of the country, women were molested, raped and burnt for dowry with greater impunity than ever before, defying the newspapers, which angrily reported them every day. All this in spite of a Constitution which guarantees the equality of all its citizens. Perhaps the Constitution was already being seen by many as a dangerous thing. It had been framed by a Western-educated leadership, which had persuaded the provincials to accept it. Now they were waking up to the dangers of secularism, democracy and equality which were making the low castes, tribals and women demand minimum wages and equality before the law. So began the great feudal backlash in a major part of the country. Along with taming of women it included Harijan baiting and the struggle to perpetuate bonded labour—all better achieved with more freedom from the central government, the guardian of the Constitution. All over the country, a struggle began between the avant-garde of the English-knowing middle class and a large section of the rest—which included the lumpen, the feudal landlord, and the illiterate but rich contractors and shopkeepers in the urban sector, the battleground of the cinema.

Amitabh's baptism in violence came in *Zanjeer* (1973) but reached mythical heights with *Trishul* (1978), an archetypal product that mythologized the present, made miraculous, divine muscle power seem to descend from a dead mother in heaven, enabling the hero to wreak revenge, to deny the call of sexual love, and to plunge into battle for the family's honour.

Powered by mother's divine blessing from the other world, Amitabh fells a large group of musclemen obviously stronger than himself, making his prowess seem miraculous, akin to the feats of gods and godmen in mythology. In *Deewar*, the mother, the icon of family integrity, formally sides with the honest son but secretly pines for the wicked one and possibly loves him more (for his macho?). The two brothers represent the horns of the dilemma of the times haunting the self. They are the double (and are therefore is some films played by the same actor), with the split identity clothed in separate bodies.

In *Sholay* (1975), Amitabh is the hired non-hero, the gunman as coldly efficient as a machine,[54] unconcerned with the morals of a situation, with a controlled anger expressed in very few words, in much stillness, and in sudden eruptions of violent but precise action. As always, his only relationship with a woman falls outside socially accepted parameters. In *Sholay*, where it comes nearest to 'love', she is a widow whose remarriage is prevented by her suitor's timely death.

Inevitably enough, the rise of the mother cult coincides with an increase in misogyny and male camaraderie. In *Deewar*, the nightclub girl who loves Bachchan tells him her name and he retorts: 'What's the use? Girls like you change your name as often as you change your clothes.' The Amitabh brand of hero's attitude to love and romance is best expressed by him as the bandit Don in the film of the same name. By contrast, in *Samadhi*, Dharmendra, hero of the previous decade, fights for the hand of the woman he loves and the well-being of his son. In *Amar Prem*, Rajesh Khanna, the other star of the 1960s, sticks to the pure-at-heart prostitute he has loved all his life in a sentimental story by Bibhutibhusan Bandopadhyay (of the Apu trilogy fame). The 1970s' macho figure does not go after women; they roll at his feet of their own accord. Popular films require romance and Amitabh obliges as far as he can, which is not very far and usually means camaraderie with a woman on the fringes of society—a street performer in *Zanjeer*, a kotha dancer in *Muqaddar Ka Sikandar*, a cabaret dancer in *Deewar*, a remote, unattainable widow in *Sholay*. In place of the lady love, there is the mother; she motivates revenge (as in *Trishul*), makes him give his life (as in *Deewar*), drives him to crime by her absence (as in *Muqaddar Ka Sikandar*). She is the macho man's obsession. He finds more satisfaction in camaraderie with men than in dalliance with women (as in *Sholay*, *Silsila*). In *Do Anjaane*, where he does get married, he virtually rejects his wife at the end. In *Silsila*, he turns from a love relationship to the prison of a dead marriage in order to preserve traditional values. Woman is to be respected only as mother. Even some of the marginal women with whom the macho man strikes up a relationship are surrogate mothers a la the prostitute in *Devdas*, the archetypal mother surrogate of Indian cinema.

The attitudes inherent within the series of Amitabh films of the 1970s and 1980s are mostly, as we have noted, anti-constitutional: take the law in your hands because of the law's indefensible delays and because there is more satisfaction in personal revenge; grab what you can, because honesty does not pay; treat women as chattels because that is what they deserve; the family is the only valid social unit, the state counts for nought and since the state has failed, the individual must act to obtain justice for the wronged. There is no search here for the means to change society or its systems, even through violence. Instead, it is the nihilism of the lumpen and the antisocial units and groups, living outside the organized working class and waiting to grab the opportunity to become the privileged tyrants they rage against. Time and again the Bachchan figure emerges from among the oppressed to become the oppressor. The anger is not of the rebel but of the violence-seeking psyche, no matter how cool it may appear. The satisfaction of violence is greater than the purpose of it. 'We saw flashes of cold anger in Amit's early films,' reminisced Javed of the Salim–Javed team whose scripts transported Bachchan to his pedestal, 'and thought he was ideal for action films.' It was on their recommendation that Prakash Mehra gave him the historic lead role in *Zanjeer* which created a long-lasting legend at the box office.

The appeal of violence for the lumpen is a remarkable trait, developed as it is by a member of the intellectual and social elite. Bachchan was educated at Sherwood College, Nainital, and later became an executive with the British firm of Bird & Co., Calcutta. The son of famed Hindi poet Harivanshrai Bachchan, he looked, during Abbas's *Saat Hindustani* and the years immediately following it, like a student out of Tagore's Santiniketan in his white pyjamas and brown kurta. He found a conduit of identification with the social dropout, the underworld killer, the unemployed and unemployable lumpen, whose sole pastime is the cinema where he can find satisfactions that cannot be his in real life. He became the symbol of hope, the model of action for those who feel wronged and denied of opportunities that they vaguely feel are rightfully theirs, whose talents and abilities have been ignored by a ruthless, unfeeling world. His illness in 1982 brought out the enormous regard in which he is held by a vast mass of humanity. Millions of boys and girls prayed for his well-being. Thousands of people thronged the gates of the hospital where he lay fighting for his life. Like all his fights, he won this one too. After his recovery, he had to give repeated darshans to the crowds below, like an emperor of old, or a prime politician of today, assuring his people that he was alive and well and would continue to pour his blessings upon them. It was as if his devotees snatched him from the jaws of death, making 1982 the year of Amitabh Bachchan. No other film star in the world commanded a following as wide and as devoted as his at the height of his career. It is not the middle class that has made Bachchan what he is today. It is the plebeians, the lumpen proletariat that took him to the pinnacle of success. With all the popularity he has with the wide-eyed boys and girls from schools and colleges, if one of his films did not click with the lumpen, the petty trader, the semi-educated contractor, the entire social section that has been the traditional breeder and supporter of fascism, it would be a flop. Trouble arose when the rebel suddenly changed sides, donned a khadi kurta-pyjama and elected himself MP, carried along by the mammoth wave of sympathy-cum-confidence voting after the assassination of Indira Gandhi. When he later went to Assam to help the Congress (I) campaign he was stoned by an electorate who liked his rebel films, but not his new incarnation as a champion of the establishment. Few understood how the apostle of violence could suddenly speak in honeyed tones and advocate the virtues of official patriotism. When this stance continued for some time, the Jekyll and Hyde of politics and cinema began to strain his credibility in both. The contradiction between his cinematic image and his Congressite socialism in politics was becoming untenable.

Shahenshah (1988) broke the link between politics and cinema in Amitabh's image, pulled in two directions. Its failure at the box office more or less coincided with the decision not to contest in Allahabad again. And no wonder, for *Shahenshah* re-inflated the image of the violent Amitabh to bursting point. In fact, its conformity by day (Amitabh as a police inspector) and rebellion by night (when the police inspector turns into a one-man government) perfectly posed the dilemma of Amitabh's life, torn between politics and cinema. One would have thought he would essay a different kind of role, going back to the benign figure of *Anand* or *Kabhi Kabhie*. But no; perhaps neither he nor his producers would know how to cope with such a change, how to alter the colour little by little, film by film, until the blood was washed clean. *Shahenshah* turned the police station into a comic stage where the daily farce of law enforcement is played. The successful man it set up is the picture of corruption and ruthless violence against society that the police bolsters up and the honest press dies in denouncing. The case against the villain, J.K. (Amrish Puri), is dismissed despite obvious evidence of his guilt. In the courtroom itself Shahenshah proceeds to demonstrate true justice to the corrupt judge. He denounces the dreams of independent India (*azadi ke sapne*) he used to nourish in his heart; '*Ghatia log desh ke neta bante hain* (Rotten people become leaders of the country),' he declares, without stopping to think that people might construe that to be a reference to his friend, then prime minister, Rajiv Gandhi. Having torn off his police insignia in style, and harangued the judge on true justice, he then proceeds to show how it should be done and kills J.K. with his usual supernatural strength.

The anger sat well on his face. The horrible violence he perpetrated seemed for real, fully intended, not simulated for cinema. But the audience was not convinced. Something had turned sour. Under the angry film image lurked the goody-goody one of the politician. The audience wanted the Jekyll and Hyde game to end. Only when he withdrew from politics and unified his image once more did the box office slowly come back to him. By contrast MGR's image was more consciously and meticulously planned and executed than Hitler's or Stalin's cinematic strategy. Leni Riefenstahl was too talented to be useful enough to Hitler for any length of time; Stalin had no end of trouble with geniuses like Eisenstein, Pudovkin and Dovzhenko, and had no joy out of the mediocre. MGR's directors, on the other hand, served his every wish faithfully, with the result that when MGR stood before the electorate, his victory was a foregone conclusion. Indeed, his image was so strong, so completely consistent, that when anything went wrong in real life it was the bureaucracy which was blamed, not MGR.

MGR was never seen smoking, drinking or teasing girls in his films; he was, consistently, the saviour. His films always subtly projected his party ideology; its villain was clearly defined as the Brahmin north. NTR was identified with the gods of the Hindu pantheon or the noble character of the epics. Both of them used violence but for a socially, morally, and even politically defined purpose. Violence was not their credo, nor was it, as with Bachchan, their instrument of self-satisfaction, transmitting a sense of vicarious fulfilment to the vaguely wronged who wanted to be in a position to do wrong to others.

XV

It is a moot question whether cinematic divinity has a direct psychological link with dictatorship. Gods have little patience with the laws of man. DMK atheist MGR became God through the exercise of power shown to be invincible in his films; God-playing NTR just slipped into godhood; Amitabh, with his miraculous muscle power, has a simulated divinity. An MGR or an NTR or an Amitabh in power, used to the adulation of the masses praying at their gaudy temples, must find it difficult to accept democratic checks on their actions. Like their followers, they too confuse myth and reality.

Both MGR and NTR tried to curb the press, using the extra-constitutional power of their millions of fans always at hand as a dire threat, tried to keep intellectuals under control and appropriate equality with them through politically awarded doctorates, and by juggling with university appointments tried to establish the rule of the loyal mediocrity instead of the independent meritorious. Would Bachchan have been different if he had come to power? It seems unlikely.

Their followers, too, are as impatient with democracy as the stars themselves. Ever ready to take the law into their own hands, they question the right of other humans to control their stars. An MGR fan mob heckled Kannada film star Manjula for having slapped MGR in a film even though the script called for it.

Erik Erikson speaks of the attraction to totalism in those who fail to graduate from the trauma of puberty and adolescence into manhood. Since the key to such graduation lies in the psychic separation from the mother, the glorification of the mother cult and the attendant denial of honour to woman in any other role must indicate the inability of large sections of the illiterate or semi-literate uprooted urban mass audience to cultivate the sense of adult independence required in a respect for democracy. In this sense, the growth of the fan cult of star dictatorship is not unrelated to the growth of fundamentalism and intolerance of social differences. Indeed, it is possible to see a direct connection between such illusionism and fascism. Aided and abetted by large-scale unemployment among the semi-educated and its resultant frustration and anger, star adulation explodes easily from dream to reality. In Tamil-majority Bangalore, riots were sparked off by matinee idol Rajkumar's statement demanding a compulsory Kannada-proficiency test for all schoolchildren; the Rajkmar Fan Association looted shops, damaged buses and stabbed a Tamil boy.[55] It was not long after that the biggest film star of Karnataka chose virtually to withdraw from political stances and statements.

It is astonishing that the party in power at the Centre, with the entire development machinery in its hands, never understood the need to project its philosophy through popular cinema. Had it planned such a campaign as meticulously as the DMK once did, it could well have, in four decades, won over the entire urban population and its rural periphery to its point of view. Many of the dangers to the unity of India, a country that can only be called a honeycomb of religious, linguistic and regional identities, could possibly have been minimized if not averted altogether, since they are largely the product of the very classes that patronize the cinema most heavily.

Despite its reverses in Tamil Nadu and in Andhra Pradesh, where it once saw cinema take over the state, the Congress party simplistically tries, repeatedly, to capitalize on the popularity of established stars. Besides Amitabh Bachchan, it inducted Sunil Dutt, one-time star Vyjyanthimala Bali and Rajesh Khanna into the party juggernaut. Judging by the polls in Assam, in which Amitabh had tried to pull his weight, and West Bengal, where Rajesh was harnessed to the job, the effort to make simplistic use of star charisma has proved pitifully ineffective. The party never evaluated the link between the image of a star built by his films with what he might be able to achieve in politics. In the case of Amitabh it was at least an attempt to make hay while the star shone; Rajesh Khanna's glamour had faded too much to reflect glory even though his screen personality had been less at variance with Congress party ideology. Besides, the coexistence of the two in the same fold created an additional image confusion that any advertising expert would have detected at once. Khanna's intervention in the 1987 West Bengal elections proved predictably abortive in a highly conscious electorate with a large middle class and an ideologically developed, organized working class and a relatively aware peasantry.

One of the differences between the Keralite, Kannada and Bengali audiences from those in Tamil Nadu and Andhra Pradesh is in their world awareness. A.K. Ramanujan has pointed to the relative absence of modern, Western impregnation of Tamil and Telugu cultures compared to Bengal, Kerala and Karnataka as a possible reason for the cultural insularity of Tamil Nadu and Andhra Pradesh.[56] Significantly, the two states have been backward in terms of the growth of a 'New Cinema', a serious and conscious expression of the socio-political debate that has stirred the areas more stimulated by the impact of modernity, such as Kerala, Karnataka, Maharashtra and Bengal. It can be argued that the 'seeing is believing' factor worked more in Andhra Pradesh and Tamil Nadu with the merging of myth and fact in their star-politician's hold over the populace. That belief is further strengthened by the election results in recent years, which show an erosion of faith in the leadership in the cities, with the countryside remaining intact. By comparison the rural–urban ideological differentiation is much less in West Bengal, as two assembly elections have proved. The United Left Front led by the highly culture-conscious Communist Party of India (Marxist) captured a large majority of the seats. Congress politics appears to have failed to get at the grassroots either through God (and godman) as in Andhra Pradesh and Tamil Nadu or simply through man as in Bengal.

The 1989 elections in Tamil Nadu laid to rest the ghost of M.G. Ramachandran in the politics of the state. Both his wife Janaki and his heroine and party colleague Jayalalithaa initially failed to capitalize on his legacy, which each claimed to have exclusively inherited. The cinematic mantle of the extraordinary film star/politician failed to settle itself on either; it may be said that the mantle itself melted into thin air. MGR's arch-rival of two decades, M. Karunanidhi, leader of the Opposition DMK, won a thundering victory over all other forces. Since Karunanidhi's links with cinema had steadily eroded during the years of MGR rule, celluloid's power over politics may itself be on its way out. When Jayalalithaa staged a comeback, it was really without the help of cinematic charisma.

A similar diminution of cinema's role in politics took place in Andhra Pradesh. NTR's image had been tarnished nationally and within the state. His return to film acting in *Vishwamitra*, his extraordinary wealth reconfirmed behind his professions of asceticism, and his impulsive and dictatorial actions led to his downfall. The fascist and obscurantist nexus between cinema and politics resulting from the equation of myth and fact ended in disillusion. Whether the decline of the MGR–NTR mythological vision of modern India will give way to a more realistic separation of myth and fact in these two states may depend on new, dominant forces coming into play, causing a cultural revolution that would reflect itself in politics.

NOTES ON FIVE DIRECTORS

12

SATYAJIT RAY

I. The First Ten Years

It was not for nothing that Truffaut (reportedly) walked out of a showing of *Pather Panchali*; it was because he could not bear the slow rhythm. Arriving once in a rush to see *Postmaster* I was irritated beyond measure by the time Anil Chatterjee took to turn his head less than 180 degrees. But, slowly, the film cast its spell; one was lifted out of the breathless pace of middle-class life and placed in the heart of Indian reality, surrendering to the rhythm of life as it is lived by the majority of people, and has been, for hundreds of years. The waterlogged path, the little hut surrounded by bamboo groves, became real; every movement of a face took on meaning, became a personal experience.

Yet Satyajit Ray does not nostalgically idealize traditional India. The postmaster cannot stick life in the village and must go back; he is too city bred. Apu moves from his village to Benares and finally to Calcutta, inexorably drawn towards a more modern world. *Jalsaghar* records the decay of feudalism, no matter with how much melancholy. *Devi* gently points to the protest against superstition naturally arising out of scientific education. And Amulya in *Samapti* sports a portrait of Napoleon and wears tartan socks and Oxford shoes—a wayward mixture of tradition and modernity.

In India, the hiatus between modern and traditional, educated and uneducated, rich and poor, is so great that this process of identification with the rhythm and reality of the life of the people is essential to any art which is not prepared to be ephemeral. The rhythm of Ray's films is one of the finest things about his work, for the very reason that it expresses a wider reality than the one we are used to in our islands of modernity in India.

It is also intimately bound up with the contemplative nature of his style, the preoccupation with what happens in the mind rather than on the surface. Ray's work abounds in long wordless passages, in which his characters do very little and yet express a great deal. Think, for instance, of the long, slow opening shot of *Jalsaghar*, showing the old man sitting on the terrace in the twilight, his back to the camera, and his servant handing him his long pipe. It sets the note of the entire film—the passing of an order, the twilight not only of his own life, but of an age.

For those who look upon cinema as a vehicle of action and drama, Ray's work is 'anti-film'. In the one sequence of *Jalsaghar* in which he essays a sudden spurt of dramatic action—the death by drowning of the old man's wife and son—he is acutely uncomfortable, and becomes almost banal both in the symbol of the upturned boat and the manner of introduction of the dead boy. In *Jalsaghar*, as in *Devi*, he takes a story with great 'dramatic' potential and persistently plays down this element. Perhaps he feels, like Auguste Renoir, that:

> The hero portrayed at the moment when he is defying the enemy, or a woman shown in the hardest pains of labour, is not a suitable subject for a great painting, though men and women who have passed through such ordeals . . . become great subjects when later on the artist can portray them in repose. The artist's take is not to stress this or that instant in a human being's existence, but to make comprehensible the man in his entirety.
>
> —*Renoir, My Father*, by Jean Renoir

The inevitability and the direction of change are never in doubt in *Jalsaghar* or *Devi*; that is why Ray is content to express the individual in his entirety and never feels the need to take up the cudgels for social reform. In *Devi*, he has no less sympathy for the father-in-law who becomes obsessed with the idea that his son's wife is the incarnation of the Goddess, than for the unfortunate girl who gives her life to it. To Ray both are victims: one of his superstition, the other of its consequences. There is no anger, no sense of urgency, and no obvious partisanship for the forces of change.

In this sense of resignation and fatality, Ray is Indian to the core. Indian tradition views existence as a continuous line of epic sweep rather than as a tight circle of drama in which death brings tragedy. The Apu trilogy is almost as littered with dead bodies as *Hamlet*, yet the feeling is totally different. Durga dies, followed by Harihar, and then Sarbajaya; finally Aparna. But life goes on, and hope never dies. The 'tragic view of life' of Western literature is totally absent from Ray.

In today's India hope is not just an eternal tradition: it underlies the here and now. A vast process of change has been developing for more than a hundred years through the influence of Western scientific thought. Until Independence, this was largely confined to the educated middle class; now that a faster tempo of industrialization has set in, it has begun to spread more widely. The poorest or most sceptical Indian realizes today that although material prosperity and the modern age are not just around the corner, India cannot remain in its present condition forever. Perhaps in the past hope had something to do with the hereafter, or at most with the imminence of Independence; now it springs from the aspiration towards a better life in this world. Dialectically enough, the hope of material prosperity produces a sense of faith, and faith is an important element in art. Ray's work does not merely record the poverty of India: it is imbued with confidence in the human being.

The spiritual restlessness of a Bergman or a Fellini lies in the search for hopes and faiths which they cannot find. Inevitably, the difference in spirit gives rise to differences in form. The slow tempo of Ray's films reflects a deeper sense of Indian reality. In that respect, it is very different from the slow rhythm of an Antonioni film, which demands a response which is not 'natural' to the Western way of life, but rather runs counter to it and so creates bitter controversies. Ray's images are (like Antonioni's) what I would call musical in expressiveness: they send out ripples far beyond any conscious understanding of the elements contained in them. They are 'decorative', pronouncedly so in *Charulata*, but to a varying degree in other films as well. This, too, is embedded in the Indian tradition, in which *décoratif* is not a word of abuse as it is in France. In Rajasthani miniatures or classical music, decoration and expression are one and the same thing. And the deliberation of Ray's composition does not inhibit the spontaneity of the work, which flows like Indian music, improving freely within some very broad definitions. Even his background music often becomes memorable by itself, as in *Pather Panchali* and *Charulata*, and is not the 'unheard music' that background music in films is ideally supposed to be. The melodic themes are often recognizable and memorable, and emphasize the lyrical–decorative aspects of his films.

In *Pather Panchali*, Ray created his basic style and technique. It was not without its rough edges (think of the sequence of Durga's illness, with its element of theatrical contrivance), but the truth of inspiration carried it along. In *Aparajito*, his technique becomes more mature and polished and capable of subtlety. Less obvious emotions can now be expressed with more restraint (as in the death of Sarbajaya). In *Jalsaghar*, Ray made his first important film in a studio, with a professional actor and more complex resources. And *Jalsaghar* is the outstanding example of his technique until *Charulata*—in his handling of a vast set, mixing the real and the artificial. Significantly, it came out of the oldest and most primitive of Calcutta's studios. In the terrace scene of the opening, the moonlit veranda sequence, the music room in session, the ride to death, every shade of atmosphere is subtly drawn out.

Mood and atmosphere dominate, and it is because of their dominance that craftsmanship plays such an important role. From here on, Ray is completely sure of himself and uses the camera almost with the fluency of a writer using his pen. To master technique and subordinate it completely to one's will is the first requirement for individual expression; and in cinema it often becomes the supreme enemy, because of the enormous complexities and temptations. But Ray's unit (he works always with the same group of technicians) moves as easily under his hand as a well-ordered machine.

Watching him shoot *Two Daughters*, what struck me was his sheer technical fluency.

It is not the perfection of technique, however, that makes Ray's films important. The world and mind he projects are basically those of the Bengal renaissance which started in the nineteenth century. In a way he is a chronicler of the past; yet the inner assurance of hope and faith is not a thing of the past, for these feelings are buried under the surface of modern India, in the Nehru dream. Nehru stood somewhere between Gandhi and Tagore; and the truth of the Tagore value-world never quite lost its appeal in Nehru's India. In fact, it found new expression in the ideals, if not in all the realities, of the Nehru era.

The Calcutta of the burning trams, the communal riots, refugees, unemployment, rising prices and food shortages, does not exist in Ray's films. Although he lives in this city, there is no correspondence between him and the 'poetry of anguish' which has dominated Bengali literature for the last ten years. On the whole, Ray has portrayed the past evolution of the middle class as reflected in the long period dominated by Tagore. It is something that has gone into the making of himself and his generation; something he knows and understands. In a broad way, it forms the background of his experience. The experience need not be directly personal: the people, the customs, the attitudes reflected in the literature of the Tagore era become, through repetition and constant explication, part of the fabric of personal experience. A certain image of the villager, the young man getting to know the world outside, the women slowly liberated through social evolution, became crystallized in the poems, plays, novels and essays not only of Tagore but of writers of his period; and it is this image which projects itself in Ray's films. His characters are powerfully simplified, and contained within very broad outlines of the typology of the period.

Look at Ray's heroes. Soumitra Chatterjee's resemblance to the young Tagore in *The World of Apu* is far from accidental, for he reappears—without the beard—in film after film. And in the Apu trilogy Ray veers away from the novelist Bibhutibhusan's slightly dewy-eyed vision of 'Golden Bengal' to the Tagorean attitude of someone who is deeply attracted towards Western science and feels the urge to create a new Indian identity. Bibhutibhusan's wonder child never grows up: Ray's Apu lives through the experiences of childhood and youth to become a man.

In *Devi*, we meet Soumitra Chatterjee again, by now already an embodiment of Bengali youth of a certain period and type both of which are distinctly derived from Tagore. Already in *Devi* the weakness of the character has become apparent: he is a thinker more than a man of action, a bit of a Hamlet. He has read Mill and Bentham and disapproves of his father's superstitious visions, but he is not strong enough to withstand the pressures of tradition or repudiate what he considers to be the evils of ignorance. In his political thinking Tagore eschewed both the violence of the terrorist and the shrewdly practical non-violence of Gandhi; but he provided inspiration towards the general ideals of patriotism which is not narrow, individualism which is not intolerant. Ray's heroes also represent a noble philosophical outlook, but are not men of action on the plane of reality.

By the time of *Charulata*, Soumitra Chatterjee has evolved further from his earlier, Tagorean base. The Mill- and Bentham-reading character (inspired by Rammohun Roy, a nineteenth-century social reformer often described as the 'father of modern India') now belongs to the older generation, and is embodied in the bearded, pince-nez-sporting Bhupati with his affluent idealism. Amal (Chatterjee) himself stands between the pure Tagore and what is to come after. But he too is devoid of cynicism, on the whole unselfconscious, and capable of moral action, in going away when he realizes that he is about to betray his brother. Of what is to come after, we see rather more in *Kapurush*: the 'Ravindrik' (Tagorean) generation has finally revealed its failure in the weak-minded, slightly parasitic intellectual (a film writer), who is no longer made a coward by his conscience but by sheer lack of courage.

In the series of films—the trilogy, *Devi*, *Samapti*, *Charulata* and *Kapurush*—the Ray hero has emerged in a straight line from the Tagore mould of protected innocence into the contemporary world, only to find himself inadequate to contend with it. The type of hero represented by

Soumitra Chatterjee in various Ray films is no longer noble in his motives and irresolute in his actions: in *Kapurush*, he is weak without being noble. But this is an end which is surely not untypical of the romantic Bengali youth brought up under the Tagore umbrella. They have become cynical under the pressures of disillusionment in independent India. Their past idealism has become a drag on them and has made them unable to cope with a society where, whether we like it or not, the law of the jungle has acquired some currency. But even this evolution never takes the hero entirely outside the Tagore value-world; it only takes him to its farthest limits, limits which Tagore himself had explored.

Even in the working-class garb of *Abhijan*, the Tagore-oriented middle-class minds of Ray and Chatterjee show clearly through the thin disguise of the different-style beard of its hero. Soumitra has tried in many ways to play 'tough' not only in this film but in others too; but he has not ceased to represent the charm, innocence, unselfconsciousness and the accompanying weakness of the young Bengali romantic hero of the Tagore period. A sort of protected hero, with a dominating father-figure lurking somewhere in the shadows, who is not destined to battle on his own, still less to win.

In *Kanchanjungha*, the hero comes from an altogether new social class, and his line of thought is different from that of the Tagorean dreamers. He is a product of today, with an idealism that is more capable of contending with realities, because it is more clear-eyed and much more of a piece. He is not the affluent son turned idealist: he belongs more to the larger middle classes which ceased to be landlords long ago. He is not in the least ashamed of his comical uncle, would call a spade a spade any day, and even if he is attracted to the daughter of the impossible Rai Bahadur (a low-grade British title), he sets no great store by her vague promise of seeing him in Calcutta. If the liaison did not work out, he would have no hesitation in breaking it. But this different hero is only hinted at in the splendid isolation of the picture's Darjeeling setting, and this lightweight film obliquely bypasses a set of values unfamiliar to the Tagore mythology.

Another modern type, less of a hero, is presented by Anil Chatterjee in *Postmaster* and *Mahanagar*. But in both films the basic emphasis is away from him: in one on the child, in the other on the woman. As a result he is a somewhat shadowy figure, brought in to fill the place of the traditional none-too-bright middle-class individual. He has acquired the outward mental accoutrements of the Tagore world, to the extent of wanting to teach the child in *Postmaster* and counselling the wife to take a job in *Mahanagar*, without any sense of dedication to either. His relationships, his emotions, never reach the larger-than-life size achieved by other Ray heroes, especially Soumitra Chatterjee, in their representation of an epoch or an outlook.

One could say that in the films preceding *Mahanagar*, Ray's preoccupation is with man. The trilogy's heroines are the women of Indian tradition, loving and sometimes loved, providers of anchorage to the nomadic male who goes out to do battle and whose fate is therefore of greater importance. The girl in *Devi* is not much more than an object, owned by her father-in-law even more than by her husband; even Sarbajaya, patient and loving in a Mother Earth way, cannot decide either her own or her family's future. In *Postmaster*, the child is a little mother, already burdened with the responsibilities of an outgoing love. In *Samapti*, although the husband is a somewhat 'enlightened' young man, the measure of self-determination which the wife is destined to enjoy does not seem to be too great. The film does record a change in the outlook towards marriage, but more from the man's point of view than from that of the girl, who accepts, with happiness, what all others have accepted before her.

It is in *Mahanagar* that, for the first time, we come across a woman who is awakened to the possibility of determining the course of her own life. Typically enough, the awakening touch comes from the husband, for men have been traditional liberators of women. But traditionally, too, they have retracted when they have seen the consequences of their action. Arati is unable to exert herself in her brief freedom, but she has had a glimpse of a world where she is somebody in her own right. When she resigns from her job—her one act of protest—it is in obedience not to her husband's wish, but to her own impulsive fellow-feeling for the Anglo-Indian girl who is unjustly dismissed. Ironically enough, in this act she also gives up the freedom she has won. Somebody, protesting against this thesis, said that 'as for her rights, Arati is perverted'. So she is. The adjustment to a sudden inner feeling of economic independence is not easy, it comes out in little awkward ways which add to the truth of the situation.

But I find Ray's first essay on the Indian woman tentative and unsure of itself. The characters are not seen sufficiently from the inside, and there is an excessive dependence (itself uncharacteristic of Ray) on outward incident. The meeting under the doorway, when the husband says, 'Do not worry, it is a vast city and one of us is bound to find a job,' provides too pat a solution for a problem which will continue to plague us for a long time to come. And it is unlike Ray to seek such four-square solutions: his films are much better when they are what people call open-ended.

The sureness of touch is much more evident in *Charulata*, and because Ray's understanding of the character is perfect, everything falls into place. Charulata is observed entirely from the inside—obsessively so, in fact, with the result that we do not see into the minds of the men. Except when he breaks down in the carriage, Bhupati is more of a type than a character—the agreeable 'young Bengal' liberal of the nineteenth century, affluent, idealistic, touching in his innocence and lack of self-consciousness. Amal, too, reveals himself only in the scene in the press room after the robbery, where, standing in the half-light behind his brother, he awakens to the truth of his situation. His inner conflict elsewhere is so muted as to be missed almost completely by many people.

But where Charulata herself is concerned, every thought in her mind is clearly visible. In Madhabi Mukherjee, Ray found the embodiment of a certain type of Indian woman, just as he had found the man in Soumitra Chatterjee. Deeply intelligent, sensitive, outwardly graceful and serene, inwardly she is the kind of traditional Indian woman of today whose inner seismograph catches the vibrating waves reaching from outside into her seclusion. The world outside is changing, and down in the drawing-room, English nineteenth-century social philosophy and Rammohun Roy's ideas are inevitably working towards the liberation of women.

Mahanagar is a contemporary story and *Charulata* a period piece. Yet in the latter, the woman is more self-aware, and one might even call her ruthless. If her conscience does not trouble her too much, it is not merely because of her innocence: she has a strong character, she finds out what she wants, and the knowledge does not shock her. It only makes her go forward to get her man. She reminds me, perversely, of Lady Macbeth in Wajda's Siberian film. In a society which tells a woman 'here is the man that thou shalt love', she does not shy away from an impossible relationship. And, I repeat, this is only partly due to the innocent nature of her self-awareness. It dawns on her so slowly that it is hard for her to draw the line; but in that unforgettable garden scene she perceives the dark truth, without a shadow of doubt. A 'transparent' moment, and a great one at that.

I see in *Kapurush*, irrespective of the fact that it is a somewhat sloppily made film by Ray's and *Charulata*'s standards, a continuation of the theme of the woman's quest for happiness of her own making. She is the same character, as self-possessed and serene as ever; but she has herself changed, through her previous experiences, as it were, in *Mahanagar* and *Charulata*. She tasted economic independence in the first, and wanted it; in the second she found the man she loved, and longed for the right to go on loving him. In *Kapurush*, she is the woman who has lost both. She is married to a vapid tea-planter whom she has never loved; she stays married to him because that is the only way for a woman. She is almost in the same state of suspended animation as she was at the end of *Charulata*. And suddenly, to disturb her peace, her earlier love reappears on the scene. She knows already, unreasonably, that he failed once to take her away; and she knows that he will fail again—this time not out of any noble sentiment for a brother, but out of inability to defy society. Again her character is more eloquent in its silences than are the others in their long speeches. Again, the director's mind is concentrated on the woman's side of the triangle. *Kapurush* is thus a weaker restatement of the same proposition, and its importance lies only in the continuity of the theme and the sense of finality which it brings to it.

With increased freedom for the woman, the system of marriage has proved inadequate, and in Western society shows signs of cracking up.

Whether that is a good thing or not, let the social philosophers work out. But the inescapable fact is that such pressures are beginning to be felt in our country, with the progress in women's education and economic independence. It may well be that Ray never thought consciously of such a continuity. All the same it is clearly discernible, in spite of the fact that the films were not conceived in a neat time sequence.

It is typical of Ray that the most contemporary and truest statement of the theme should be achieved in the exquisite period piece rather than in the modern setting. In the first place, contemporaneity is not something that belongs to the story of a film, but to the outlook the director brings to bear on it. Ray's contemplative, lyrical style is symptomatic of a remoteness from the immediate problems of the day. And if he had not been able to stand back and look at what has happened in our country in the last hundred years, he could not have made the trilogy, or projected so completely the Tagore era, the nineteenth-century Bengal renaissance, and taken in even the fringe of the post-Tagore period.

Where Ray's apprehension of character tends to falter is in dealing with characters (the capitalist of *Jalsaghar*, the tea-planter of *Kapurush*) more or less unfamiliar to the typology of the Tagore era. Its idealism often underplayed unpleasant truths of character and the contradictory urges inevitable in human beings. Biographies of this period, for instance, never bring out the man in his total psychology; they select the more pleasant, publicly displayable traits. Tagore himself never reveals his personal life in the way of Gandhi. Gandhi's outlook was not contained within the framework of the rise of the middle class in India; Tagore's was. At its best, the Tagore trend resulted in the emergence of noble images of character; at its worst, it was hypocritical, a little puritan, a little afraid of Freud. It was never suited to the depiction of life in the raw. The furthest that it goes in revealing human weakness is the delicate and forgiving treatment of it in *Charulata*.

Neither the more violent and ugly aspects of our society, nor the 'poetry of anguish' generated by the struggle of the Tagoreans to cope with them, are reflected in Ray's films. In fact, whenever he has taken a tentative step towards them, he has tended to burn his fingers. Take *Abhijan* for instance: the attempt to enter the underworld of the working class results in total failure. And the reason for this failure is that it cannot be drawn from the myths and types of the Tagore world. One is not surprised to hear that the film was originally to have been made by someone else from a script by Ray, until at the last moment he decided to take it on. Even the atmosphere of the office in which Arati works in *Mahanagar* is just not complex enough. It never quite exudes the dankness, the monumental indifference, the cynicism and self-seeking, which make up the fabric of such inelegant reality. It is strenuously woven, and the clear-cut characters in the office situation carry no suggestion of unseen depths.

Here the powerful simplifications of Ray's earlier films tend towards oversimplification. In other words, he fails to enter the post-Tagore world, in which the young idealist has either turned cynical, or has turned away from patriotism, politics and social reform because all this proves too dirty for him and makes him take refuge in the 'poetry of anguish'. It is a moot question whether the later generation brought up on Tagore in the pre-Independence era of hope was toughened enough in its training to cope with the pressures of disillusion, greed, corruption and ruthlessness released in the post-Independence era. Even the rural scene today has changed, and the typology of the past no longer fits. The image of village life conjured up for so long by literary habits has at last become untrue. New types are being created by the incursion of planned investment into the countryside, the invasion of the radio, the block development offices, family planning drives, the commercial cinema, the money generated by soaring food prices, the opening up of communications. The old myths are no longer adequate: they provide a rich background to the middle-class mind, but the need to translate these values into a tougher outlook and language has become painfully clear.

The post-Tagore age has finally caught up with us. It is an age that might call for a passionate involvement on the part of the artist, and the film is an art which, willy-nilly, must in some way reflect these changes in social reality. Whether Ray will enter into another phase of development to do so, or new artists will arise out of these new and less serene urges of the times, it is impossible to say. Or will the most significant expression of intellect and sensibility—which in the years of Ray in Bengal has been the domain of the cinema—move to another medium? In his documentary biography about Tagore, Ray does for the man what his films as a whole do for the Tagore age: accept a value-world created by another, and proceed to illuminate it brilliantly, to project and extend it in terms of the cinema.

II. Modernism and Mythicality

The modernist enterprise in Ray's films is easily discernible. The trilogy takes the young Apu from a traditional village to a liberal modern education in the humanities; *Devi* and *Ganashatru* expose the dangers of blind faith; *Mahapurush* and *Joi Baba Felunath* satirize India's godmen; *Sadgati* directs a cold anger at the country's age-old caste hierarchy—the list is long and its modernism unmistakable. The nineteenth-century Bengal renaissance makes itself evident at every step in his long career. Its rationalism and its propaganda for the cultivation of the 'scientific temper' are obvious in his writings; his detective stories, his stories for children, the children's magazine are clearly all many-coloured essays on a rationalist positivism he inherited from his father and grandfather. Despite his unique ability to treat children as equals, which invests the children in his films with a living character and an authenticity rare in Indian cinema, his urge to teach them to grow up as rational, secular and democratic human beings is instantly detectable. On the face of it, therefore, the mythopoeic seems to be far from his concerns. But is it really so?

The relationship of what an artist says about his work and what the work says about him has always been an intriguing one. To define the contours of what is consciously formulated and what rises from within the depths of the psyche has ever proved a contentious area not only in itself but particularly between the artist's view and the critic's. Even where a film director selects a certain option overtly imposed by the exigencies of the situation in an art which manipulates reality to the extent of cinema, the selection is often traced to psychological predispositions hotly denied by the director himself.

Satyajit Ray considered himself an eminently conscious artist, well aware of what he was doing and why. He was given to a great degree of meticulous planning and subdued the improvisatory elements to the minimum. Thus when I once stated that Ray's *Mahanagar*, *Charulata* and *Kapurush* formed a continuous line of thought on the condition of woman in today's India, Ray instantly countered that he had thought of the second film long before the first and therefore the formulation of such a sequence would not be valid. The idea that the chronology of the thought was less important than the sequence that actually emerged did not endear itself to him at all.

In his writings, interviews and pronouncements, Ray frequently endorsed the modernist element in his mental make-up; he repeatedly emphasized his agnostic indifference to religion. What is more, he acknowledged his debt to Hollywood and to Western classical music with its fully pre-composed dramatic structure as opposed to the improvisatory linearity of its Indian counterpart. In a letter to me (27 September 1989) he said:

> I don't think Indian art traditions have had anything at all to do with my development as film-maker . . . I am firmly of the opinion that cinema is a product of the West—where the concept of an art form existing in time has been prevalent for several centuries. Indian culture shows no awareness of such a concept. If I have succeeded as a film-maker, it is due to my familiarity with Western artistic, literary and musical traditions. Add to that my observation of Indian life and you have my prescription.

But whether he liked it or was aware of it or not, Ray inherited, from his grandfather, his father and Rabindranath Tagore as well as his school at Santiniketan where he studied art for two and a half years, their modernist–social–reformist tradition on the one hand and a religious–philosophical Indianness on the other. Both became distinctly discernible in his films.

The dominant religious orientation in his ambience was derived from a modernized and selective version of the Upanishadic and Buddhist wisdom of the late second to the middle of the first millennia BC, the first imbued with a sense of an intelligence permeating the universe and the second with non-violence and compassion. Both ingrained in him a feeling for India's spiritual tradition—something he hardly ever talked about. Besides, he acquired from his cultural heritage a sense of the unity of the country in the midst of its diversity which Tagore enunciated with much influence on the country's leadership. As we shall see later, these strands manifest themselves in Ray's work in counterpoint to the Western form of the construction of his films. Of Santiniketan itself he says, after bemoaning the absences he felt in his city-bred self and the lack of films to see:

> It was a world of vast open spaces, vaulted over with a dustless sky, that on a clear night showed the constellations as no city sky could ever do. The same sky, on a clear day, could summon up in moments, an awesome invasion of billowing darkness (during the monsoon) that seemed to engulf the entire universe. And there was the *Khoai* (soil-eroded edges of downgoing land) with its serried ranks of *taal* (palm) trees, and the Kopai (a river), snaking its way through its rough-hewn undulations. If Santiniketan did nothing else, it induced contemplation, and a sense of wonder in the most prosaic and earthbound of minds.
>
> In the two and a half years, I had time to think, and time to realize that, almost without being aware of it, the place had opened windows for me. More than anything else, it had brought to me an awareness of our tradition, which I knew would serve as a foundation for any branch of art that I wished to pursue . . . Santiniketan taught me two things—to look at paintings and to look at nature.

The contradiction between the Western form of cinema he consciously pursued and thought of as his own, and the invisible that took over the background of his films is discernible from more of his Santiniketan experience recounted by himself:

> It was Santiniketan which opened my eyes to the fact that the kind of painting that I used to admire that provoked the reaction 'How lifelike', should be a preoccupation that lasted only 400 years. It started with the first awareness of perspective in the fifteenth century,

> and ended with the invention of photography in the nineteenth. The first representations of nature by man are believed to be the Stone Age cave paintings of 20,000 years ago. What is 400 years in a span of 200 centuries?
>
> Neither Egyptian nor Chinese, Japanese or Indian art ever concerned itself with factual representation. Here the primary aim was to get at the essence of things; a probing beneath the surface. Nature was the point of departure for the artist to arrive at a personal vision.
>
> Two trips to the great art centres of India—Ajanta, Ellora, Elephanta, Konarak and others—consolidated the idea of Indian tradition in my mind. At last I was beginning to find myself, and find my roots.

Obviously, what we have here is markedly different from what he asserts in the excerpt from his letter to me quoted earlier. The letter almost claims the status of a foreigner (Lord Macaulay's 'Brown Englishman') making films in India. What his thoughts on Santiniketan convey is a quintessential Indian who borrowed the medium of cinema from the West along with its grammar if not all of its idiomatic structure.

It is not only in association with Bibhutibhusan Bandopadhyay that Ray's most Indian traits can be discerned in his films. We see them even in *Devi*, ostensibly a film of protest against superstition. In the 'Postmaster' segment of *Teen Kanya* the heartlessness of the postmaster's casual departure, unaware of the feelings of the little maidservant who has grown so fond of him, interpreting his casual gestures of kindness and interest in her welfare as signs of a close personal bond, is as much a part of the forces of nature and the inexorability of change as the father-in-law in *Devi* who victimizes his son's young wife without any knowledge of the forces acting within him. In *Aranyer Din Raatri* one cannot but feel the sense of the young men and women caught at a given point of time and place in the inevitabilities of courage and cowardice, mindlessness and lust. Tomorrow everything will change, but today they exist, and somehow, must behave as they do. Ray is miraculously able to always make us conscious of this at the back of our minds. Even in the dance sequence in *Shatranj Ke Khiladi* while the king's minister waits for the exquisite dance to be over before informing his Lord of the British usurpation of his throne, there is the same sense of the inexorability of what has to happen. The delicate, fugitive beauty of the dance emphasizes the evanescence of the moment, a critical moment in the history of the land. The same sense emanates from the very character of Nikhilesh in *Ghare Baire*. At the back of our minds, the thought impinges on us that all these characters could have been at some other time and place, caught in entirely different situations, but are at this moment where they are, not by choice but by the play of forces beyond their control. This contemplation of time and fate is forced on us even as we think of the foolishness of the two aristocrats who are obsessively playing chess while their world is collapsing around them without their knowledge (curiously, it is the women in this film, one trying to get her husband to make love and the other trying to conceal her lover from her husband, who seem to be more in control of their actions and to will them).

Ray's creation of a contemplative space for his audience is one of his prime characteristics and a very Indian one at that, running counter to his claim of not being influenced by Indian art traditions. The proposition he presents us in his writings is the somewhat questionable one that as a person he is completely Indian, firmly rooted in his own soil, but his films are Western in form, structurally based on Western classical music. Apparently he belongs to one culture but produces the art of another. The question: is it possible for the form to be that independent of the culture within which its content exists? A revealing sidelight on this problem comes through in Stanley Kaufman's comment on the faulty sense of timing of *Aparajito*:

> There is still a bit of difficulty with Ray's sense of timing; a few scenes are brushed off too quickly, a few dwelled on too long. But ideals of timing vary from culture to culture and whether Ray is adhering to the standards of his country or has not mastered timing as practised by the western artists from whom he has learned so much else, it is difficult to say. The Brahmin looking for a wife, Apu's

visit to the temple of the privileged monkeys—are novelistic material, discursive in a film.

Obviously Kaufman does not see that such apparently irrelevant details produce a sense of flow of life going on regardless of the events, the ups and downs, in the life of individuals. The musclemen on the ghats of Benares, the widows in white listening to the reading of religious scriptures or discourses upon them are, he could have added, equally irrelevant. Yet it is these surrounding non-events that give the central event of the growth of Apu's mind and of his father's impending death their uniquely non-Western quality. At Harihar's death, a flock of pigeons fly away all of a sudden: the allusion is obviously to the traditional thought of the soul leaving the body like a bird. In *Aparajito,* the tank by the side of which Sarbajaya would sit in the evenings under a tree, reflects the Orion, bringing in a suggestion of infinite time and space within which human life is lived out. In *Apur Sansar*, Apu playing the flute by the riverside evokes the mythological image of the young God Krishna on the banks of the Yamuna; when Aparna's (Apu's bride-to-be) mother sees him, she remarks that she has seen that face before, in folk paintings of the gods; when after Aparna's death, Apu grows a full beard and goes away into the wilderness, throwing away the pages of the manuscript of his much-beloved novel, any Hindu will think of God Shiva who, in mythology, put his dead wife's body on his shoulder and roamed the mountains of the Himalayas. Ray's work is thus replete with the evocation of ancient myths.

By contrast, Ray's treatment in *Devi* has a much more Western, tight and well-shaped structure than the trilogy's relaxed and meandering, discursive form close to the style of Indian classical music in its linearity. In *Devi*, the sense of the premeditated bears strongly upon the viewer. Russian silent cinema techniques with broad spaces and static compositions predominate, helping to establish the period, the formality of relationships, without establishing the geography of the village or any attempt to recreate the period details in the exterior in any depth. The shot of the meandering line of the sick coming to the Goddess to be healed recalls Ivan standing with his staff looking at the vast plain across which his subjects are coming. The howl of jackals suggests the darkness not only of the night but of the age, an age of darkness when human sacrifice to the Goddess was not uncommon. The sound of the wooden clogs on the father-in-law's feet creates a sense of menace and doom. Grand formal gestures like this predominate in the style. There are no sub-plots; the concentration on the grim central tale is absolute.

In the trilogy, he took pains to retain the sense of spontaneous flow of the original; in *Devi*, he deals with much inferior literary work on whose spiritual and artistic qualities he feels obliged to improve in order to bring it up to his own level. For the feel of the film he does not have to rely on the author. In this he succeeds to a degree obvious in the extreme to those who know the rather simplistic original in Bengali. He imposed on it a sense of formality, design and distance to emphasize the universality of the mindset in Hindu society, its propensity towards rationally insupportable beliefs, and the lack of sufficient self-awareness to detect self-deceit and avoid the promotion of that self-deceit to religiosity.

It is essential for Ray here to project an innocent unawareness of the self in order to contrast it to the more modern consciousness represented by the young husband and to prevent the wife's transition into a more modern mindset. Ray feels motivated to propel this change forward through his medium. The enterprise was in no way unique to him; modern Bengali literature has been doing so well into this century. It was only given a further lease of life by the Marxist movement which gained ground in the immediate pre- and post-Independence periods, and has been marginalized only recently with the collapse of international socialist power structures and the rise of a cynical consumerism. Of course the modernist project was not confined to Bengal; Ray's two Hindi films, *Sadgati* and *Shatranj Ke Khiladi*, were both based on Premchand's short stories and took him out of the geography of the Bengal renaissance.

There is another, rather curious route to the discovery of the strand of mythicality in Ray's films and its connection with Indian art tradition: it is through the costuming of his women.

Since the story of *Pather Panchali* is obviously placed somewhere in the late nineteenth or early twentieth century, the natural dress for Sarbajaya would have been a simple cotton sari, an unstitched stretch of bordered cloth wrapped round her frame without a petticoat or a blouse. The modern Indian manner of draping the sari—which consists of a petticoat underneath to make the sari opaque to the view and a blouse to cover the torso fully, particularly the back and the upper arms which the sari does not adequately hide especially when the body is in movement—was introduced by the Parsi community in Bombay. In Bengal, it was nicknamed the 'Brahmika sari' after the name of the reformist Hindu community to which the Tagores and later Satyajit Ray himself belonged. By the early decades of the twentieth century, the style had begun to spread among the urban middle class but took much longer to reach the village where older women still dress in the traditional way.

It should also be noted that there was in fact a socio-religious injunction among the Hindus against the wearing of stitched clothes to which an exception had been made for men who served the government in any way or were in business or belonged to the zamindar class. The probable reason for this prohibition could be the fact that according to tradition (and the majority of historians) the 'Aryans' wore unstitched silk clothes (to this day Hindus are enjoined to wear unstitched silk clothing at all religious ceremonies). Cotton, although traditionally associated with the 'non-Aryan', was allowed for daily use perhaps because silk was too expensive. Especially among Brahmins, stitched clothing was rarely worn. As a Brahmin wife, it would have been improper for Sarbajaya to be in anything other than a sari, and a wrapper for the torso for going out of the house, if she could afford it. Stitched clothing on a woman would in those days indicate a Muslim or a Christian.

It is interesting to ask why Ray, who was quite meticulous about the accuracy of such period detail, chose to dress Sarbajaya in clothing that belonged to a later period (except in a few scenes of *Aparajito*—to supply an oedipal undertone to the relationship between mother and son?). Indeed the problem arises not only in the case of Sarbajaya but that of all Ray's women in his period films. It is also interesting to note that he allowed the bare arms and back in the case of very young girls such as Durga in *Pather Panchali*, Ratan in *Postmaster*, Mrinmoyee in *Samapti*, but not Sarbajaya in *Pather Panchali*, Aparna in *Apur Sansar*, Doyamoyee in *Devi*. The only exception in a woman in any period film is Ananga in *Asani Sanket* which in fact belongs to a late period—that of World War II—by which time stitched clothes had become somewhat more acceptable in rural Bengal. Even Charulata in the film of the same name is a doubtful case as it is placed in 1879.

The only possible explanation appears to lie in Ray's sense of how much sexuality to allow in the presence of a woman in a particular situation. By and large, his tendency was to cover them, regardless of the period. Only in Ananga in *Asani Sanket* do we see a slight departure. It is in this film that the women, who form an almost secret group in their camaraderie shielded from the menfolk, have a degree of sexuality in them, apart from the two Muslim noblemen's wives in *Shatranj Ke Khiladi* whose bodies are of course fully covered, in very period-correct stitched clothing designed by Shama Zaidi (in Ray's other period films there are no dress designers as such). The exposure of a woman's body appears thus to have weighed heavily in Ray's consideration of how to clothe them.

In *Pather Panchali* and the early part of *Aparajito*, Sarbajaya is still a young woman, but in his anxiety to depict her as only the mother, Ray denies her the sexuality natural to her age and circumstance as a married woman. She does her wifely duties towards Harihar but there is never the faintest suggestion that the two have a marital life in physical terms.

Similarly in *Apur Sansar*, Aparna must be seen as the innocent young girl. The warmth of her sexual life we are allowed to deduce, but to show her arms and back bare would bring out her sexuality too stridently for Ray's taste. She is to him an embodiment of the mythical Aparna, God Shiva's wife, whose death would later find her forlorn husband wandering in the forest like Shiva himself. She is an *idea* manifested in a temporal and spatial context. Stressing her flesh-and-blood presence would take away from her mythicality, her embodiment as the traditional wife with whom her husband would fall in love after marriage. It would make her too much of an individual, appropriate her excessively into a particular time and space and destroy her status as an ideal being, a type embodying the entire history of the ideal feminine in the context of a race and a civilization. 'The mythic in the ordinary' consists of a powerful compression of historical image, even an action like that of a woman sweeping a floor, into a living, believable figure or the repetition of an age-old action in a freshly individuated manner.

It is interesting here to recall what the painter Nandalal Bose, Satyajit's teacher at the art school in Santiniketan, says in an essay on Indian art, 'The Image of the Buddha is not the image of a man; it is an image of the idea of meditation, the image of dancing Shiva, of the idea of universal rhythm.'

Coming to *Devi*, Doyamoyee, also played by Sharmila Tagore with the shadow of Aparna hovering over her, is the embodiment of mythic innocence about to turn into the Goddess. Although she is just married and we have seen a peck of a kiss between husband and wife half hidden by the mosquito curtain, Ray cannot afford to invest her with sexuality because that would obviously in his eyes come in the way of her elevation to divinity.

The twin motivations that emerge to incline Ray away from women's sexual expression through their bodily presence, to the extent of ignoring the essential period detail, are thus interlocked. One may well be his Brahmo puritanical self disinclined to entertain the suggested presence of the flesh implied in the correct period clothing (rather the brevity of clothing); but more importantly, it is his treatment of woman as an embodiment of certain virtues, differently emphasized in different films, in a mythic way which can often be traced to actual mythical figures such as Shiva and Parvati (in her various aspects, including that of Kali) in Hindu mythology. No wonder Pauline Kael, with the habitual keenness of her intuition, found in his work a way of seeing, and showing, 'the mythic in the ordinary'.

What would have been the consequences if Ray had allowed the innate sexuality natural to Sarbajaya or Doya in their less crisis-ridden moments to emerge? Obviously Ray's task in establishing their characteristics in the situations in which they are placed would be more complicated and make the characters themselves more full of natural contradictions which he would have had to allow for. The relationship of contradictory strands in a character would have had to be explored deeply and made credible. In other words, he would have had to fill in more of their naturalistic detail on the lines of a somewhat Western–modern realism. In terms of painting, his evasion of that type of detail, shot with contradictions and yet forming a whole, would have dimmed the simplicity and strength of outline which goes back 2000 years to Ajanta Bagh cave paintings enclosing a flat space within well-defined lines (and dependent on linear expressiveness like Indian classical music; though Ray repeatedly refers to Western music, yet his treatment is unique in its linear flow), or say Bankura or Kalighat (Calcutta) folk painting of the nineteenth century or perhaps more properly to a *folk*-derived style such as Jamini Roy's *The Mother*, *The Wife*, *The Worker*, and similar portraits of typicality enshrining traditional, uni-linear and uncomplicated views which nonetheless compress age-old visions and invest them with a somewhat nostalgic gentleness and charm, a touch of the utopian, in which there is no place for evil. Even the Kalighat style of semi-Western shading and modelling of the body is absent in Jamini Roy who at once refines and simplifies his subjects into two-dimensional ideas. Bibhutibhusan's own vision was markedly similar to this; indeed it may have launched Ray in the same direction, a vision that lasted till *Charulata* and then went on adapting itself to the assessment of contemporary reality through the eyes of a changing, modernizing, despairing and beleaguered Apu, the Apu of *Apur Sansar* caught in a vicious latter-day world. Underlying this simplified vision, there is simple musicality, a detached observation and an absence of the complex interplays of contradiction which create the Western type of drama of conflict and resolution in which there is less of a place for compassion and more of involvement in the events moment by moment. In a sense, Ray's world is timeless, even though the films chronicle change; Ray does not throw himself into the welter of things, passionately taking sides. He remains the distant observer who sees the whole being of his characters in a flattened perspective without tonality, volume or mass.

In comparison there is more agony in the work of Ray's contemporaries such as Mrinal Sen or Ritwik Ghatak. Ghatak is particularly relevant here because, despite his more conscious involvement with myths, they choose to encounter the characters at a moment of the loss of the mythic in their lives. His protagonists cry out, as it were, for what they are about to lose or know they have lost. Because the moment claims them, the reality wrenches them out of the mythic and throws them headlong into the present. The protagonists of *Subarnarekha* (Ghatak, 1962) are bereaved souls faced with stark reality where goodness has already given way to cynical, survival-only situations.

Ray is far more concerned with the transition of society and his characters from one state of being to another. In *Devi*, he does represent blind faith, unrelieved by rationality whose lack he does emphasize; but what is surprising is that he does not in the process either oversimplify the superstition or lose sympathy for the characters caught in a predicament whose origins and reasons are apparent to their creator but not to them. The father-in-law who deifies his son's young and beautiful wife and thus takes her away from his son is gloriously unaware of the fact. There is not a trace of malice in him. In fact he is as much a victim of circumstances—history, tradition, beliefs handed down from ancestors, given beliefs in a given place and time in which he was born and which were not of his choice. Ray's keen awareness of this aspect is enshrined in his treatment of the song for instance which the old grandfather sings sitting on the steps of the temple of the Goddess with his dying grandson on his lap. It is set in a traditional tune and there are numerous extant songs by the author Ramprasad in the eighteenth century of the same intent from which Ray could have chosen one. But he chose to write the song himself in the style of Ramprasad. The only motivation one can see in this is that he wanted to enter deeply into the spirit of the song and of the faith with which it was sung and was careful not to trivialize it. Composing the words of the song was a way of orienting himself into it as it were. The mise en scène bears this out; the attitude of the forlorn old man, the way he sits, the way in which he sings and is portrayed on the screen, are all entirely sympathetic; they reflect fully the state of *his* mind, not the director's. There is here no insolent attempt to dismiss the old man's simple faith with modernist disdain. Similarly, when the father-in-law prostrates himself before the young woman as the Goddess, it is with full faith which is in no way marginalized or made ever so faintly ridiculous. His son studies in Calcutta at a time when rationalist ideas are being inducted into him. That too is a fact of life, not an ideal state prescribed for society. It is the tragedy of the outcome that is emphasized, not the rightness or wrongness of action. Doya is caught between the old and the new and her identity is destroyed by the tension; the truth, the indivisible process through which it happens is what most concerns the director. Ray is in fact here much more detached than, say, in *Jalsaghar* where he displays a shade of wicked delight in the old landlord's disdain for the young upstart capitalist. At the end of *Devi*, Ray makes one of the many significant changes in the literary original he employs to adapt it to his ways of thinking. One of the most beautiful, most Indian, is the last shot of Doyamoyee running, disappearing, into a misty field of flowers; going back, as it were, to her Mother Earth, making it faintly reminiscent of Sita in the Indian epic Ramayana for whom the earth had opened up at the moment of her ultimate humiliation. In Prabhat Mukhopadhyay's short story, she commits suicide by hanging herself by her sari from a girder on the roof.

However, from a formal point of view, the most important non-Western feature in Ray is the slowness of the tempo and what has been called the contemplative space his cutting always provides despite its basically Western style. Another is his use of the camera, in which there is a preference for the natural human vision (the 40mm lens) and the general avoidance, with some exceptions, of the big close-up which, he once told me, gave him the sense of the head falling off the screen, something that seemed hyped and false to him. How very different this is not only from the Hollywood style in general but even say Bergman, possibly the greatest votary of the close-up in cinema. As Liv Ullmann says:

> I love close-ups. To me they are a challenge. The closer a camera comes, the more eager I am to show a completely naked face, show what is behind the skin, the eyes; inside the head. Show the thoughts

> that are forming . . . Closer to the audience than in any other medium . . . the human being is shown on the screen. The audience, at the time of the identification, meets a person, not a role, not an actress.

Here there is a celebration of the individual, not the type, not even the type slowly becoming an individual for the purpose of the audience. It is not content with the broad contours of folk art, the flat surfaces, the two dimensionality of virtually all Indian art, classical or folk, even including sculpture in the round which is best seen from one point of view. Western photographers have tried to photograph overhead figures in Indian temples by getting up to their height only to discover how this distorts the image actually meant to be seen from below. What Liv Ullmann is saying of Bergman's close-ups is also utterly different; unlike Indian art, it is all perspective, completely Western, showing all details, all tonality within the human being, the whole human being, and not just one aspect of him, the particular person, going even beyond the actor's identity into the person that he is. Sarbajaya in *Pather Panchali* is first a type, a mother, a timeless myth, before she is a person. There are aspects of her personality that are carefully hidden from us, as in the case of her sexuality which we know must be present somewhere in her but which, if shown, would reveal her in not the outline stressing one aspect of her character but the entire complexity of her being, full of shading, perspective and tonality. It would divest her of her timelessness, her musicality and fix her into a particular time and place and a single personality. Perhaps this is also the reason why Ray depended so little on rehearsals and so much more on spontaneous expressions of the natural self of the actor.

Leaving Bergman alone as a unique phenomenon, we find in the Hollywood product of any quality, a liberal use of the big close-up in order either to emphasize glamour or to dramatize details of the acting, or both. The Hollywood style of acting more often than not demands the spilling of the guts of a performer in order to create drama. It calls for big close-ups because emotion has to be wrung out of the juices in the actor's system in order to bathe the audience in them, as it were. Hollywood gives its actors the hyped rhythm of the audience's own world; Ray, like Bergman or Antonioni, imposed his own rhythm on the audience. He would himself emphasize the rhythm as a product of the subject itself; but behind this justifying philosophy would lie the rhythm sought by Ray's own feeling which he was anxious not to bring to the fore.

Altogether, much of the impact, the interiority and the sense of timeless mythicality are achieved in Ray's style by a process of holding back the emotional expression in what he once named, talking about Asian cinema (and, in a way, identifying himself with it), as 'calm without, fire within'.

13

RITWIK GHATAK
Cinema, Marxism and the Mother Goddess

In the twenty-two years of his life in cinema, Ritwik Ghatak (1925–76) made only eight feature films and a few documentaries. Yet he made a profound impression first on the Bengali intelligentsia, and later on film buffs all over India. Working during a period dominated by Satyajit Ray, he struck out on a completely original path—not by design, but by the distinctive nature of his genius. He began as a committed Marxist playwright, actor and short-story writer; and only then, in search of communication with large sections of the people, did he move to cinema. In 1964–65, he was vice principal of the Film Institute of India in Pune where, within a brief period, he deeply influenced a group of students who were later to become notable film-makers themselves: Mani Kaul, Kumar Shahani, Saeed Mirza, besides film theorists Ashish Rajadhyaksha and Arun Khopkar. His films never won an award, either national or international. He never went abroad (except to make a film in Bangladesh). He died in 1976 of alcohol abuse and a host of allied maladies, after alternating spells of work and hospitalization. Yet today he is a cult figure, an anti-establishment hero for many film-makers and film buffs in India, and is beginning to engage serious attention among film scholars abroad. Judged by the small volume of his work, its influence is strikingly significant.

In discussing the cinema of Ritwik Ghatak, I would like to consider three basic ingredients in the formation of his outlook and his style: the influence of Rabindranath Tagore, the involvement with the IPTA of the 1940s, and the impact of the partition of Bengal at the time of India's independence. I wish to explore the ways in which these three factors gave rise to the basic characteristics of his work in cinema; and finally, how the internal conflicts generated by them led to an untimely end to his career.

Like Satyajit Ray, Ritwik Ghatak was born and bred under the cultural umbrella of Rabindranath Tagore. Rabindranath himself came in the wake of a century-old renaissance of the middle class which sought to break out of the defensive prison of Hinduism of the Mughal and early British periods: out of the dark age of human sacrifice, the burning of widows, female infanticide, the fear of crossing the seas, and a caste system rigid to the point of rigor mortis. He took the movement to its peak, helping to give the country a new sense of oneness, an openness to the world, a dynamic synthesis of modernity and tradition and a new rationality and universality of outlook. In common with the Brahmo movement for the social and religious reform of an atrophied Hinduism, he reinterpreted tradition and revised the selection of elements from within it to strengthen the forces of change that seemed most urgent to him, at the same time establishing a new stability of moral values.

Tagore's sensibility and his world view are encapsulated in his 2000-odd songs, gathering the threads from his poetry, fiction, essays, religious sermons and political speeches, and even his paintings. Ghatak made intensive use of this Rabindrasangeet. In *Meghe Dhaka Tara* (Cloud-capped Star), the effect of a long sequence is designed around the song '*Jay raatay more dooaargooli bhaanglo jharray*'.[1] It is used as a passage of deep internal dialogue to lead to self-assessment, and the framing of new positive values out of the process of introspection. In *Subarnarekha*, '*Aaj dhaaner khetay roudrachhayar lookochoori khela*'[2] is a recurring motif, reinforcing, at the end, the sense of hope even at the edge of disaster. The use of the song recalls Tagore's statement: it is a sin to lose faith in man. Time and again, Ghatak's films take us to the brink of despair, and retrieve us—often with a Tagore song.

The quotations from the Upanishads that abound in the revelry scenes of *Subarnarekha* and the Vedic hymn '*Charaiveti, charaiveti*' (move on, move on) at its end, were favourite quotes of Tagore; most of the Upanishadic ones appear in the compilation *Brahmo Dharma*, made by Rabindranath's father, Maharshi Devendranath. There is, besides, a Ravindrik reticence about sex, almost Victorian, in Ghatak's films. There is never an embrace, not to speak of a kiss. Only in *Titas* does he show some physical intimacy in a highly sublimated, mythologized manner. Ghatak played King Raghupati in Tagore's play *Visarjan* (The Sacrifice), produced by the IPTA. The book which he read out most to his son was *Raj Kahini* (Princely Tales of Rajasthan) by Abanindranath Tagore. The song in *Subarnarekha*, '*Aju ki ananda, jhulata jhulanay shyamara chanda*', is taken from one of the *Raj Kahini* stories.

His films, with the sole exception of *Titas*, are about the middle class. Marxist as he was, he spoke of the class which he understood and to which he belonged, instead of indulging in shadowy, derivative abstractions of the working class in which many writers of his time indulged. One look at Bimal in front of the photographer's camera in *Ajantrik*, as he delicately holds the end of his dhoti gathered like a flower, in the tradition of the aristocrats of nineteenth-century Calcutta, is enough to reveal his middle-class origins. Gaur Mistri, who repeatedly warns him about his folly in trying to keep his ancient car running, is typical in his speech and manner of a small-town lower-middle-class man. If Tagore epitomized the highest reaches of the Bengali middle class, Ghatak was very much a part of it. When Bhabani Sen, a senior Communist Party intellectual, once described Rabindranath as a reactionary writer, Ritwik was one of those who protested emphatically. To an interviewer he said of Tagore:

> I cannot speak without him. That man has culled all my feelings long before my birth. He has understood what I am and he has put in all the words. I read and find that all has been said and I have nothing new to say. I think all artists, in Bengal at least, find themselves in the same difficulty. It just cannot be helped. You can be angry with him, you can criticize him, you may dislike him, but ultimately, in the final analysis, you will find that he has the last word.

But Ghatak's inheritance contained many elements that arose from outside the mainstream of the Tagore tradition. The author of *Religion of Man*, the leader of the Brahmo Samaj and the writer of sermons in Santiniketan, seldom addressed God as Mother. As in the Upanishads, God is always the Father: *Pitanohsi pita no vodhi* or *Vedaham etam purusham mahantam / Adityavarnam tamasah parastat.*[3] Rabindranath had an instinctive distaste for the mother cult. Some of his songs do have the mother image in them, but his prose, a product of rationality, almost never does. In *Ghare Baire* there are sharp barbs aimed at the mother cult. The novel was a counterblast to Bankim Chandra Chatterjee and his somewhat anti-Muslim resurgent Hinduism in the novel *Ananda Math*, which celebrates the country as the holy mother. Tagore never liked the cry *Vande Mataram*: if he had had his way he would probably have changed it to *Vande Pitaram*.

The Brahmo movement and the Bengal renaissance switched their spiritual allegiance from the Puranic pantheon, around whose mythology Hinduism's darkest beliefs in its defensive phase under the Mughals had crystallized themselves, to the Upanishadic literature, free of ritualism in its philosophic quest of universal truth. It was a part of the rationalist revolution; the reformists found in it the nearest correlative to their modernist beliefs within the Hindu tradition. It was their counterpoint to revivalism.

Rabindranath, one might say a bit fancifully, was the Aryan, the Upanishadic interpreter of an invisible, indivisible universal spirit of which we are all elements. Bankim and other neo-Hindus, as well as traditional Hindus with their mother goddesses, were perhaps more tribal Bengali in their cultural derivations. (Here it is important to remember that the tribal, pre-Aryan strand is basic to Bengali ethnicity.) Rabindranath wrote lovingly about the Santhal tribals around Santiniketan, did a great deal for their welfare; but his basic culture was Upanishadic, Sanskritic, Aryan, into which the folk was subsumed. Ghatak's affinities were obviously with the tribal element in Bengal, whose fertility goddesses later acquired many forms and replaced Vedic faiths with a fusion of the Aryan and the non-Aryan in Bengal, as indeed all over India.

Ghatak seems to have been torn between the two strands: the Ravindrik, rationalist, Marxist, secular, world embracing on the one hand, and the tribal, magical, nostalgic, and regionally self-contained on the other. It is perhaps due to this that he embraced the Jungian notion of archetypes and Eric Neumann's idea of the Great Mother, seeking a modern, scientific correlative to what may have come from the depths of a specifically Hindu consciousness. Ghatak celebrates this mother worship in many of his films, most directly in *Titas Ekti Nadir Naam*. It is a curious phenomenon, because the film explores a Hindu concept in a Muslim country, for reasons I will discuss later. Before doing so, let me turn to the second formative element in Ghatak's outlook: his involvement with Marxism and the IPTA.

II

As he came of age the Bengal that Ritwik inherited was in a state of turmoil. The country as a whole had been hit by the shortages of World War II and bloodied by the battles of political independence. But Bengal had its special share of misfortune. The 1943 famine was engineered by the British in aid of their war effort; in a year of very good harvest, five million people died because their food had been sent away to the armed forces of the empire. On the eve of independence came the Hindu–Muslim riots, and with it, the partition of Bengal, causing one of the largest and most traumatic migrations in history, much bigger in scale than that in the Punjab. Culturally, the effect of these events was to shake the Bengal renaissance and its 150-year-old faiths to their roots. The transition from Tagore had been spelt out by the poet himself. As war clouds gathered over Europe and Asia, he wrote:

> Hissing serpents poison the very air,
> Gentle words of peace sound hollow,
> My time is up; but before I go,
> I call out to all to prepare in every home
> To fight the demons of the dark.[4]

Ghatak was sixteen when Rabindranath died, eighteen when the Bengal famine came, and twenty-two in the year of Independence. His eldest brother Manish belonged to the Kallol group of writers who struggled to get out from under the Tagore umbrella—even though they revered him—to cope with the raw realities of a changing situation. An all-India movement was born in response to the impending threat of fascism and war. The Progressive Writers' Association was formed in Lucknow in 1936. Among the writers who became part of it were Munshi Premchand, Mulk Raj Anand, Sajjad Zaheer, Josh Malihabadi and many others. For the first time in the history of modern India, an organized attempt was made by the middle-class intellectual to reach out to the people. In spite of the disillusion of the Russo-German Non-Aggression Pact and the Soviet invasion of Finland (which Tagore bitterly criticized), the movement survived. It was reinforced, both in the nature of its concerns and in its physical spread, by Hitler's declaration of war upon the Soviet Union in 1942.

Within months of it, the Anti-Fascist Writers' and Artists' Union was founded in Calcutta and attracted novelists Manik Bandopadhyay and Tarashankar Bandopadhyay, poet Bishnu Dey and many others. The Union made a determined bid to reach the working class. Benoy Roy, for instance, made a great impression by singing rousing political songs among industrial workers in Calcutta and other large centres. These songs were especially composed for the purpose, but they included a Bengali version of the *Internationale* (sung at the end of Ghatak's *Nagarik*). All this soon led to the founding of the IPTA in 1943, whose purpose was to revitalize folk art, and inform it with a revolutionary consciousness. The year 1944 saw the staging of Bijan Bhattacharya's *Nabanna* (The Harvest), co-directed by Shambhu Mitra and Bijan Bhattacharya, which had a tremendous effect on the cultural scene in Bengal. Bengali theatre, once realistic and revolutionary, had degenerated into conventional technical virtuosity, played out against painted backdrops and heavily made-up faces.

Nabanna suddenly brought out on the stage the appalling realities of famine, in a language that people could understand and a vivid realism that shook them. At one stroke it swept away the cobwebs that had enveloped Bengali theatre. Its realism was at once technically innovative and emotionally powerful. Its author, co-director and major actor, Bijan Bhattacharya, was later to appear in Ghatak's *Meghe Dhaka Tara* and *Subarnarekha*. *Nagarik* had IPTA's Shobha Sen (Utpal Dutt's wife) and Geeta Shome (later Geeta Sen, Mrinal Sen's wife) acting in it. Practically every major writer in Bengal in this period was in the Progressive Writers' Association; practically every major figure in the performing arts was in the IPTA. Among the participants of the IPTA who became famous later on were Ritwik Ghatak himself, Mrinal Sen, Utpal Dutt, Hemanta Mukherjee, Balraj Sahni, K.A. Abbas, Salil Chowdhury, Jyotirindra Moitra (who directed the music of *Meghe Dhaka Tara*), to name only a few. The IPTA sought to harness the power of folk forms in the cause of class struggle. In Bengal there was the example of the Gambhira of Malda district which the IPTA put to good use. The form was traditionally devoted to the praise of Shiva, but used also for commentary on contemporary local events. It was also a way to revitalize the folk arts at a time when they had started to become unfashionable under the impact of a rising urban, westernized culture.

Ritwik wrote several revolutionary plays, became leader of the Central Squad of the IPTA in Bengal, acted, directed plays and staged agit-prop poster-theatre shows in the cities and the districts. But the euphoria of the IPTA did not last long. Within a year of the staging of its most successful play, *Nabanna*, the IPTA 'ceased to function as a coherent organisation'.[5] The political leaders and the artists came into violent conflict. Bijan Bhattacharya refused to write doctrinaire plays in which 'good and evil, capitalism and slavery, freedom and oppression were treated in black and white'. An unpublished piece of Bijan Bhattacharya's writing, translated by Samik Bandopadhyay, about the impact of the Bengal famine on his mind states:

> I spotted in a Calcutta street a crawling baby fumbling over the corpses, searching for its mother's breast. The mother was already dead. Even while we organized gruel kitchens to feed the starving people, I felt the need to do something meaningful. Only when I wrote my play *Nabanna* and staged it did I have the feeling that I had at last become a mother to that hungry child even as I mothered my play to make it grow into a performance for the people. That image of the crawling child has haunted me ever since. Whenever in my creative quest I miss the crawling baby, I shift my position endlessly until the child comes into view again.[6]

Like Bijan Bhattacharya and Shambhu Mitra, Ritwik Ghatak's idealism also found it impossible to tolerate either the dogmatism or the realpolitik of a communist revolutionary process. This was largely directed from England through the British Communist Party. Both Bijan Bhattacharya and Ritwik Ghatak were too intimately Bengali in their temperament, affinities and experience to continue to respond to the dictates of a leadership on whom the stamp of Western models was too clear. They were too concerned with the individual human being for the 'people'-oriented communists. Ritwik was forced to appear before a one-man commission and was promptly dubbed a Trotskyite.[7] The fragmentation of the IPTA never ceased to trouble Ghatak's mind. His nostalgia for its early ecstasies and his regret over its factionalism is reflected with autobiographical truth in *Komal Gandhar*. What remained with him from those days was his desire to communicate with the millions—which in fact made him turn to cinema.

He began his career in it by acting in Nemai Ghosh's *Chhinnamool* (The Uprooted, 1951), a film of raw realism on the predicament of refugees from East Bengal. The film was a failure, and is remembered mainly as a prelude to Satyajit Ray's *Pather Panchali* for certain aspects of its realism. As for Ritwik's own films, none but *Meghe Dhaka Tara* fared well at the box office; his passion for communicating with large audiences remained unfulfilled. In the same period, Ray established a far greater measure of rapport with the Bengali audience. *Pather Panchali* was an instant and resounding success; *Apur Sansar*, *Teen Kanya*, *Mahanagar* received public acclaim. *Charulata* was the second biggest hit of 1964. The problem of communication began to haunt Ritwik Ghatak and preyed upon his spirit till the very end. It made him a loner, a refugee.

III

Which brings us to Ghatak's umbilical cord with East Bengal, where he was born and bred and which he loved with all his heart. It gave him his feeling for nature, for the great rivers of East Bengal, its many dialects with their varied music, and its people with their natural forthrightness.

Nature, to Ritwik, was not a means of reflecting human emotions, but a great force of which the human being was a humble part. East Bengal was the El Dorado he lost when Partition took it away from him. In *Bari Thekay Paliyay* he refers repeatedly to a book on the El Dorado which, his biographers tell us, he and his twin sister used to read. In his refugee trilogy, the trauma of Partition is deeply imprinted. Perhaps because of his experience, Ghatak never shared in the euphoria of India's independence and the atmosphere of hope thereafter that many of the writers and artists reflected. Ray's early films, for instance, are imbued with a faith in man and a silent hope for the future; looking back over a hundred years, he saw an arc of change that he chronicled lovingly. His disillusion came in the 1970s, beginning with *Aranyer Din Raatri* and climaxing in *Jana Aranya*, also seen in *Pikoo* and *Sadgati*. Ghatak's agony of Partition launched him directly into the here and now of unemployment, destitution and the disintegration of the family. His vision shot prophetically beyond the immediate post-Independence optimism, into the disaster that the collapse of moral values would bring.

In the refugee trilogy—*Meghe Dhaka Tara*, *Komal Gandhar* and *Subarnarekha*—one can hardly find any reference to the economic realities of Hindu zamindari dominance over the Muslim peasant in East Bengal, to which Rabindranath made such pointed reference in *Ghare Baire*. In *Titas*, it is not his central concern, which lies in evoking the power of the Mother Goddess. Curiously, just about the time of the making of *Titas*, Atin Bandopadhyay came out with his epic novel on Partition, *Neelkantha Pakhir Khonjay* (In Search of the Bird with the Blue Throat). This depicts with great vividness and poetry the central economic reality of the Hindu exploitation of East Bengal Muslims and the slow and inexorable division which it created between the two communities. I have often wondered if Ritwik was at the time familiar with this novel, and how he might have turned it into the great but different film that it could have been.

For well over 200 years, the socio-political configuration of Bengal had the Hindus of the west as zamindars and the Muslims of the east as ryots living under their hegemony, making the Partition in 1947 a sort of culmination of a historical necessity, a revolution against the overlordship of the Hindu majority of the west.

In his early youth, Rabindranath Tagore had been sent by his father to get acquainted with the administration of their zamindari. One day he noticed a wooden platform on the veranda of his kachheri or administration building. On enquiring about its purpose he was told it was meant for well-to-do subjects to sit on. The platform had a carpet spread on it, a corner section of which had been folded back, leaving the bare wood visible. Upon asking about this he was told that the bare section was meant for well-to-do Muslims among his subjects. As a measure of the hegemonistic relationship between the two religious communities, the young poet's observation was significant.

The very concept of the Bengali bhadralok or gentleman is embedded in the apparel worn by the landed aristocracy of western Bengal. The hallmark of the Bengali bhadralok, visible to this day, lies in the fine-textured, shining white of the dhoti and kurta (called Panjabi by Bengalis) which is worn at formal occasions by most and regularly by people of political importance, including Marxist ministers of the state government. Pondering over the bias for immaculate white, one might conclude that it signifies the cultivated avoidance of manual work on the part of the wearer, a little like a sign saying: 'I do not work with my hands and dirty my white clothes.'

But where did this nostalgia leave the committed Marxist that Ghatak was? It seems highly improbable that he should not have been aware of the Hindu–Muslim economic divide; it is more credible to think that he chose to ignore it. As was customary with Ghatak, he made an explanatory statement later on, which is not detectable in the film (*Titas*) itself: '. . . the main force behind all this conflict and tension is the economic structure.' He goes on to inveigle against the zamindars, describing all of them as 'inveterate scoundrels' (see Haimanti Banerjee's monograph on Ghatak published by the NFAI). But even in this post facto verbal commentary, he does not as much as mention the communal divide between Hindu landlords and Muslim subjects.

In the absence of an underlay of politico-economic analysis, Ghatak's sentiment comes perilously close to Hindu nostalgia for a lost kingdom, and his enthusiasm for the Mother Goddess to the brink of Hindu fundamentalism. It cannot be without significance that in Ghatak's films there are no major Muslim characters, not even in *Titas*, shot in Bangladesh.

However that may be, there is no doubt that his nostalgia for East Bengal planted another seed of agony in him that was to torment him all his life. Other writers and artists around him had forgotten the Partition, and were immersed in the problems and prospects of a truncated India. He was almost alone in continuing to suffer from the wounds of the parting. He hardly ever made a pronouncement on the partition of the Punjab; it was East Bengal which continued to beckon to him.

The unresolved dilemma of reconciling Marxist rationalism with Hindu nostalgia, compounded further by Ghatak's expulsion from the Communist Party, resulted in the confession of failure in his last film, *Jukti Takko Ar Gappo*. The name Ritwik gave himself in *Jukti Takko Ar Gappo*, Neelkantha, is significant. Neelkantha, or the blue-throated one, is one of the names of Shiva because he drank the poison that came up alongside the nectar when the gods and the demons churned up the ocean, and the poison endangered the lives of the gods. Shiva's throat went blue, but the gods were saved.

The piling up of this lonely nostalgia—for the lost purity of revolution, the disintegration of the IPTA's unifying vitality, the splitting of Bengal into two, and the failure of his films to reach a wide audience—caused him agony. But some of these concerns also contributed to his craft.

IV

Much effort has been expended by some critics in detecting portents of future greatness in Ghatak's first film, *Nagarik*. Its theatricality has been blamed on the IPTA legacy but the fact is that *Nagarik* was still wrapped up in the conventions of Bengali cinema which was itself largely an imitation of the theatre. The long-suffering mother, the violinist, the humiliations of unemployment were all staples of the convention-bound Bengali film. Except for a few low-angle shots and some interesting sound effects, the film has little to distinguish itself from the general run of contemporary Bengali cinema. It shares little with his second, and very striking, film, *Ajantrik*. Indeed, it is difficult to imagine that it was made by the same person.

When he made *Nagarik* (1952–53), Ghatak was directly under the spell of the IPTA style of theatre, already conventionalized, merging it with some of the devices of Bengali cinema and inventions of his own. The conceptual conventionality of the film, apart from its stylistics, can be traced partly to the IPTA but mostly to the shibboleths of traditional Bengali cinema. Its young men are totally unable to conceive of alternative ways of survival to clerkdom, whose centrality is made into the pillar of middle-class existence, unshaken by the sound from the garage next door. Educated unemployment at the time of *Nagarik* was not nearly as comprehensive as it is today, when you find millions, including the middle class, devising ways of survival through other means—small trade or the vending or pursuit of culture, for example. If *Nagarik* did not think of such possibilities, it is because it functioned conceptually within the tight framework of the IPTA's theatrical hype. In *Meghe Dhaka Tara*, by contrast, one brother makes it to success through music, the other through football, 'declassing' himself to become a factory worker, much to the chagrin of his father who is a retired schoolteacher. Kali Banerjee's youth showing through his white hair, Keshto Mukherjee gesturing as the supplicant are lifted from the theatre. The street violinist playing at critical moments, the peeled plaster on the canvas walls are in the classic tradition of New Theatres; but the powerful close-ups and two-shots, the depth-of-field despite poor resources, the treatment of levels in the use of the staircase are original Ghatak and pure cinema.

Yet there is an overall poverty of cinematic conception in *Nagarik*, as compared with *Ajantrik*, that cannot be explained merely in terms of poverty of resources. It seems far more probable that the cinematically revolutionary departures of Ray's *Pather Panchali* (1955), *Aparajito* (1956) and *Parash Pathar* (1957) which appeared in the years between *Nagarik* (1952–53) and *Ajantrik* (1958) triggered a quantum leap in Ritwik's consciousness—even though he was never influenced by Ray. *Pather Panchali* shook Indian cinema to its foundations by its stark realism, its treatment of detail and its total freedom from conventions. Undoubtedly, its boldness sparked off Ghatak's striking departure from *Nagarik* to *Ajantrik*. At the same time, it must be noted that *Ajantrik* is completely free, like the rest of his work, from any influence of Ray, despite the latter's domination throughout Ghatak's career from *Ajantrik* onwards. In fact, with the characteristic force of his vision, Ritwik transformed the clearly theatrical into the stuff of cinema, unlike any other Indian film-maker. The Kali Banerjee father-figure of *Nagarik* is repeated by Bijan Bhattacharya in *Meghe Dhaka Tara*, and in *Subarnarekha* as the leader serving as a surrogate father. Each bears the unmistakable imprint of the IPTA, but they are by now subsumed into a distinctive cinematic style.

Ghatak's extraordinary use of the wide-angle lens can perhaps be traced to his East Bengal experience of wide rivers and open spaces, whose vastness was not to be invoked by anything less than the 18mm lens. The nostalgia welling up in him needed a heightening of the reality, and bred an impatience with the confines of the normal lenses. In the vast spaces of *Ajantrik* there is a tranquillity (absent in later films) and a meditative response to nature, holy in itself—making man seem small by contrast. Partha Chatterjee has remarked on how Ritwik juxtaposes the extreme wide-angle lens with the telephoto in *Jukti Takko Ar Gappo*. In *Titas*, Ritwik makes dramatic use of the 18mm lens towards the end, in a close shot of a heroic Basanti seen from below—breaking a cardinal rule in the use of this lens. The extreme close, the extreme wide, both heighten the reality and introduce theatre into cinema by ignoring realism, making it larger than life, bursting with a passion to expand beyond the limits of the medium itself, sometimes resulting in transcendence, sometimes in a kind of emotional hype as in the voiced-over songs of *Subarnarekha*.

Ghatak's hallmark in the use of close-ups is in the treatment of Nita's face in *Meghe Dhaka Tara*, and Sita's upturned face struck with agony in *Subarnarekha*, shot low angle, the tautness in the area below the chin heightening the effect. The backlighting of Nita's hair as she pauses on the staircase recalling her lover's perfidy is Hollywood via New Theatres. Yet how powerfully it contributes to our understanding of her! Some would say the halo around her head in this scene crowns her as Jagaddhatri, the benevolent Mother Goddess. But of that, later.

In discussing Ghatak's craft, it is necessary to note his extraordinary use of sound. I shall confine myself here to two examples. In *Meghe Dhaka Tara*, the sound of the whiplash is a conventional literary simile for humiliation, transferred to the cinema in an oddly effective manner. We become aware of the device because we know it from literary experience (it is one of the very few alienated, intellectualized moments in Ghatak's work) and have to draw a parallel between the humiliation and the sound of the whiplash. Ghatak first uses the sound as Nita comes down the staircase from her lover's room with the knowledge that he is going to marry her younger sister. He repeats it in the scene after her brother teaches her a Tagore song that echoes her own feeling, again on the staircase, with great effect, because this time we know what it means and do not have to deduce it from literary experience any more. He uses it a third time, with less effect, because this time we know the intent of it a little too well.

My second example is from *Titas*, where the young fisherman (later compared to Shiva) gets married to his girl (later compared to Parvati), and is alone with her for the first time. The two stand there in the room, regarding each other intensely from a slight distance. At this point, Ghatak introduces a sound of heavy breathing, clearly suggesting sexual union, builds it up to a climax and *then* has the young man pick her up and lay her on the bed. Here the device is not literary because the sound is directly related to the action; only it is displaced, the sound coming before the action. The displacement intensifies our sense of their desire and yet alienates us, making us observers, totally removed from the possibility of identifying ourselves with their desire for our vicarious satisfaction, as most films would do.[8]

Turning to music, the most interesting use of it in Ghatak's films is in terms of the song. It is used to heighten, expand and elevate reality to the plane of powerful emotion, extending, sometimes hyping it, in the same way as the wide-angle or the telephoto. No one has taken a conventional device of the popular Indian cinema, and of the Jatra and other folk forms, and turned it into effective cinema so often. It is at its most successful where a character first sings and then the melody is picked up by the instruments, or repeated in voiceover as in *Meghe Dhaka Tara*. Really daring is the way in which he opens that film with off-key singing as the beginner Shankar sits in the open and practises. As the film develops, the music does too, heightening by emphasis, or by counterpoint, the effect of a statement. The Tagore song in the film is sung in the most direct manner possible. Nita asks her brother, at a very emotional moment in her life, to teach her a song. But it creates some of the most effective moments of the film. It is in the pure voiceover songs, unanchored in realism, that sometimes one sees an overindulgence, stretching out a film and reducing its cohesive force as in some passages of *Subarnarekha* and *Titas*.

Ritwik also follows the commercial cinema's convention of instrumental accompaniment to songs where it is not realistic, that is, its source is not indicated. Besides, he often ignores tonal perspective not only in songs but in dialogue as well. Thus in *Meghe Dhaka Tara*, Shankar's singing, whether far or near, retains the same loudness in some scenes or is exaggerated. When he talks to the nurse in his dying sister's sanatorium, the volume level of the dialogue remains the same as they go away from the camera. Another curious thing is the way he uses classical music in rural scenes where others would employ folk tunes, again ignoring the needs of realism. Partly these may be traced to his beginnings in the theatre; but the element of deliberate choice cannot be ignored.

V

I must confess here that I find some of the theories spun around Ghatak's unorthodox marriage of Marx and Jung, by his more ardent disciples, rather overblown.[9] The exegesis often overwhelms the text. Ritwik Ghatak wrote and spoke volubly in explication of his own work. But as with many others, 'what an artist says about his work and what the work says about him are not the same thing'.[10]

In *Ajantrik*, there is a rather unconnected sequence of a tribal procession that erupts resplendently upon a serene sky without any previous indication or later link-up. There is no scene showing any interaction between the tribals and modern industry. As though filling this gap, Ghatak talks about the childlike acceptance of the incursion of machines into their lives: 'They [the aboriginals] are constantly in the process of assimilating anything new that comes their way. In all our folk art the signs of such assimilation are manifest . . . [They] have the same attitude to externals which is the emotional thesis of the story.' Plausible enough as these generalizations are—anthropologists have made similar observations—

the fact is that on screen they are not borne out. Neither the tribal ability to assimilate nor the examples of folk art are presented at all, except in post facto exegesis.

In *Meghe Dhaka Tara*, the idea of the Bengali traditional courtyard as the yagna mandapa or sacrificial space, of Nita as Mother Goddess Jagaddhatri and her mother as the destructive Kali can be largely dismissed—without reducing the importance of the film either as art or as social statement. Anyone who has seen conventional Bengali films of the 1940s and 1950s knows that inevitable courtyard with a long-suffering female in the middle of it. The daughter as bread-earner and the mother as selfish guardian of the family, ready to sacrifice the daughter's happiness at the family altar, are equally familiar figures. Particularly, the comparison of the mother with Kali, the destroyer, runs counter to the evidence of the film.

In at least three major statements, the mother places her understanding of and sympathy for the daughter beyond all doubt. First, she scolds her singer son for scrounging off his sister. Second, she is distinctly annoyed when the younger sister shows an excessive eagerness to bring tea for her elder's lover when she is sitting with him. Third, when Shankar, now a successful singer, discovers that Nita has tuberculosis, she is extremely sympathetic even though she no longer needs Nita's money; and she regrets that Nita, in her reserve, had not told her about her affliction. In mythology, Kali's destruction is a motiveless cycle, not born of the earthly want to which the poor mother is subject. Ghatak's film-making is sharp and his feelings so acute that he elevates these stereotypes to real people whose lives are distorted by want. If there are shades of mythological archetypes, they are, at best, his own theoretical overlays, at worst, mere conjecture on the part of his disciples.

The mere fact of an event on the screen having a mythological parallel, or a reference to some traditional archetypal image, may not by itself strengthen the impact of what emanates from the screen. Nor is it entirely original. The comparison of the coming of the Mother Goddess at the time of the autumnal harvest festival with the married daughter visiting her parents is common enough in popular songs and in literature. In cinema it was first employed possibly in a docudrama, *Panchthupi*, by Harisadhan

Das Gupta, well before Ghatak. The over-elaboration of such ancillary intellectual structures sometimes has little to do with the actual images in the film. It is the outcome of a temptation for over-explication, of spinning out possible theoretical analogues and associations, from which the film-maker often suffers as much as the film critic. Ghatak himself was not totally unaware of this pitfall, for he says, as a preamble to his own statement on the theoretical significance of *Meghe Dhaka Tara*: 'Without being over-articulate, I can claim . . .' All he does, however, is to give some pointers to common enough parallels between reality and mythology.

As one who was deeply concerned with access to large audiences, Ritwik was disturbed that people did not see the connection between the tribals and Bimal and his old car the way he himself saw it in *Ajantrik*. He was fully aware of the fact that a superstructure of ideas in his mind had not in fact emanated from the screen and it frustrated him that the film was 'disapproved and finally rejected by the people'. It turned out to be 'esoteric', he said, because the connections had not been clearly enough established. *Meghe Dhaka Tara* was a success with both select and large audiences even though they did not interpret it on his own lines, at least not consciously.

In the context of Ritwik's longing to be understood by large audiences, it is interesting to quote Utpal Dutt, who has made highly popular use of the Jatra form for the purpose of revolutionary theatre: 'The Brechtian style interferes with our people's responses because they are used to another kind of theatre, and *all forms must come from the people's understanding* . . .' Dutt proceeded to cut out the *juri* and *vivek*, two traditional elements of Jatra, because he found that they no longer worked with today's audiences.

Ghatak's style of work, as Saeed Mirza points out, was very intuitive ('Keep a bottle of liquor in one pocket and your childhood in another') and not as deliberate as has sometimes been made out.[11] There is also a point to be made about the Jungian archetypal interpretations of his films: the sheer arbitrariness of imposing a Hindu cosmic scheme upon a society that has lived with Islam and Christianity for many centuries and has been changed by them in many respects, the position of woman included. Some of Ritwik's own writings and statements on this subject may have been made in retrospect during his academic sojourn in the Film Institute. What seems more important is the heroic strength with which the role of woman is invested in his films, particularly *Meghe Dhaka Tara* and *Titas*. There is a social and moral insight here that is more free of male chauvinism than any film director one can think of, including some women directors. *Meghe Dhaka Tara* undoubtedly has a significant repetition of motifs and continuity of social patterns, as in the replacement of one Nita by another at the end; but to read cosmic significance in them is to suggest that exploitation is perennial and inevitable. Ritwik's humanism and purist Marxism ran counter to such a conviction of inexorable sacrifice. In almost every film, he leaves a hopeful pointer for the future through a child: in *Ajantrik*, the little boy who plays with Jagaddal's horn, in *Titas*, the boy playing on a paper flute, and so on.

Here it is necessary to note some of the ways in which Ghatak differs from Satyajit Ray since Ray dominated the serious cinema during the entire period of Ghatak's film-making from *Nagarik* onwards. Ray, the Tagorean Brahmo rationalist, has a cosmic view of a very different kind—free of mythology, yet completely Indian. Ghatak's pattern, if we were to accept it as a theory, would be a cyclical one of creation and destruction; in Ray, it is replaced by a sense of the cosmic flow of time that invests all human activity, however small, with a significance beyond its immediate meaning. Besides, Ray's Indianness also lies in its innate sense of the limits of human endeavour, of an area of freedom circumscribed by given circumstances beyond one's control, such as the place of one's birth, the period and the family one is born into. We see this in *Devi*, a film on the superstitious aspect of the worship of the Great Mother that Ghatak would never have made. The exploiter and the exploited are both victims; they happen to be born at a certain time, on certain sides of the divide between superstition and rationality. Ray's sympathy is with the rationalist but he never condemns the religious delusions of his protagonist. Significantly, the story had been conceived by Rabindranath who asked Prabhat Mukherjee to write it, for he did not want it to be seen as a Brahmo attack on Hindu beliefs.

Indeed one can, and should, see Ray and Ghatak as two complementary aspects of the Indian mind, one embodying the contemplative, inward principle in which the calm without and the fire within make for an intense clarity of vision; the other representing the active principle going forward into the here and now, with all the power of passion and yet aware of an inner order. One is primarily a poet; the other a dramatist. One, to use Andre Bazin's formulation, turns reality into spectacle; the other makes spectacle seem real. One is a highly disciplined classicist,[12] the other childlike, wayward, romantic.

VI

Ghatak shared with fellow film-makers of the New Cinema a puritan streak in the depiction of sexual relationships. Sometimes there are powerful but indirect suggestions as in *Meghe Dhaka Tara*, where a woman steals her elder sister's lover, or in the displaced sound effect of sexual congress in *Titas*, but the approach is never frank and free to any extent.

However, *Subarnarekha*'s confrontation of brother and sister in a brothel, leading to the gory suicide of the sister, remains one of the most shocking scenes in Bengali, indeed Indian, cinema. It marks a unique departure from the unwritten convention, probably derived from Greek and Sanskrit drama, of leaving the action to take place offstage and putting the contemplation of it onstage. A subsidiary reason for its prevalence is that it suits the resources of low-budget productions. We find it as an effective principle in most of Ghatak's other films.

Ghatak also had a penchant for juxtaposing sharply contrasting elements to create an apotheosis of irony, reaching into emotions. In *Subarnarekha*, the two friends go to a bar festooned for Christmas. Once they get thoroughly drunk, one of them begins to recite verses from the Upanishads in Sanskrit, indicating the true nature of his concerns and his self-mockery.[13]

VII

One of the subjects that writers on Ghatak have not probed is the alcoholism that brought his career to an untimely end. Psychologists will agree that alcoholism is not a cause, but a symptom, of inner problems. As I have tried to show, Ghatak's mind was buffeted by his failure to break out of his middle-class confines, to reach a mass audience, by the alienation he suffered when he was thrown out of the IPTA, and the disintegration of revolutionary purity not only in that organization, but in the communist movement in India, as he saw it. He also suffered, very probably, from the conflict between the secularism of the Marxist faith and his nostalgia for the mother cult which he rationalized under a Jungian garb—itself unacceptable to Marxist dogma. Allied to these was the loss of his El Dorado, with which he could not reconcile himself. Even the prospect of a cultural unity which arose after the liberation of Bangladesh was lost very soon, shattering his hopes once more. It is thus a moot question whether Ghatak's alcoholic disintegration was due to outward difficulties, or to inner conflicts between intellect and sensibility, cultural inheritance and conscious orientations, intuitive urges and theoretical approaches.

It seems simplistic to put down alcoholism as an inherited genetic problem unrelated to the workings of a person's mind. Such biological determinism would be abhorrent to the Marxist faith; what is more, it could be set up as a safe haven for murderers and paedophiles and others like them whose failings could be attributed to genetic disorders with equal ease, divesting them of all moral responsibility for their actions.

An uncompromising artist, Ritwik neither made films to suit the demands of usurious middlemen, nor did he permit intellectual gout to affect his creative powers. Anguished by the sufferings of his people and their betrayal by their leaders, thwarted by the collapse of his political ideas on the one hand and the apathy of his audience on the other, Ritwik drove himself to a sort of self-destruction. Caught up in the toils of dejection, caused by the poor reception of his films—both in intellectual and financial terms—Ritwik had been taking refuge in alcohol. His statement 'Somehow I feel, alcohol is the final salvation,' probably provides a glimpse of his state of mind.

It also seems possible that he was drawn to the myths and archetypes because he felt himself bound by them, that he was trying to exorcize a traditional–bourgeois ghost within his Marxist self, and he did not succeed. In its inner recesses, did his highly moral and sensitive mind question his Tagorean inheritance and his bonds with the middle class (with which his films are so preoccupied), and did they bear a familiar Marxist sense of guilt on account of it? Some such explanation has to be sought for his disintegration. Perhaps he would not have been so self-destructive if he had been able to identify with social classes other than his own. His niece, Mahashweta, was later to do this in her extraordinarily powerful stories and novels about proletarian women and tribal heroes, without mythologizing them. To those who had known him over the decades of his career from the days of the IPTA, and followed it from theatre to film, Ritwik's greatness seldom seemed to lie in the consistency of his meaning or the sustained creative level of his work. It seemed rather to rest in his grand passion, in the peaks of expressive power he reached and his intense effort to find an order within. The search for a conscious and constant application of theoretical ideas in his work may thus be less rewarding than it at first seems. Ghatak was much more of a Fellini than an Eisenstein, although both influenced his work in their different ways. He bares his soul in the centre of the stage in *Jukti Takko Ar Gappo* and gives us a glimpse of the ghosts tormenting him. It is the moral height at which his inner battle was fought, his refusal to compromise, and the nobility of his failure, that made him unique.[14]

14

ADOOR GOPALAKRISHNAN
The Kerala Coconut

Adoor Gopalakrishnan (b.1941) came to film-making through the film society and film institute route, reinforcing enthusiasm with training. Besides, his early experience of both traditional and modern theatre as well as of classical dance, especially Kudiattam and Kathakali, provided a rich background for his creative fulfilment in cinema.

Kerala is deeply regional in its culture and close to classical learning and tradition. Adoor's family deity is Krishna, the village in which his *Kodiyettam* was shot is dedicated to Duryodhana, a character in the epic Mahabharata. Kerala's synthesis of classical tradition and modern thought, of simplicity in lifestyle and richness in culture, make it remarkably different from many other states. Yet, Marxism has been a major element in its social and political make-up. The accent on education and health care in the 'Kerala Economic Model' has made this state relatively free from harsh urban–rural contrasts—most of Kerala is semi-urban. The economic model has developed its cultural coordinates. As a result, Kerala provides appropriate soil for the growth of a serious cinema.

The impact of film society activity in these surroundings no doubt gave Kerala's intelligentsia a potent combination of regional depth and international awareness, plus an understanding of the universal language of cinema. It seems improbable that, without such a milieu, Adoor's talent would have blossomed as it did, or his audience come to have the loyalty it does towards his work.

Adoor was the prime mover of the film society movement in Kerala and one of the earliest products of the Film Institute of India in Pune, established by the Government of India. As such he can be regarded as one of the earliest talents to be discovered and brought to the fore by the process of social engineering in newly independent India.

Adoor Gopalakrishnan stands out in his independence from Marxism, particularly in its orthodox and thoughtless, superficial and imitative manifestations. This is particularly significant as, like in West Bengal, Marxism has been a powerful political and cultural force in Kerala, from which to stay away is difficult and not entirely without hazards. The communists, besides commanding a large following, have often been elected to power and controlled the bulk of state subsidies to the arts, including the parallel cinema. With his fame as a film-maker, Adoor, like Ray in Bengal, has maintained a formidable distance from political pressures as much as from consumerist forces. His humanism has never been overpowered by ideological pressures from political forces. Unlike Ritwik Ghatak, and others in Bengal, his films do not bear the marks of a struggle against official leftism or party ideologies to emerge independent; he withstood these pressures from the very beginning of his career. This also bespeaks the tolerance of the Marxist rulers, perhaps induced by the formidable reputation Adoor so quickly acquired.

Adoor is the name of the small town from which Gopalakrishnan came. The town is known for its Kathakali dancing troupes and it is customary for the players—and the villagers—to prefix their names with that of the village from which they come. Hence the name Adoor Gopalakrishnan, known to his friends, all over the country and abroad, as just Adoor.

II

Adoor's work shows an affinity to Kathakali's extreme formality of style. Kathakali's totally reconstructed image of the human figure when he appears on the stage, with the face painted in emphatic colours and the body draped in innumerable angles and folds of cloth that hide his form, make him only a Kathakali artist. It is through this complex cloak of artifice that one has to recognize a character in a Kathakali performance. The individual human being is wiped out; a character in the play possesses him, inhabits his body. In this respect, Kathakali is akin to Japanese Noh; the clothes hide the man and make the character. The sounds, the cries, the staccato gestures too are stylized, artificial. Each character is known by its costume and make-up; the quality of acting is judged by the degree of approximation to what is decreed by tradition, and by the force, vigour, as well as the subtleties of the performance.

It is tempting to think that Adoor's films have a similar dimension of masking reality behind artifice, challenging the audience to discover what it may. The movements of the characters are often, as of Unni and Rajamma in *Elippathayam*, slow, deliberate, stylistic. Does this have to do with his childhood ambition to become a theatre director? It is not altogether surprising to know that he first considered entering the National School of Drama in Delhi but could not because he has no knowledge of Hindi.

Consistent with this theatre background is the fact that Adoor uses camera movements very sparingly; the bedrock of his filming is the steady shot more often than not at eye level. It is very different from those who resort to the tracking shot as soon as object movement within the frame ceases, so as to keep things moving and thus keep the spectator's eye engaged. Adoor's object is to keep the screen full of realistic details and yet eliminate all minor movements, demanding from his audience complete concentration on the central action. In films like *Kodiyettam*, the absence of music also heightens this concentration.

III

In thirty years, Adoor Gopalakrishnan has made only nine films. He chips away at his scripts for years, until he has arrived at a lean, muscular form in which nothing is expendable. His films are like Kerala's ripest coconuts; their hard shells have to be broken if one is to relish their substance. Part of this shell is formed by his style of severe understatement, his refusal to explain.

To compound the problem, what one finds inside the Kerala coconut is often a powerful absence. *Elippathayam* and *Mukhamukham* are both powered by silence, the frequent absence of words where they are expected. His reticence throws a challenge at the very start of the game; it forces the audience to concentrate on the image and to pay extra attention to the words when they come. In *Mathilukal*, the two protagonists cannot see each other, separated by the wall that stands between the men's section of the jail and the women's. There is thus an intense concentration on the words. 'My films are for an enlightened audience,' Adoor declares blandly, despite the consumerist made-easy pressures building up rapidly, as much in Kerala as in the rest of his country.

Adoor's early films seem to see reality from the right end of the telescope, as it were; the middle period, one might say, sees it from the reverse end of the telescope, which pushes the characters out to a distance, where their relationships and behaviour patterns stand out in clear relief. Thus, *Swayamvaram* or *Kodiyettam* describe more than they analyse; *Elippathayam* and *Mukhamukham* are more concerned with analysis than with narration.

In *Elippathayam*, little is spoken to express an attitude. The laziness of the rural rich menfolk, their total inability to act is apotheosized in the landlord's inability to bathe himself, indeed to do anything other than sit in an easy chair, endlessly staring at newspaper headlines. His most active moments find him snipping off grey hair from his moustache. One by one he quarrels and gets rid of his sisters; the eldest, foiled in her attempts to get her share of family property, departs; the second dies of stomach pains without medical attention; the youngest, fed up with her life of slavery to the lazy elder brother, leaves the house. Unable to fend for himself, the landlord confines himself to the bed, resembling the rat inside a trap carried to a tank and drowned by the youngest sister at the beginning of the film. This is the rat trap he has created for himself.

Silent repetition of daily chores is used to build up an anticipation of some kind of unknown tragedy lying ahead. Yet it is not a means of creating suspense; indeed, it is the very opposite because it emphasizes the fortitude of the women, the dullness of their chores, the uselessness of the man they serve as unpaid servants rather than sisters. They are not the only ones to behave the way they do, nor are they the only ones trapped in a prison; it is obviously symptomatic of the rottenness of the society around them. Well after the audience has got the idea, Adoor goes on piling the repeats so as to drive the idea home. Each time Sridevi, the youngest sister, goes to dip the rat trap in the pond, she repeats the full action without the progressive abridgement that other directors would have used. It is only at the end, and well after it, that we find the images stuck in our minds. Just as the *bādi* in a raga in Hindustani classical music is dinned into the ear, Adoor's basic images are firmly grounded in the mind's eye through the long-held steady shots and their repetition. This makes his films structurally very different from the Hollywood narrative model, giving them a stamp of individuality.

There is intense pressure in *Mukhamukham* for the revolutionary released from jail to break into a torrent of words, about his jail life, the changes in his ideas, his relationship with his party and his future plans—about all of which he maintains a stony silence, creating a powerful tension. The lack of explanation infuses an ambiguity; the audience is induced to speculate, decipher meanings on its own. Its presumptions, set ideas, knee-jerk reactions, are all shaken off one by one until the audience has to face the last alternative, the true one, however unacceptable: that the man has had enough; he just wants to be left alone with his drink.

Even in Adoor's first film there is an unwillingness to be over-explicit, so as to leave room for the audience to fill in the gaps. We are not told why Viswam and Sita in *Swayamvaram* have to elope, or why, when they run out of money, they cannot raise it from relations or friends. Such mundane details are left to our imagination. The young couple is on the bus and the bus moves, the film begins.

Adoor's silence in *Mukhamukham* brought him the same kind of trouble that Mrinal Sen had faced when he refused to explain where the girl had been all night in *Ek Din Pratidin*. Marxists read all kinds of explanations into the silence, mainly the rejection of their policies—everything, in other words, except the human and obvious one. Inscrutability is not beloved of the leaders of 'The People'. Predictability is more useful.

However, unlike Mrinal Sen in the instance I have quoted, Adoor has provided profuse commentaries and interviews after the film was released. The audience cannot avoid seeing the disintegration of Sreedharan the revolutionary into Sreedharan the drunk. Adoor tried hard but unsuccessfully in his many interviews to fend off this view.

> Sreedharan's reappearance is a 'fiction'. It is a product of the concretization of the intense desire of a people caught in a particular situation to get back the 'man image' of a hero called Sreedharan . . . In an important scene of the film I have used Lenin's quotation, 'The proletarian movement passes through various stages of growth. At every stage a set of people stagger, stop and are unable to continue the forward march.' This film concerns one such moment . . . Sreedharan was a 'messenger'. He had delivered his 'message' and gone. His message is still with us. The mistake is in calling the messenger back and expecting him to fight our battles for us.

Despite this very articulate explanation, Iqbal Masud, in a perceptive essay, said:

> Sreedharan is built up in the second half with such specificity that he is no mere image of fiction. He is an individual in the process of disintegrating and this is conveyed so powerfully that one sees in Ganga's (the actor) ruined face and body, the ruins of a once-bright communism.[1]

Cinematically, the most interesting aspect of the film is the power of silence which reaches its pinnacle here. Adoor's first film had been by far more definitive. Its rebel couple, who run away from family and tradition, face a grim fate. After a long, brave struggle, the man dies, on a stormy night, and the woman, child on lap, is left staring at the bolted door, outside which wait the patient men who would make a whore of her. 'The trip from illusion to reality', as Adoor himself calls it, is complete. Film by film, Adoor moved towards the inscrutable, demanding more and more from his audience.

All of this makes him an outstanding creator of unpopular cinema.

IV

Adoor's visuals are very Keralite. They breathe the very air of his region, its lush greenery, its moisture settled on every surface, human or vegetable, investing every movement with a slow and languorous grace. There is much palpability in the images; rain keeps pelting down on the dense vegetation, bare bodies glisten with a moist immediacy.

At the same time, they suggest a Japanese way of looking at space. They make subtle use of the architectural similarities between Kerala and the Far East—China, Japan and Korea, particularly the last two. The eye-level shots of doorways and horizontal lines of the tiled roofs often suggest Ozu, and the fast, low-angle lateral shots of movement in front or behind trees and shrubs faintly echo Kurosawa. Like Ozu, he emphasizes the ordinariness of the ordinary. Eye-level mid-shots predominate, and foregrounding, so common with other directors and so remarkable in Ghatak, is somewhat rare in Adoor's work. The formal compositions, the steady shots held for long moments, the long stretches of a single texture, also recall some silent film techniques.

Cast in the Ray mould, Gopalakrishnan writes most of his own stories, looks through the lens to check every frame and is in every sense the auteur of his works, in control of all aspects of film-making. Asked why he uses the word 'realisation' instead of 'direction' Adoor replied: 'Film-making is not mere direction. My film is the realization of my concept. The word direction is inadequate to describe that process. The director merely directs. The term does not connote creativity.'

Adoor shares with his compatriots in the parallel cinema a reticence about depicting sexuality, but sometimes he has used a kind of coarse appeal with fat folds of bare flesh as in Unni's neighbour out to seduce him in *Elippathayam*. Earlier, in *Swayamvaram* and *Kodiyettam*, the seducing women, similarly endowed, behave in similar fashion, swaying and thrusting their folds at the man. Some characters are free from this—the more independent or modern ones like Sridevi in *Elippathayam* and Shobana/Nalini in *Anantaram*. Does this indicate Adoor's own dislike for the assertion of sexuality as such? Of course it is possible that he was at first forced to work with unsuitable actresses because, as he says, 'I spent two years looking for non-actors, but to no avail. Girls won't come forward—they think acting is tantamount to becoming a prostitute; the boys are keener on respectable jobs and don't want to interrupt their studies.'[2]

The puritanical streak may nevertheless be part of him because he does avoid all close encounters among men and women, even in his later films, when the social prejudices against cinema had died down. Unlike Ray, he would perhaps rather avoid a slightly explicit scene than go in for the kind of sanitized lip-to-lip pecking of *Ghare Baire*.

Beginning with *Anantaram*, one sees a shift in Adoor's work towards the visually beautiful. This is as true of the lighting and composition as the looks of the actors and actresses. Adoor seems to have mellowed, grown more amenable to accessibility. Shalini in *Anantaram* obviously belongs to a later generation in which girls were less prejudiced against cinema and actresses less so towards the parallel screen.

Talking of early times, it is worth noting that the innovations of *Swayamvaram* caught Kerala and its cinema unawares. They even went one up on the Ray model of complete creative control of the film. In Adoor's own words, '*Swayamvaram* was a kind of revolt by a young and idealistic group of enthusiasts who remained outside the framework of commercial cinema . . . I went against most of the conventions of commercial cinema. There were no songs in *Swayamvaram*. The entire film was shot on actual locations. I used natural ambience recorded from the location. Barring Sharada who belongs to Andhra Pradesh, no actor or actress dubbed the dialogues.'[3]

But here his resemblance to the Ray-model directors ends. The rest is Adoor. The power of silence, the quasi-Japanese sense of space, the stolidity of the steady image, the force of repetition—are all his.

The earlier films are composed in a more severe fashion with straight lines, squares and rectangles predominating, the colours restricted and not much of a factor in themselves. *Anantaram* onwards, curves, circles play their part, colour is more relaxed and pleasant, lighting more flattering to the skin. It is further softened by the undercurrent of nostalgia in the autobiographical element. The accent shifts from the judgemental in *Elippathayam* and the contentious in *Mukhamukham* to a more compassionate, nostalgic mood in *Vidheyan* and *Kathapurushan*.

With *Nizhalkkuthu* (Shadow Kill, 2005), Adoor reaches new heights, bringing together various strands developed in earlier films. For the first time in his work, there is a lyrical passage of deliberately emphasized, declared, visual charm in the love scenes, in the faces and bodies, in landscapes. A remarkable story, written by Adoor himself, leaves us thinking more than ever before. The many strands of the story, especially the story within a story, make the film rich in ambiguities. What makes it more intriguing is a curious coldness in recounting the love story; it is as though we have seen it all before, and will do so again. That it is obviously a replay of the Radha–Krishna legend is only a small part of the feelings it arouses in us.

The hangman is a deeply religious person, given to drinking, affectionate towards his family and friends and altogether the opposite of any image that the word hangman might conjure up in us. All facile assumptions are challenged. The picture that emerges is of a man caught in the meshes of his time and circumstance which makes us rethink all assumptions, and in fact seeks to rid us of the very habit of making ready assumptions. We are forced to think of the more universal meanings hinted at, of numerous ordinary people who must often act as hangmen of sorts, handing out punishments, deserved or undeserved, to people for whom redemption comes too late, in supreme irony.

What the film brings home to one in the end is that it is not individual moral choice that controls human destiny but the network of social and genetic circumstances that determines all conclusions. The hangman's devout worship of Kali does not deliver him from sin; nor does his son's deliberate moral choice of Gandhian non-violence absolve him of the necessity to hang a possibly innocent man. Adoor had for long struggled against the political determinism of communist orthodoxy; now he substitutes it by moral determinism.

15

MRINAL SEN
Loose Cannon

For over half a century, Marxism has been the dominant ideology in Bengal. It has, however, been so tempered by the profound humanism of Tagore as to acquire a local form reminiscent of what was once dubbed Eurocommunism in Parisian leftist parlance. The Bengali's innate love of literature and his preoccupation with culture in general provided the soil on which the seeds of Marxism were sown, giving a very middle-class orientation to the mix of the two. Both strands promoted, among other things, an internationality of outlook to which the cinema, a West-born medium, eminently lent itself.

Furthermore, the film society movement, primarily motivated by the British example, warmly embraced European creative innovations and South American revolutionary fervour. Satyajit Ray's films and his leadership of the film society movement created an umbrella that accommodated a variety of tendencies. Hollywood narrative techniques, Italian neo-realism, German Expressionism, and a sovietique glorification of The People in the abstract, became grounded in the Tagorean world view, yielding an attractive form of cinema. This mix has its ambiguities and caused subterranean conflicts between individual creativity in cinema with an agit-prop restatement of the Marxist class struggle formula. This continued till the early 1980s which saw the beginning of a reassertion of the worth of the individual who, until now, had been regarded by the dominant ideologues as a cog in the wheels of social engineering.

No Bengali director reflected the diverse strands in the social and political fabric of India as widely as Mrinal Sen. All through the 1960s and 1970s, even extending into the 1980s, there was the dominance, not merely in cinema but in the ambience of the high culture of Bengal, of the triumvirate of Satyajit Ray, Ritwik Ghatak and Mrinal Sen. The enormity of Ray's reputation surrounded him with a halo; Ghatak's students at the Film Institute in Pune developed a cult around him.

Mrinal Sen stood alone. Unlike other spokesmen of the Nehruvian world view, he is not a chronicler. He does not accept the prevailing humanist view of things and weave his films around them. He is nothing if he is not a critic, analyst, commentator, rebel—all rolled into one. Almost from the beginning, every film has been for him a challenge thrown at prevailing ideas, an adventure, an unusual encounter, not an exercise in craftsmanship. Sen has mostly been perceived in two ways: the first sees him as a political film-maker, a product of the broadly Marxist movement; the second as something of a loose cannon, powerful in his blasts but unclaimable for any ideology or group. It is more difficult to define what he stands for than what he is against. He always asserts that he is not, has never been, a member of any political party, and does not obey any party diktats. His writings are of little help in this regard because he does not specify his own ideology nor describe his particular utopia. Perhaps he has none. Almost all his films oppose certain goals more than they define alternative scenarios. This view of his work tended to congeal over the period dominated by Ray. As he came out of that shadow, Sen gained a new visibility.

Mrinal Sen has worked in many languages in various regions of India. This may be a simple factor of the variety of opportunities that have come up in his career; but opportunities also choose their favoured protagonists. Evident in his work is a readiness to embrace the plural, multicultural aspects—the aspects that make for the living quality, the rich texture of Indian society. Hence his *Mrigaya* (The Royal Hunt, 1976) with tribal folk, *Oka Oorie Katha* (The Outsiders, 1977) with Andhra labourers, *Matira Manisha* (Two Brothers, 1966) with Oriya farmers, *Bhuvan Shome* (1969) with Gujarati villagers and so on. This without doubt expresses a pan-Indian awareness, a consciousness that extends beyond Bengal, as also an adventurousness of the spirit, a readiness to face challenges, undaunted by the possibility of imperfection. It is a part of Sen's indifference to the concept of a masterpiece, at least in this period of his career.

The first thought that occurs on a revaluation of his films is that too much of a leftist aura has been read into them. In his early films he tried, predictably, to find himself and his métier. He avoids showing or even talking about *Raat-Bhor* (Night's End, 1956), his first film, made a year after *Pather Panchali*, obviously considering it too amateurish. His second, *Neel Aakasher Niche* (Under the Blue Sky, 1958), tells the story of a Chinese vendor in conventional terms but with adequate narrative skill. It is content to create a sympathetic portrait of a Chinese vendor in the streets of Calcutta without any ideological goals or social analyses lurking behind.

His third film, *Baishey Sravan* (Wedding Day, 1960), which established his reputation as a film-maker, is again a realistic, descriptive film. It minutely examines the disintegration of a couple's relationship under the pressures of unemployment and poverty, without seeking ideological reasons. The focus is on the husband's leg injury that disables him and makes it impossible for him to continue to vend cosmetics on railway trains. Famine is shown and war suggested, but both remain minor narrative props.

But artistically, drastic change came with *Baishey Sravan*. Suddenly, Sen's touch is sure, deft and neo-realist, suggesting a late reaction to Ray's first film. A middle-aged travelling salesman of country cosmetics on a suburban train, newly married to a charming young woman, has a fall from his bicycle and gradually goes to seed. The story of love in the time of famine is told perceptively and with compassion. The man's decline and the souring of the relationship with his wife are subtly observed. The long-suffering mother is clearly reminiscent of the old woman of *Pather Panchali*; so is the style of narration, but not without suggesting original talent. War and famine supply the background but are not analysed politically to the extent that ideological loyalties could have mandated.

Except for the comic flair of the first half of *Abasheshey* (And at Last, 1962), three rather listless films that followed did not betray any remarkable traits in their explorations of middle-class life. However, as exercises in narrative skill they must have contributed to Sen's growth.

Suddenly, inspiration visits him and Sen makes *Akash Kusum* (Up in the Clouds, 1965), obviously in reaction to his first viewing of the French nouvelle vague in Truffaut's *400 Blows*. Sen lavishes his sympathy on a young man who keeps building castles in the air, refusing to come to grips with the realities of his life. In society, such a man would attract ridicule, rejection; but Sen invests him with warmth, freshness and enthusiasm, without any suggestion of political direction. *Akash Kusum*'s freshness set the tone for later films, making a landmark in his career. In some of the scenes of *Matira Manisha*, there are sparks of the same nouvelle vague inspiration, without any particular emphasis on the break up of the pattern of landholding.

The next film, *Bhuvan Shome*, touches the high water mark of this wave of bravura, one in which the director is not driven by the medium's impulses but gets on top of them. An inscrutable impishness lies at the base of the film that first brought him all-India success. A top-notch bureaucrat of the Indian Railways, one of the biggest railway networks in the world and India's largest employer, who is known for his honesty and his severity in dealing with corruption in others, goes bird hunting to a small village in Gujarat. Here he faces an irate buffalo and nearly dies of fright. Worse, he meets the young wife of (this he does not know) a lowly employee of his who is given to taking bribes. She feeds him, gets him to wear native Gujarati dress so that the birds should not fear him, shows him around an abandoned mansion on the beach, tells him to look after her husband in the railways who takes small bribes due to him by the laws of nature, and sees him off on his journey back to work. Only work does not suit him any more. Thrilled by the novelty of his holiday experience, the brutish bureaucrat tears up the papers on his desk in a gesture of nihilistic glee.

It is difficult to think of another Indian film director who would be as attracted to this material as Mrinal Sen was. The film brings together two people of social classes that are hermetically sealed off from each other, in a comic encounter bordering on the absurd. It treats the theme of petty corruption as a fact of nature, and it strips the pompous official of the masks of social class, making a villager out of him for the time being. There is also his pitiful ineptitude at the use of the gun. Nothing falls into any revolutionary pattern; even though the elements were there,

there is no attempt to enlist them for a political or otherwise edifying purpose. Sen is content to have fun, revelling in the impish and the absurd. By dint of sheer drive and plenty of noise, Sen turns a scene actually showing man chasing bull into one ostensibly showing bull chasing man. Even when you are on to the subterfuge, it is merely amusing.

But there are underlying oppositions—against conventional morality over corruption, against pompous authority, indirectly against the work ethic. The undercurrent of naughty nihilism lies there, without being overemphasized.

II

The early 1970s in Bengal saw a grave if short-lived challenge to what left extremists saw as the Communist Party of India's abject surrender to the ruling bourgeois–democratic forces. While it lasted, it unleashed a Pol Pot-like terror regime in Bengal, most visibly in Calcutta. It became impossible for a sensitive film-maker to ignore the events overtaking his environment. It is in this context that one needs to see Mrinal Sen's political trilogy.

No wonder the films of this middle period show a broad inclination towards the socialist idea. But unlike the sovietique agit-prop films of Russia that had once set the pattern for officially blessed political films, and despite the murder and mayhem that prevailed in the name of revolution, *Interview* (1970) takes an impulsive, serio-comic swipe at the establishment with its story of the trials of an unemployed youth struggling to get a job but foiled by sartorial problems. The date set for a job interview to be stage-managed by a relative, turns out to be a public holiday and the young man is unable to get his suit out of a cleaning shop. He is obliged, after many a failed adventure in search of a suit, to wear a native-style dhoti. The relative's stage-management is foiled and the young man fails to get the job. At the end he avenges defeat on a mannequin in a men's wear shop window dressed in the kind of suit that could have got him the job, or so he thinks and we are asked to believe.

The irony and the futility of such a revenge is a part of Mrinal Sen's design and not a fortuitous by-product. Caricature is a familiar part of his vocabulary; he mixes it freely, sometimes unexpectedly, with realistic narrative and other storytelling devices.

Interview hangs a big tale on a single hook, a suit upon a suit hanger. It is 'sixty per cent improvised' and bears the stamp of a loosely connected tale. In this sense it is the polar opposite of, say, *Kharij* (The Case Is Closed, 1982) with its brick-by-brick connectivity. However, it contains some tightly integrated passages as well, such as the one in the bus, where the young man standing in a bus addresses the audience and refers to his hot pursuit by the director of the film. Such incursions of American Direct Cinema of the 1960s, considered gimmicky at the time, today seem to be one of its most engaging set pieces. Another is the young man's ten-minute address to the audience at the end.

Light and airy, the film hangs by a thin thread, yet lets fly sharp innuendoes against a society that regards the show of clothes as more important than the substance of a man. Its job interview scene, unlike the one in Ray's *Pratidwandi*, shot at the same time, is totally improvised, exaggerated, caricatured, and seems interesting today for those very reasons.

In *Calcutta 71* (1972), Sen presents three essays on poverty and frames them with direct comments on the dehumanizing effect of poverty. Although Sen is known to admire Satyajit Ray's Apu trilogy very much, he seems to have a chip on his shoulder about its 'lyrical realism'. In Sen's own words, 'As long as poverty is presented as something dignified, the establishment is not disturbed. Our attempt is to define poverty in terms of history.'

As the rain pelts down into the ramshackle hut of a family, its fury certainly washes out all dignity from the lives of the poverty-stricken people who abandon their huts and take to the waterlogged streets in search of shelter. The entire episode is frighteningly real, producing a sense of shock. As the mother keeps moving her baby to shield it from the water, we are made to realize that it is not the fury of nature but the machinations of man that have paralysed their lives.

Fearful too is the picture of the boy who smuggles rice from one district to another by train. The boy's lack of sentimentality and his street-smart realism, his indifference to the severe beating he receives from a muscular passenger are shattering. Both the stories are political perhaps because they are not lyrical, shocking more than sympathy evoking in the humanist manner. Poverty is seen as dehumanizing, devoid of dignity. The film is effective because it is bereft of lyricism for one thing and preachy purpose for the other.

Padatik (The Urban Guerrilla, 1972) is an even and consistent work, driven more by reflection than passion. The young revolutionary harboured by a socialite woman presents a piquant source of tension which Sen handles with skill, using this backdrop to dramatize the discourse on revolutionary strategy in the foreground. Personal history and psychological factors humanize the bourgeoisie who would otherwise remain a class enemy. This helps to take the debate beyond the level of the obvious. However, Sen avoids, just as Ray or Ghatak would have, the sexual resonances that such constant proximity between a handsome woman and a personable young man within the confines of an apartment would inevitably suggest. On the other hand, the revolutionary's new understanding of his father and his resolve to begin his struggle anew, eliminating past mistakes, strike a credible note.

Sen's reaction to the conditions of the time is unusual although deeply felt. Even the direct address by the protagonist of *Interview* does not divest the film of its multipolarity. The independence of his thought and his interest in cinematic innovation are too strong to permit such a simplistic course. His style, even in the three films regarded as his most directly political films—*Interview*, *Calcutta 71* and *Padatik*—is never altogether free from a playful buoyancy laced with a contradictory neo-realism.

He is more concerned with the human condition than with the particular political impulses of the time. Sen's films of the period do not paint the horrors of the present in order to replace them with the promised land. At the end of *Interview*, the frustrated young man throws a stone at a shop window housing the suit that he thinks could have got him a job. In *Calcutta 71*, we sympathize with the poverty and deprivation of the characters, and in *Padatik*, we bear with an ideological discourse. The essays on poverty as a human condition in *Calcutta 71* are presented without giving shape to the action resulting from the hatreds they might arouse against the social classes that thrive on the poverty of others. In fact, the only attempt to demonize the rich, at the dinner party to exhibit artistic skill in paintings of poverty, falls flat. Its exaggeration is too cartoonish, too unreal, to have any effect. It is the satire of a man who does not know the subject of his attack well enough to hit where it hurts. On the other hand, there are no promises of the rosy dawn revolution would bring. The extent of the poverty shocks but does not rouse enough anger to make action unavoidable. And this at a time when murder and mayhem were raging in Calcutta with extremists trying to overpower the ruling order through maximal, brazen violence on both sides.

Only *Chorus* (1974) comes close to the early sovietique agit-prop model. But the sloganeering is diluted by the ultra-fast pace and the technical bravura, raising the medium above the subject (putting the cart before the horse, as a hardliner might say). For the most part, Sen's films stand defiantly against pompous clichés, shibboleths and ready-made solutions. An outstanding, astonishing example is in *Oka Oorie Katha* which tilts against the windmills of the work ethic itself.

Considering that both capitalism and communism glorify the work ethic—one for the good of the individual, the other for the social good—Premchand's story, on which the film is based, is no candidate for either. Vengkaiyya, the irritable old protagonist with his stringy white hair and missing teeth, is a veritable anti-hero of the work ethic. Only fools work, says Vengkaiyya, because work benefits only those who order it. When his son marries and the young wife brings some order into the decrepit household, no one is more unhappy than the old man. When she dies, father and son borrow money for her funeral but spend it on drinks.

Mrinal Sen was obviously powerfully drawn to the story's innate nihilism. It came nearest to his posture towards the world, one of defiance of virtually all authority and all traditional prescriptions—classical or modern. Sen could easily have turned the story in the direction of resistance to the local landlord's wiles for making money on the labours of the poor. But he does not take this high road; he prefers the low road of the maverick who defies everybody and every ism.

In retrospect, one can see that Mrinal Sen chose this time to speak of poverty in general, about which there was no difference in the rhetoric of right and left, rather than specific problems marking out the period. Nor did he concern himself with the inter-party clashes and the killings going on to impose one interpretation of Marxism on the others and on the entire population. This enabled him to express anger without attracting either governmental censorship or the deadly wrath of the extremists. None of the powers that be could either claim him as theirs or reject him. The only way to make a political film at that point of time was to make it apolitically, by choosing the commonalities and ignoring the differences. In his own words:

> I made *Calcutta 71* when Calcutta was passing through a terrible time. People were getting killed every day. The most militant faction of the Communist Party—the Naxalites—had rejected all forms of party politics. At the same time, they had a host of differences with the other two communist factions. These in turn led to inter-party clashes and invariably ignored the main issue of mobilizing forces against the vested interests, the establishment. This was the time I felt I should spell out the basic ills of the country, the fundamental ills we were suffering from and the humiliations we had been subjected to. This was the time to speak of poverty—the most vital reality. I wanted to interpret the restlessness, the turbulence of the period that was 1971 and what it was due to.

The major device which works here for the politics of Brechtian alienation, and against narrative illusion, is the direct address to the audience in *Interview* and *Calcutta 71*, making this device his trademark, as it were, rarely to be found in any other director, Marxist or not. It is an anti-narrative device designed to break the illusion of the story and impose on the audience a need to think. But apart from this, there is little in the political films that could be seen as serving a political purpose.

Sen's determination to break down the Bengali's literary barriers to cinematic understanding never deserts him altogether. Every now and then he springs surprises to jolt the mind of the viewer. This is not to underrate the strength of Sen's social commitment, which was at its height at the time, but to emphasize the polyphony he always seems to attempt.

Unlike Satyajit Ray, he is not supercraftsman seeking perfection in a singular mode; unlike Ritwik Ghatak, his other illustrious, equally Marxist-inspired contemporary, he does not seek the objective correlative of a set theory of cinema. In Sen we find a welter of narrative illusion, Brechtian alienation, irony, anger, lyricism, expressionism, naturalism and the French nouvelle vague. He throws all these balls into the air and juggles with them with great verve, without caring if one misses a turn here or there as long as the play is alive and engaging.

In later films, beginning with *Ek Din Pratidin* (And Quiet Rolls the Dawn, 1979), linearity of construction, which he often berated earlier, becomes a carrier of his humanistic pursuit. The individual is at the centre of the stage, important for his own sake; the Marxist ghost has been fully exorcized. The middle period may be called the period of struggle with it, at the end of which he emerges as master of himself.

III

Ek Din Pratidin marked an important third phase of his film-making. From here onwards, Sen is more deeply concerned with the human condition and less with ideology, iconoclasm or experimentation, making the revaluation of the totality of his oeuvre a pressing need.

In *Ek Din Pratidin*, Sen's ire is directed at the conventional morality that informs family domination of young women, abridging their freedom and unheeding of their compulsions. A young working woman is late in coming home one night; in the minds of everyone surrounding her—family, neighbours—there is only one unspoken thought, that of sexual escapade. Throughout the speculations, imputations, suspicions that are voiced or insidiously suggested through the night, nobody is worried about her physical well-being or her own compulsions. When she returns after the long family vigil, nobody wants to know what problems she had or dangers she had faced or where she had spent the night. Nobody, that is, except her younger sister, who might one day be in the same situation. The audience would of course dearly love to know where she was all night, but Sen resolutely holds out, making the absence of the woman her powerful signature. It is the director's unfailing weapon for foiling the moral platitudes hurled noisily or silently against her. To all enquiries on where the girl was all night, Mrinal Sen's steadfast reply was the same: I don't know. In fact, Sen tells the following story: Satyajit Ray rang him up after seeing the film and asked, 'Where was the girl all night?' Sen replied, 'I don't know.' Ray's retort: 'You are the director, it's your business to know.' The story spells out more clearly than anything else the difference between the two directors.

In *Ek Din Achanak* (Suddenly One Day, 1989), a successful professor is found missing one day for no apparent reason. He has not left a note; he has not eloped with his attractive girl student. We can only conclude that domesticity became too much for him. Mrinal Sen rejects one of the holy cows of Indian society—family life.

Thus the humanist, the maverick individual, has an overweening presence in the films of Mrinal Sen. A sidelight to his humanism is cast by Sen's penchant for nostalgia. In a number of films—*Baishey Sravan*, *Akaler Sandhanay*, *Khandahar*, *Antareen*—he dwells on old buildings belonging to the feudal era with affection and without any trace of Marxist analysis. In this he is very akin to Ritwik Ghatak. Why the fondness for decrepit old mansions? In *Baishey Sravan*, the hero wallows in the pride of family history as he shows his wife around the decayed building; in *Khandahar* (The Ruins, 1983), the camera roams lovingly over the weather-beaten structure in which lives the young woman whom the world has forgotten; in *Akaler Sandhanay* (In Search of Famine, 1980), much that happens revolves round the old mansion. Like Ritwik Ghatak, does Sen too have a streak of nostalgia in him for the bad old days of feudal landlordism, lost forever with the partition of the country?

IV

Sen is unique in his fondness for the medium and his passion for exploring its possibilities. He would sometimes seem to proceed from the medium to the subject as in *Akash Kusum* or *Chorus*, instead of the opposite which was usual with his contemporaries. No other director seems to have so consciously played around with the medium as a thing in itself and not merely as a derivative of the content.

It is for these reasons somewhat unsatisfactory to separate Mrinal Sen's so-called 'political' films from the totality of his work. It is only in relation to the times that they can be viewed as political, not by themselves. In the end, it is his humanism and his love of the medium that seem to matter.

In terms of creative technique, Mrinal Sen's signature is most visible in his genius for improvisation. No other Indian director seems to have depended so much on the inspiration of the moment, on improvisation. The classicists hold this against him; many see it as his individuality. But here too it is difficult to stick a label on Sen; *Bhuvan Shome* and *Akaler Sandhanay* are full of on-the-spot inventions not by compulsion but by choice. While shooting *Bhuvan Shome*, he discovered an abandoned mansion and promptly worked it into the script, making it into an attractive scene which proved quite effective. In the midst of shooting *Akaler Sandhanay*, he suddenly remembered how, when they were shooting *Baishey Sravan* twenty years ago, a woman whose husband had just died in the village refused to part with his body until their daughter came to see her father for the last time. At Sen's request, his producer sent a car to fetch the daughter. Sen was reminded of the incident while they were shooting *Akaler Sandhanay*'s remarkable film within a film. He at once wrote it up as a new scene and shot it. It became a memorable scene that fitted into the story perfectly. The method works because he is able to integrate his inventions into the existing texture of the script with uncommon ease.

The script for *Akash Kusum* had already been written when Mrinal Sen saw Truffaut's *400 Blows*. He is said to have rushed home and rewritten the whole thing. The film that resulted was full of jump cuts and freezes, promptly attracting the label of gimmickry for its maker. But, in retrospect, the film is not as reckless as may have then seemed to many. In fact, it has, like *Bhuvan Shome*, an enduring, endearing freshness. The shock cuts and freezes seem to suit the subject and its temper. However, the devices here were not stamped political like the direct address to the audience in the 'political films'.

V

Sen's post-Marxist agenda consisted of a revaluation of the worth of the individual. Starting from *Ek Din Pratidin*, he virtually gives up his fixities of political direction and the restless inventions that had prevented his political statements from becoming posterish. He more or less announced this with the story of the single working woman whose late return home places her in the dock before family and neighbours. This concern for the individual runs through practically all later films, particularly *Kharij, Khandahar, Ek Din Achanak, Antareen* and climaxes in *Amar Bhuvan*.

Except that he takes time off to attack the comforts of creativity, the dramatic exploitation of poverty in *Akaler Sandhanay*, one of the best films ever made in the film on film-making format. A film director, obviously belonging to the unpopular cinema, comes to a village with his unit to make a realistic film on a famine, encounters opposition and has to go back in order to shoot it in the studio. The attempt to get a local woman to play in the film ends in disaster. In a superb scene of Smita Patil acting the role of a village woman during the famine, a woman in the audience is too moved by the acting not to intervene and spoil the shot. In other words, the realities of village life become too much for the film director to bear. The film unit's presence sets up ripples, stirs hidden animosities, brings prejudices into play. Sen is now turning against his own tribe and thereby upon himself, for what anthropologists today call the politics of observation, the effect that the observer's presence and the act of observation itself have on the subject he has come to study.

Kharij shares the enhanced consistency of the later films. Its characters and events are developed brick by brick with a fine connectivity, suggesting more premeditation and less improvisation. It is shot at close quarters, television style, emphasizing the denseness of middle-class life in a block of flats and the restrained play of reactions on the faces of the actors, who, it must be noted, rise to the needs of close scrutiny. Sen's exploration of the thoughtlessness and the self-absorption of the protagonists busy keeping up appearances, is compelling on all counts. The film is more concerned with the reality of the general indifference towards the well-being of the juvenile domestic servant than the condemnation of the couple who employ him. The end could have been strident, even violent; but Sen is content to show the gentle forbearance of the dead boy's father and his belief in the inexorability of fate. The restraint lends a rare poignancy to the end of the film.

The mood of poignancy turns into the dominant note of the next film, *Khandahar*. In the entire Sen oeuvre of twenty-seven feature films, there is no film more unlike the others than *Khandahar*. Its lyrical realism has a consistent depth and stylistic integrity. What is more, he does not judge his characters or question their political correctness. They are important simply because they are human and they are there. Sen steeps himself in nostalgia, in the angst of remembrance, in this story of city youth visiting the ruins of a mansion that still houses a dying old woman and her spinster daughter. There is an unspoken whiff of a romance with the possibility of one of the young men taking her away—a wisp of a mirage that disappears almost before it appears. This potentially cloying tale becomes an exquisite gem of a film.

It is impossible not to remember Satyajit Ray's *Aranyer Din Raatri* despite the difference in tone. Sen is more concerned with the portrait of the girl left at the end to her life in the collapsing mansion rather than the analyses of relationships to elaborate the comparison with Ray's film. Sen's is nostalgia that leaves the delicate scent of a woman, and a place, in the air. The film is remarkably free of political connotations, however nuanced. The camera moves with a quiet grace, matching the exquisite poise of Shabana Azmi as the fading spinster. The tonal difference in the visitors' speech from that of the inmates is exactly observed.

If this foray into the realm of poetry seems to mark a departure from the collective ethic in Sen's work, the impression is somewhat dispelled by the philosophic concern with what might be called Marxist cosmogony in *Genesis* (1986). Innocence in a ménage à trois is disrupted by the intrusion of a businessman with his quest for profit. But the film has a warmth and freshness that go beyond sociological formulae. The location in Rajasthan has the primal character of paradise created by three refugees from disaster. In fact, there is a rather engaging portrait of happiness in this relationship of two men and one woman, suggesting that it could be a valid form of social organization. Indeed, the philosophic and poetic appeal of the film transcends whatever ideological concerns it might evoke. Thus it is not far removed from the humanism of Sen in the 1980s.

In *Mahaprithivi* (World Within, World Without, 1991), the inner world counts for more than the outer. We are told about but shown nothing of either the protagonist's life in Germany which included the fall of the Berlin Wall, or the depredations of the Naxalites at home. While this made the film somewhat claustrophobic, it showed the nature of Sen's humanist concerns of this period. So did the next film, *Antareen* (The Internees, 1993) which consists mostly of telephone conversations between a man and a woman who do not know each other even when they brush past each other by accident. The choice of stories of the period shows a minimalist trend imposed by the financial pressures on the Bengali unpopular cinema of the time. But it also shows an increasing concern for the individual and less and less for the collective.

Unlike, say, *Kharij*, whose protagonists represented a common, uncaring middle-class attitude towards domestics, the characters of *Amar Bhuvan* (My World, 2001) bear no mark of their social class. *My World* is a world without conflict between individuals, not to speak of classes. We know that Noor is rich with Gulf money, that Meher is a peasant; but that does not define them as individuals functioning within a class. To propose this, Sen creates a utopia within a set of relationships between a Muslim woman and her previous and present husbands—two men who should be in adversarial position but are not, because they behave like individuals. The look of the film embodies the utopian idea. It is not overeager to stress realism; it only proposes the possibility of gentleness in all circumstances. If anything is the opposite of class struggle, it is this.

Indeed, the apotheosis of a conscious choice of humanism is reached in *Amar Bhuvan* which, like some extraordinary Iranian films, seeks to weave magic out of a world without evil. The wheel comes full circle in this tale of a divorced couple, both remarried, steeped in a gentle, nostalgic remembrance of what once was. When all parties meet in full knowledge of the feelings of all concerned, there is no rancour. Sen places this gentle utopia in a Muslim society and holds it up to an India with its terrible memory of the Gujarat riots still fresh in its mind. In this context, the film becomes a pained cry for peace and tolerance, for live and let live. The film is based on a long-spun short novel by a Bangladeshi writer and shows an image of society rare in West Bengal. It simplifies the many strands of the story and the film-making has a limpid quality reflecting the simplicity of the story as told by Mrinal Sen in what one hopes is not his swan song although it has the air of one.

16

SHYAM BENEGAL
Official Biographies, Personal Cinema

If Ray reflected the Tagorean enlightenment, Benegal is undoubtedly the chronicler of Nehruvian India. He shares its 'socialistic' bias and its foundations in secularism, pluralism, democracy, equality of opportunity, human rights, women's rights and all their concomitants. His all-India identity is pronounced, obvious. Compare him to Satyajit Ray and Ritwik Ghatak and the difference leaps out. Ray was a Bengali and an Indian; Ghatak was only a Bengali; Benegal is only an Indian.

His upbringing may provide a clue to the nature of his identity. Originally from Konkan in south Kanara, he was brought up under the Nehruvian umbrella. Besides, he must have internalized the values of the nineteenth-century reform movement directly and through the cinema of Satyajit Ray. The Ray model of realism dominated the cultural avant-garde cinema in India for nearly two decades before the appearance of Benegal's first film. The film society movement, beginning with the founding of the Calcutta Film Society by Ray in the year of Independence, spread a new awareness and a new concept of cinema. It was Benegal's period of self-education, developing his world view and his view of cinema.

No wonder he was eventually drawn to the making of Nehru's *Discovery of India* for television. It is important to realize that for the generations brought up on a West-oriented education, alienated from the traditional face of India, a self-propelled, intensely personal, discovery of India was a must for any form of creative work. The paintings of Amrita Sher-Gil and Jamini Roy, the revival of classical music and dancing outside the domain of the temple, the princely courts and the courtesans, the rapid expansion of the media, the spread of Marxist awareness of the underprivileged among other things, created a new ambience for the arts. Cinema, by the very nature of its recording of reality, provides an ideal medium for this cultivation of sensibility towards the changing environment. What Ray said of himself, Benegal could well have said too: '. . . film-making is exciting because it brings me closer to my country and people. Each film contributes to a process of self-education, making me conscious of the enormous diversity of life around me.'

The Benegal who emerged from these new encounters was exceptionally clear-eyed about ideology, untrammelled by the self-doubts and admonitions of the collective that often trouble many of his Bengali or Malayali counterparts. He grew to become steadfast in his broad ideological persuasions, refusing to be buffeted by changing influences in his environment.

One only has to look at the range of subjects of Benegal's films to see where his heart lay at the time he came to cinema. His first feature, *Ankur*, was concerned with oppression generally and the oppression of women in particular—a concern carried into the next film, *Nishant* (Night's End, 1975), and picked up again and again through his career. An early exemplar of this is in *Bhumika* (The Role, 1977), which deals with woman's dilemma of finding both security and freedom. *Mandi* (Bazaar, 1983) went into the prostitute's struggle to survive and her inscrutable relationship with a society that at once needs her and rejects her. Later in his career came the three remarkable portraits of Muslim women in *Mammo* (1994), *Sardari Begum* (1996) and *Zubeida* (2001), exploring an area seldom visited by the Indian film-maker.

Ceaseless exploration in between also propelled him towards films like *Kondura* (1978), an essay on superstition reinforced by myths. In *Junoon* (1978), *Kalyug* (1981) and particularly *Trikaal* (1985), he showed a sense of history and a depth of interest in the interactions of past, present and future.

II

But the strand central to Benegal's ideology and his oeuvre is of the documentary. His feature films turn fact into fiction; they grow out of the documentary approach. One should first look at his Fabian semi-documentaries on the theme of the cooperative movement, best illustrated by *Manthan* (milkmen and women), *Susman* (handloom weavers) and *Antarnaad* (fisher-folk). To this group one should add *Samar*, a full-length feature sponsored by the government to reduce caste exclusivities in the distribution of water in some areas. All four films analyse social relationships and the human condition produced by them. Add to this the long semi-documentaries, *Discovery of India*, *The Making of the Mahatma* and the full-length film on freedom fighter Subhas Chandra Bose, and you have as many as seven major films overtly centring on the biographies of certain individuals and institutions. Intense social and political activism must obviously underlie such abiding concerns. The preoccupation also shows a refusal to recognize the customary and rather persistent distinction between documentary and feature film-making. The two together make up his voyage of discovery, long, varied and purposeful, and map out its course before us.

Manthan (1976), *Susman* (1987) and *Antarnaad* (1991) also represent a unique approach to film funding and to the involvement of people with films made about them. In these three films, Benegal solves the problem of alienation of people from films about them that has always plagued parallel cinema, by making his audience part of the film. The men and women of the Khaira milk cooperative who made *Manthan* possible by contributing money must have seen the film made about them—which is more than one can say about other films made to highlight the condition of common people, not only in terms of their suffering but of their efforts to pull themselves up by their bootstraps.

The problem with making such markedly purposive films is that weighty purpose can stifle the film under its own load and end up being what somebody called 'UNESCO Cinema', politically correct but lifeless. Whether the film is a success or a failure, the mere act of making such a film may be charged with a feel-good factor for its makers and contribute to the integrity of the group; but the living quality of the final product, the artistic worth of the film, must remain a separate issue. It is here that Benegal shows a unique ability to invest an official biography of an individual or an institution with the quality of personal cinema. The magic behind this is the film-maker's total identification with the subject and its emotional outreach. Of this, *Manthan* stands out as an outstanding example.

The film has a unique charm. The director's sense of oneness with the efforts of the milkmen and women never flags. It remains warm to the touch till the end. The observation is never cold and detached. The milkmen and women are handsome, colourful, and humane. There is a unique, subterranean awareness of sexuality that spreads a mild glow on their faces. This extends to the relationship of the local village women with the men who have come from the city to help them build the cooperative. Only once does this secret tension break through to the surface (and is quickly controlled); the rest of the time it is a mild, invisible undercurrent.

Much of the charm of the film emanates oddly from this tension between the villager and the city bred, categories that do not normally interact with each other but have been thrown together by an unusual identity of purpose. The standard equation between the townsmen and the villagers has been, for ages, one of exploitation in one way or another; their working together to achieve a common purpose is an altogether new factor, at first regarded by the villagers with some suspicion. The process of overcoming this wariness is the real human story underlying the film.

The other quality that makes the film irresistible is that the problems and conflicts on the way towards the making of the cooperative are never underplayed. They have all the reality of passionate personal experience. At the many stages of the conflict, the ending is not predictable; the narrative sustains interest throughout. The acting has unusual warmth and the film will remain a unique memento of the personality of Smita Patil. Perhaps no Indian actress has expressed such subtle identity with traditional, illiterate and poor village women through her looks, acting and body language.

Benegal's other films based on rather similar pattern strive to reach the warmth and the subtle charm of *Manthan*, without equal success. They are expertly made but somewhat schematic. The weavers of *Susman* do not emerge as living human beings to the same extent despite the precision of the writing, acting and film-making that marks all of Benegal's films.

All the song and dance of *Samar* (1999), attractive in themselves, cannot save it from this fate. Nonetheless, all these films illustrate Benegal's facility in turning fact into fiction, taking the 'official' material into the domain of personal cinema. Of course, no film-maker is charged with inspiration uniformly through his career; too much should not therefore be made of variations in this respect. These films in any case served to help him to hone his skills. 'The important thing,' as John Ford said when pestered with questions on his Art, 'is to go on working.'

Antarnaad (The Inner Voice, 1991) is distinguished by another element that it adds to Benegal's identity—the spiritual. The film was commissioned and funded by Swadhyay, a voluntary organization devoted to self-development. Swadhyay means the study of self, an aim that few film-makers have made their subject. The founder of the movement, Pandurang Shastri Athavale, took his message of devotion from village to village for some forty years. 'Today,' says the publicity brochure, 'the silent revolution has grown, embracing over 15,000 villages involving about 5 million people who are now part of the Swadhyay parivar or family.'

Having launched himself on this daunting task, Benegal sets out to capture the spirit of the movement in a two-hour-forty-minute film with a large cast and widely spread-out locations. The film was shot in two villages and was based on real-life experiences. A village full of dacoits is won over, villagers contribute a day's wages towards the purchase of a trawler for cooperative use.

This experiment in Gandhian microcosmic cooperation reaches such a height of success in self-help in an age of globalization that the task of making the urban audiences believe in its reality is a monumentally difficult task that few would even think of attempting. But Benegal had huge satisfaction from the five million Swadhyayees who funded the film; they saw it and were inspired by it. An extraordinary achievement on the sidelines of the mainstream cinema. As I sat in a Bombay cinema amongst a house full of fisher-folk from the Swadhyayee villages, I realized something of the kind of private satisfaction Benegal must have received from the making of this film and the showing of it to precisely those for whom it was made and who made the making of it possible.

III

History is among Benegal's other preoccupations. In *Trikaal*, he is once again faced with the task of translating fact into fiction in the same way as in his co-op films. Yet the unique flavour of Portuguese India comes through in ample measure without the camera ever visiting Portugal. Benegal has a rare sense of history and period that he lavishes here on one of the quaint slices of Indian history. It is a remarkable part of the discovery of India that film-makers from various parts of the country in the parallel cinema must make. Benegal wrote the story and screenplay himself and perhaps this comes through in the unity and charm of the film, the compassion for the characters, however quaint they may seem. The concept of the matriarch ruling over a large extended family with as much despotism as affection is perfectly realized by Leela Naidu.

Trikaal is unmistakably reminiscent of Garcia Marquez in its grasp of the climate of a time, of history, religion, customs, character, family, all enmeshed together and unfolded with unfailing humour. A sense of distance is created, and made nostalgic, with the device of flashback as an expatriate revisits the deserted family mansion. Naseeruddin Shah adroitly pilots us into its absorbing past. The film is expertly constructed with its multiple strands roundly proportioned into an epic tale. As the grieving matriarch, Leela Naidu is altogether unforgettable and so is the natural daughter (Neena Gupta) of the departed patriarch. The texture is rich with its invocation of the visual and aural atmosphere and its interplay of the farcical and the dignified.

The nostalgic, elegiac undertone is drawn less from Marquez than from Guru Dutt, particularly in *Sahib Bibi Aur Ghulam*. Candlelight glows on the faces and the interiors, giving them the mellowness of age and wisdom. *Trikaal* is arguably Benegal's richest, most fascinating work.

The three portraits of Muslim women in *Mammo*, *Sardari Begum* and *Zubeida* also mark out the position of women in a moment of history. They are, on the one hand, an extension of the portraits of women seen earlier in *Bhumika* for instance; on the other, they mark a virtual waking up to the mute existence of Muslim women, of which Indian cinema is by and large blissfully unaware despite the shining participation of so many Muslim stars. The older genre of so-called 'Muslim socials' was flawed by its remarkable incarceration, its total absence of interaction with other communities. In Benegal's own work, there were Muslim women and men in *Junoon*, but its interest was more in the picaresque storytelling than with character and society. As a result, the group of three films stand out as a new factor to be reckoned with. Although the films are specifically about the women, their observation takes in the entire community, as seen through its least visible, most intimate, most vulnerable section, located at the centre of family relationships.

In a way *Mammo* is the most important of the three because it is the only one concerned with ordinary women as distinct from performing artists. It therefore has a special significance in exploring the Muslim predicament. Its connection with Pakistan makes it all the more real in its preoccupation. Mammo is a Pakistani woman on a visit to India who, like hundreds of others, wants to stay on with her relations in India and dodges the law as long as she can. Just when she has once again merged with her sister's family, she is caught and deported. In a memorable piece of fantasy, she comes right back, not as a ghost but in flesh and blood, proving all political divides to be false, brutal, and incapable of wiping out the bonds of family. In her fantasy return Mammo becomes the representative of all the divided families who want to reunite, as human beings, not as political entities. Benegal ventures into an area untouched by others and fraught with hazards that he manages to evade. The fact that governments are insensitive to the need for people-to-people relationships and, more often than not, discourage them, makes a film like this desperately important. It is one of the very few instruments available to cut through the divides created by politicians and military bosses.

The extraordinary performances put in by Surekha Sikri as the Indian woman and Farida Jalal as her Pakistani sister make the film come to life. They are themselves made possible by the realism of Khalid Mohammed's script. Known as a film critic and not a scriptwriter, Mohammed makes the two characters stand out in relief by making one a compulsive talker forever speaking nineteen to the dozen, and the other quiet, practical and otherwise undistinguished. Both have very good screen presence and sharply different acting techniques. For a while in the middle stretch, the storytelling, the script's inventiveness sag a bit but the early sequences, and later the trip to the Haji Ali mosque in search of the sister, and the ending are absorbing. The mosque by the sea in which the unwanted sister takes refuge acquires extra meaning; religion is the last refuge of lost souls.

Writing about the status of women in ancient India, Sukumari Bhattacharya, the Sanskrit pundit, remarks that the only women to enjoy relative independence in ancient India were the courtesans; for they were the sole custodians of their right to love whomsoever they pleased. Up to a point, it may be argued, the situation is the same in modern India in the institution of the tawaif. Benegal is fascinated by the problem; he started out on it in *Bhumika*, with which *Sardari Begum* and *Zubeida* are connected by an umbilical cord.

Both films were scripted by Khalid Mohammed, buoyed by the success of *Mammo*. Sardari is a professional singer of repute and financially sufficiently secure to retain her independence throughout her life. The film begins with her death caused by stones thrown by street rowdies and the rest is a flashback returning at the end to the scene of her death. Her struggles to stick to her musical training and her career as a singer make up the bulk of the story. Music remains the love of her life; men only betray her. A woman journalist digs up the details of her life and pieces them together. This device serves to give a documentary flavour to the story and firmly anchors it in a contemporary point of view, one that endorses her lifelong pursuit of music as entirely worthwhile. It is important to see this in the context of the ambiguity and indeed the falsehood by which the place of the tawaif in the history of Indian classical music has been enveloped. It is perfectly well known but seldom acknowledged that it is the tawaif who, with the patronage of the princely states, kept classical music alive through the British period. This was an era during which classical music did not enjoy the official favour of the empire and was in fact viewed with some suspicion. The appellation given by the rulers was 'the *nautch* girls'. It was only during the run-up to Independence and the years thereafter that the era of the 'music conference' began with the great singers among the tawaifs. A ticket-buying audience freed the singing girl from the vagaries and often the ignominy of the patronage of the rich. The music world became part of the democracy of public and governmental support. Gone were the days when a singer of the calibre of Kesri Bai would have to sing standing in the princely court because mere performers were not allowed to sit in His Highness's august presence.

Although much of what was popular in the tawaif's salons came to be placed under the rubric of light classical music of northern India—thumri, ghazal, etc.—more severe and purist forms such as dhrupad and khayal were also practised behind the shutters of the kothas. Many stalwarts who made their reputation in the period around Independence had indeed found both refuge and training in the tawaif's quarters—a fact that few of them would later acknowledge and some would vociferously deny.

All of this is not in the film. But it helps to understand the cloud under which classical music lived despite the greatness of its tradition. It also prepares us for the rigours of the life of the singing girl that the film maps out, particularly one aspect of the performing artist's problem—the buffeting she has to endure between the need for security and the desire for independence. Sardari Begum's experience is an exemplar of unshaken loyalty to music. What she sings carries an angst of the erotic; yet we are not treated to the personal aspects of it in her life. Whether this is entirely satisfactory or not is difficult to say; there is perhaps an essential interplay between love in real life and the passion a singer pours into the songs of love. Perhaps that is the source of the romantic agony. Again and again, the film has Sardari sing the line *Chali pi kay nagar* (I will go now to where my lover is). Perhaps without this personal dimension, a film on a singer like Sardari becomes a little too much of an official biography of a fictitious person.

Actually, the film is not based on the real life of a singer; it is more of an amalgam of many rolled into one. In places there are shades of Begum Akhtar, but expectations of conformity on this score are dispelled at the very start. But the quintessential tawaif grown into famous singer, who is conjured up in the film from the lives of many, has no love life. Looking at the sensitive face of Kirron Kher who plays Sardari, we sense a tragedy somewhere in her life and expect to get to know more about it, to give the music a body, as it were. Perhaps the most expressive shot of her is the one showing her cooking and singing at the same time. Indeed, one could wish for more such moments in the film.

The accident with which the film opens has shades of the reality outside her shuttered existence. The street brawl starts from what looks like Hindus smearing coloured powder on Muslims—the kind of fracas that would not normally ruffle the calm of Sardari's routine. Was the stone thrown deliberately at Sardari standing at the balcony? It does not seem so. But the violence to her, leading to her death, leaves disturbing ripples in the viewer, hinting at larger problems lurking in the milieu. The tawaif tradition was largely a product of Muslim society, incarcerating the family woman and creating a pleasure garden outside, ringing with music and dance, sophisticated wit and clever turns of verse.

Zubeida is a landmark film that calls for probing because here Benegal comes closest to the norms of mainstream cinema. Apart from the casting of box-office stars Karisma Kapoor and Rekha, its emphasis, like mainstream cinema's, is on the fixed outlines of character and relationship rather than their psychological development.

Zubeida began as an actress in the cinema. But essentially, hers was a continuation and extension of the tawaif tradition—of a woman who earns her relative independence by dint of her seductive persona and her ability to sing and dance. Zubeida does not have Sardari Begum's commitment to music; at any rate she has no chance to even test it out, being forced into marriage as the second wife of a prince. Her love affair with royalty is essentially rootless and breaks down as soon as it faces the realities of the prince's power base embedded in his family and his subjects. In contrast to her uselessness, the senior queen (convincingly played by Rekha) is more stable, unruffled by the superficies of the prince's love life. The prince himself is not unduly bothered when his lecherous cousin makes advances to his newly acquired wife. When the moment of truth comes, the junior wife is thrown aside as a toy. Issues of succession, of election to the country's parliament on the strength of popular loyalty to the traditional ruler, suddenly assume the importance due to them. Zubeida refuses to give up her claims to the prince's heart and practically causes his aircraft to crash on its way to Delhi, killing both of them.

As a character, Zubeida is the weakest and most vulnerable of Benegal's women. Prevented from sticking to her professional life, she clings to the illusion she has embraced and is yet unable to live with it. The Hindu–Muslim aspect of the marriage counts for little; the princes were used to acquiring wives and concubines from anywhere they fancied. Zubeida could well have been a Hindu. Indeed, the only reality of the film is not in the love life but in the politics: the ruler and the ruled, the remains of princely power and the residual loyalty of the people to the royal family, the reorientation of the princes to the new political bosses and elections. The fragility of princely power is mirrored in the aircraft sailing across the blue sky and the yellow-green landscape with Zubeida struggling with her husband over the controls, ignoring the hazards. The metaphor can hardly be missed; princely power is like a gas-filled balloon destined to crash. The aircraft, like Zubeida, is no more than a toy.

It is in the second half that the film acquires reality. The large open spaces of the landscape, the vaulty, windy interiors, the impressive palace front, spell the unreality of the princely dream fostered by the British to drain the so-called martial races of all powers of resistance. Whatever the original purpose, the film becomes an essay on the illusory nature of princely raj.

IV

Shyam Benegal must have realized early in the day that the best training for acting in cinema, contrary to the popular notion, is in the theatre. No wonder most of his discoveries of new acting talent come from the stage—Anant Nag, Amrish Puri, Kulbhushan Kharbanda, Mohan Agashe, Surekha Sikri and others. He has an unfailing eye for casting; his discovery of perfect new faces has benefited much of Indian cinema. Rows of new actors, many of them drawn from the theatre, have moved from his films to those of many others both in the parallel cinema and the mainstream.

In Benegal's approach to acting, Amrish Puri occupies a special place. He is at one end of the scale of which Surekha Sikri occupies the other.

Puri is the embodiment of evil whose presence is mandatory to the laws of life. He is the tyrant owner of the women in his home and they the objects of his lust. From *Nishant* to *Zubeida* he is the man you love to hate, the apotheosis of patriarchal authority, the devourer of beautiful women, the chastiser of children. He stands out as a mythical character in this universe, a reincarnation of Kamsa of the Krishna legend. He is also the repository of oppressive traditions. His dialogues are eminently predictable; the moment you see him in a situation, you know how he is going to react, what words of wisdom he is about to deliver in stentorian tones. He is to Benegal what Pran was to commercial cinema for decades together. His is the melodramatic strand which Benegal weaves together with the naturalistic represented by actors like Shabana Azmi, Naseeruddin Shah and Surekha Sikri to name only a few. It shows Benegal's openness to melodrama as a legitimate device for the so-called art film.

At the other end of the scale is the unforgettable Surekha Sikri. If Amrish Puri is always the type, Sikri is always the individual. As the sister in *Mammo*, the old singer in *Sardari Begum*, the mother in *Zubeida*, she is completely convincing. No matter what age she represents—sometimes she wears a lot of make-up to go back in age, sometimes she does not to remain herself—she never stops being convincing in anything she does, any stage in life she represents. Her acting technique is so refined that when she sings in *Sardari Begum* for a few brief moments, she transforms herself into a veteran performer, surrounded by an aura of thumri, as though she has been steeped in it all her life. Such depths of mobility are summoned up by ever so slight bends of the neck, or minute expansion or contraction of the eyes, and the manipulation of little muscles. Her acting vocabulary is rich in variety and in depth. It is interesting to see her in action opposite Amrish Puri, their techniques are so different.

One look at Karisma Kapoor's acting, and you see that she has no background in theatre. The senior queen says of Zubeida that she is a free spirit whom everyone wants to capture. It is the most perceptive comment on the character, but it places a weight on the personality and character of Zubeida that Karisma Kapoor is incapable of carrying. Her performance is too brittle and lacking in levels of feeling to measure up to what is required of her. She works entirely on the surface of the character; her knee-jerk reactions to every situation leave her character without any ambiguity or depth. To justify the Maharani's observation, she would need a great deal more mystery and unattainability. There is more of remoteness and intensity in Rekha as the Maharani; Karisma's performance is drawn straight from the one-dimensional cut-outs of commercial melodrama oblivious to the logic of character development. But the style of direction is far removed from the melodramatic; it sticks to the realistic manner customary with Benegal. It is possible that in this respect the script and the direction worked at cross-purposes, resulting in the brittleness and obviousness of the character of Zubeida.

In another way the film conforms to the melodramatic form; its use of music is extensive, perhaps designed to heighten Zubeida's performance and fill up its gaps. Yet there are some very effective passages, for instance in the use of the wedding music as a counterpoint to Zubeida's desperate efforts to escape from the marriage. At other points, music becomes a load on the credibility of the film. Indeed, in this film, Benegal probably comes closest to the ways of commercial cinema without totally accepting its terms.

V

Most of Benegal's films set up an objective truth—a historical fact, a given situation, character or a class—to which the film-making approximates closely, with order, discipline, craftsmanship. The making of passionate personal films is not his forte. In this respect he is the very opposite of Ritwik Ghatak who was nothing if not passionate. A close second is Mrinal Sen for whom objectivity means little. Benegal's ruling principle is his rationality, from which he rarely seeks to free his imagination or emotions.

Two outstanding exceptions to this are *Suraj Ka Satvan Ghoda* (1993) and *Trikaal*. In both, the underlying feeling is of nostalgia overlaid with comedy. They represent the farthest point to which he moves from his documentary base and from which he retreats before getting entangled.

Suraj Ka Satvan Ghoda is a rare commodity in Benegal's oeuvre—a love story or rather a clutch of interrelated love stories revolving round the same characters. The shades of *Rashomon* are confined to the discovery of the same characters in various could-have-been situations whose truth cannot be determined. Manek Mulla, the raconteur, is something of an intellectual and the stories are all made up from his recollections. This and the setting of adda with his friends oblige him to put on an air of self-deprecation and detachment from what is actually close to his heart.

The nostalgic, self-deprecatory multi-narrative of *Suraj Ka Satvan Ghoda* is unique in the world of Benegal. It is here that he comes closest to personal cinema and, judging by its uniqueness, shies away from it, going back to the safety of the objective, the linear and the severely connected narratives of his other films. Indeed, the underlying dichotomy that defines Benegal's oeuvre seems to lie in what might be called the official biography and the personal cinema. In this inner conflict, he seems to pull himself back from the brink of the personal for fear of being self-indulgent, of losing control. Otherwise one would perhaps have seen many more films of the *Suraj* variety.

NOTES

CHAPTER 1: OF MARGI AND DESI: THE TRADITIONAL DIVIDE

1. An unavoidable distinction between the two arises from the fact that folk art is created by the people themselves through interaction among themselves within the specificities of a place; pop is manufactured in the cities and marketed impersonally to an audience spread out across the national or international marketplace.

2. *Outlook*, 25 November 2002.

3. Peter Colaco, *Indian Cinema 1979–80*, Directorate of Film Festivals, New Delhi.

4. For a detailed discussion, see Chidananda Das Gupta, *The Painted Face: Studies in India's Popular Cinema*, New Delhi: Roli Books, 1992.

5. In conversation with the author, June 1981.

CHAPTER 2: SEEING IS BELIEVING

1. Rudolf Arnheim, *Art and Visual Perception*, Los Angeles: University of California Press, 1954.

2. B.V. Dharap, 'The Mythological, or Taking Fate for Granted', *The Indian Cinema Superbazaar*, eds Aruna Vasudev and Philippe Lenglet, New Delhi: Vikas, 1983.

3. Ibid. From 70 per cent in the 1920s, the share of mythologicals out of India's total annual film production has come down to 20 per cent.

4. For a discussion of the relevance of *Jai Santoshi Maa* to contemporary urban Hindu society, see Veena Das, 'The Mythological Film and its Framework of Meaning', *India International Centre Quarterly*, Delhi, March 1980.

5. B.V. Dharap, 'The Mythological, or Taking Fate for Granted', *The Indian Cinema Superbazaar*, eds Aruna Vasudev and Philippe Lenglet, New Delhi: Vikas, 1983: '. . . so long as ignorance, illiteracy, poverty, superstition rule the large mass of people in this country . . . such pictures will always have an audience and the sway of mythological films will continue.'

CHAPTER 8: FILM AS VISUAL ANTHROPOLOGY

1. Lawrence A. Babb, *Redemptive Encounters: Three Modern Styles in the Hindu Tradition*, Berkeley: University of California Press, 1986.

2. Frits Staal, *Agni: The Vedic Ritual of the Fire Altar*, Delhi: Motilal Banarsidass, 1983.

3. Richard Schechner, 'Wrestling Against Time: The Performance Aspects of Agni', *Journal of Asian Studies*, February 1986; 'Vedic Ritual in Quotation Marks', *Journal of Asian Studies*, February 1986.

Chapter 9: The Crisis in Film Studies

1. *Taittiriya Upanishad*, Chapter IV.

2. Bill Nichols (ed.), *Movies and Methods: An Anthology*, Berkeley and Los Angeles: University of California Press, 1976.

3. Ibid.

4. In conversation with the author, 1948.

5. Susan Sontag, *Against Interpretation and Other Essays*, New York: Farrar, Strauss & Giroux, 1966, reprint Picador, 2001.

6. Umberto Eco, *The Aesthetics of Thomas Aquinas*, Harvard: Radius, 1988.

7. Terry Eagleton, *The Ideology of the Aesthetic*, Oxford: Blackwell, 1990.

8. T.W. Adorno, *The Culture Industry*, London: Routledge, 1991.

9. Andrew Bowie, *Aesthetics and Subjectivity: From Kant to Nietzsche*, Manchester: Manchester University Press, 1990.

10. J.M. Bernstein, *The Fate of Art*, Cambridge: Polity Press, 1992.

11. Dave Beech and John Roberts, 'Spectres of the Aesthetic', *The New Left Review*, No. 218, 1996.

12. Ibid.

13. Ibid.

14. J.M. Bernstein, *The Fate of Art*, Cambridge: Polity Press, 1992.

15. Ibid.

16. Ibid.

17. *Kathopanishad*, II, ii, 15.

Chapter 10: How Indian Is Indian Cinema?

1. Lothar Lutze and Beatrix Pfleiderer, *The Hindi Film: Agent and Re-Agent of Cultural Change*, New Delhi: Manohar, 1985.

2. Ibid.

3. Sarangadeva, *Sangeeta Ratnakara*.

4. Richard Schechner, *Performative Circumstances from the Avant Garde to Ramlila*, Calcutta: Seagull Book, 1983.

Chapter 11: Cinema Takes Over the State

1. *The Sunday Observer*, Bombay, 1967.

2. Robert L. Hardgrave, Jr., 'The Celluloid God: MGR and the Tamil Film', *South Asian Review*, Vol. 4, No. 4, July 1971.

3. Marguerite Ross Bennett, *The Politics of Cultural Nationalism in South India*, New Jersey: Princeton University Press, 1976. Most of the historical data in Sections I and III are based on this book.

4. Ibid.

5. Gregory Possehl (ed.), *Ancient Cities of the Indus–Harappan Civilization*, New Delhi: Oxford and IBH, 1982.

6. RGK, 'Rediscovering Tamil Nadu', *The Illustrated Weekly of India*, 16 January 1983.

7. Ibid.

8. Sivathamby Karthigesan, *The Tamil Film as a Medium of Political Communication*, New Century Book House Private Limited. The phenomenon described here was not confined to the Tamils but was an all-India phenomenon among the Hindus. The division between margi (classical) and desi (folk) in Sanskrit treatises on the subject, such as the *Sangeeta Ratnakara*, was similar in nature; so was the restriction of entry into the temple a divide between the privileged and the underling in north India.

9. Ibid.

10. Ibid.

11. Ibid.

12. Ibid.

13. Ibid.

14. Interview with S. Krishnaswamy.

15. Interview with 'Film News' Anandan.

16. Interview with S. Krishnaswamy.

17. Robert L. Hardgrave, Jr., 'The Celluloid God: MGR and the Tamil Film', *South Asian Review*, Vol. 4, No. 4, July 1971.

18. *The Sunday Observer*, 11 July 1982.

19. Robert L. Hardgrave, Jr., 'The Celluloid God: MGR and the Tamil Film', *South Asian Review*, Vol. 4, No. 4, July 1971.

20. *The Illustrated Weekly of India*, 16 January 1983.

21. Brian Laul, *The Illustrated Weekly of India*, 16 January 1983.

22. S. Viswanathan, Editor, *Industrial Economist*, writing in *The Illustrated Weekly of India*, 16 January 1983.

23. Ibid.

24. Cho Ramaswamy in *The Illustrated Weekly of India.*

25. Ibid.

26. *Indian Express*, 26 September 1983.

27. Sivathamby Karthigesan, *The Tamil Film as a Medium of Political Communication*, New Century Book House Private Limited.

28. *The Sunday Observer*, 11 July 1982.

29. Ibid.

30. Although the present tense has been used in mentioning the economic

indicators in this section, the reference is to conditions within MGR's lifetime and not later (he died in 1987).

31. Another version of the story is that this episode brought to a head an already incipient resolve.

32. V.S. Sharma, *Indian Express.*

33. Ibid.

34. *The Times of India*, 24 August 1985.

35. *The Statesman*, 4 February 1987.

36. *Indian Express*, 12 February 1987.

37. *The Times of India*, 9 October 1986 and 13 October 1986.

38. Ibid., 31 August 1985.

39. *Indian Express*, 23 May 1983, and *The Times of India*, 31 August 1985.

40. *The Statesman*, 7 December 1983.

41. *Indian Express*, 8 February 1987.

42. Binod John, *Sunday*, 25–31 January 1987.

43. *The Hindustan Times*, 15 April 1987.

44. Binod John, *Sunday*, 25–31 January 1987.

45. *India Today*, 1–15 May 1980.

46. This essay was published in Chidananda Das Gupta, *The Painted Face*, in the year 1992. Rajkumar died in 2006. He never did become chief minister.

47. *India Today*, 1–15 May 1980.

48. Ibid.

49. *Filmfare*, 1–15 August 1986.

50. *Indian Express*, 18 June 1982. Note the similarity of this statement with NTR's utterance after assuming office.

51. See translation of song from *Pyaasa* in 'Why the Films Sing'.

52. Chidananda Das Gupta, *Jibanananda Das*, Sahitya Akademi, 1972.

53. Conversation with the critic Monojit Lahiri.

54. Kishore Valicha, 'How Amitabh Changed Commercial Cinema', *The Sunday Observer*, February 1987.

55. *The Statesman*, 6 March 1984.

56. In conversation with the author.

Chapter 13: Ritwik Ghatak: Cinema, Marxism and the Mother Goddess

1. 'The night the storm broke down my door.'

2. 'Today sun and shade play hide-and-seek in the rice fields.'

3. 'I know the great *Purusha* (male) whose colour is of the sun and who rests beyond all darkness.'

4. Translated by Chidananda Das Gupta.

5. Rustom Bharucha, *Reversals of Revolution: The Political Theatre of Bengal*, Calcutta: Seagull Books, 1983.

6. Ibid.

7. Haimanti Banerjee, *Ritwik Kumar Ghatak*, Pune: National Film Archive of India, 1985.

8. In *Meghe Dhaka Tara*, the younger sister, Geeta, is supposed to be an irresistible sex object; but Ghatak represents this in isolated shots with exaggerated gestures reminiscent of Eisenstein's silent cinema, strictly as an *idea*, and in awkward contradistinction to the style of the rest of the film.

9. Ashish Rajadhyaksha, *Ritwik Ghatak: A Return to the Epic*, Screen Unit Bombay, 1982, offers the most orderly and detailed consolidation of these theories.

10. Chidananda Das Gupta, *The Cinema of Satyajit Ray*, Third Edition, National Book Trust.

11. Speech at the seminar on Ritwik Ghatak at the India International Centre, 18 April 1985. Mirza, a student of Ghatak at the FTII, Pune, recalled Ghatak talking about how to make a good film.

12. I use the word classicist here in the sense of the individual finding his fulfilment in belonging to a given order of values; Hamlet, the romantic loner, sees something rotten in the state of Denmark and considers himself 'born to set it right'.

13. A piquant situation arose during the censoring of this scene because what Ghatak had originally used was the holiest mantra of the Brahminical order, the Gayatri mantra: *Tat savitur varenyam/Vargo devasya dhimahi/Dhiyo yo nah prachodayat*. Some members of the censor panel were outraged. They included Pandit Gourinath Shastri, one of the foremost Sanskrit scholars of the time and a devout Brahmin at that. I was asked to speak to Ghatak, who was waiting outside as customary, and explain the objection. Ghatak agreed to my suggestion to use a Vedantic verse in place of the Gayatri mantra.

14. This article is a slightly revised and enlarged version of the lecture delivered at the India International Centre on 26 April 1985, under the auspices of the National Film Heritage Programme of the Centre for Development of Instructional Technology, and the National Film Archive of India.

Chapter 14: Adoor Gopalakrishnan: The Kerala Coconut

1. Iqbal Masud, 'Requiem for Lefty', *Indian Express*.

2. Darryl de Monte, *The Guardian* (UK), 5 January 1973, quoted in 'The New Generations', *Film India*. 1981.

3. *Close Look Magazine*, Vol. XXII, No. 5, June 2002.

COPYRIGHT ACKNOWLEDGEMENTS

'Seeing Is Believing': First published in *The Painted Face: Studies in India's Popular Cinema*, New Delhi: Roli Books, 1992

'Why the Films Sing': First published in *The Painted Face: Studies in India's Popular Cinema*, New Delhi: Roli Books, 1992

'Cinema: The Realist Imperative': Lecture at Kala Bhavan, Santiniketan, Visva-Bharati University, 25 February 1989

'Woman, Non-violence and Indian Cinema': The Smita Patil Memorial Lecture, Mumbai

'A Word on Awards': First published by the Directorate of Film Festivals, Government of India, 1982

'Film as Visual Anthropology': Paper published by the Seminar on Visual Anthropology, INTACH, Jodhpur, 1987

'The Crisis in Film Studies': First published in *Summerhill*, Indian Institute of Advanced Study, 1997

'How Indian Is Indian Cinema?': First published in *The Painted Face: Studies in India's Popular Cinema*, New Delhi: Roli Books, 1992

'Cinema Takes Over the State': First published in *The Painted Face: Studies in India's Popular Cinema*, New Delhi: Roli Books, 1992

'Satyajit Ray: The First Ten Years': First published under the title 'Ray and Tagore' in *Sight and Sound*, British Film Institute, winter 1965–66

'Satyajit Ray: Modernism and Mythicality': First published in *Iconics*, Japan Society of Image Arts, Volume 4, 1998

'Ritwik Ghatak: Cinema, Marxism and the Mother Goddess': Lecture at the India International Centre, 26 April 1985

'Adoor Gopalakrishnan: The Kerala Coconut': First published in the official publication of the Mumbai International Film Festival

'Mrinal Sen: Loose Cannon': First published in *Cinemaya: The Asian Film Quarterly*, 63–64, New Delhi, 2004

'Shyam Benegal: Official Biographies, Personal Cinema': First published in *Cinemaya: The Asian Film Quarterly*, 61–62, New Delhi, 2004

INDEX